Cooperative LEARNING

WHERE HEART MEETS MIND

Barrie Bennett

Carol Rolheiser-Bennett

Laurie Stevahn

An Interactive Resource Book

About the Authors...

Barrie Bennett and **Carol Rolheiser-Bennett** are Assistant Professors, University of Toronto, Ontario. **Laurie Stevahn** is Staff Development Consultant and Director, Professional Development Associates, Bothell, Washington.

Art on pages 14, 15, 24, 27, 28, 46, 69, 89, 90, 97, 98, 99, 100, 107, 109, 110, 113, 114, 119, 121, 123, 132, 133, 150, 156, 158, 169, 184, 185, 187, 188, 189, 197, 200, 202, 204, 205, 208, 215, 226, 248, 262, 274, 277, 298, 299, 300, 308, 330, and 331 used by permission from "*Outrageous Clip Art for Youth Ministry,*" copyright 1988, illustrated by Rand Kruback. Published by Group Books, Box 481, Loveland, CO 80539.

Art on pages 12, 214, and 269 used by permission from "*Children's Ministry Clip Art,*" copyright 1990, illustrated by Mary Lynn Ulrich. Published by Group Books, Box 481, Loveland, CO 80539.

Art on pages 23, 30, 35, 40, 41, 43, 44, 45, 49, 64, 68, 71, 94, 102, 125, 134, 135, 136, 137, 139, 155, 173, 186, 205, 243, 247, 249, 253, 259, 283, 284, 304, 316, 321, and 339 used by permission from "*Youth Ministry Clip Art,*" copyright 1987, written and illustrated by Dave Adamson and Steve Hunt of The Church Art Works. Published by Group Books, Box 481, Loveland, CO 80539.

The illustrations on the following pages 12, 16, 20, 21, 22, 32, 42, 55, 60, 61, 68, 73, 75, 79, 101, 118, 128, 142, 145, 148, 150, 165, 170, 172, 175, 181, 190, 194, 201, 212, 217, 228, 238, 244, 256, 279, 312, 313, 318, 319, 320, 324, 333, and 338 are reprinted from "*Youth Specialties Clip-Art Book,*" copyright 1985, by Youth Specialties Inc., 1224 Greenfield Drive, El Cajon, CA, 92021. Used by permission.

The illustrations on the following pages 20, 21, 22, 38, 39, 53, 58, 61, 68, 77, 87, 88, 92, 93, 96, 103, 106, 117, 129, 141, 144, 159, 162, 163, 164, 167, 168, 170, 171, 177, 178, 183, 193, 196, 197, 198, 209, 210, 222, 230, 260, 314, and 336 are reprinted from "*Youth Specialties Clip-Art Book Volume II,*" copyright 1987, by Youth Specialties Inc., 1224 Greenfield Drive, El Cajon, CA, 92021. Used by permission.

Cartoons on pages 264, 265, and 266 are used by permission of John Migliore, Hamilton, Ontario.

The authors have made a comprehensive effort to sight and credit sources. Any omissions detected are not intentional. The authors welcome information to correct any oversights in subsequent editions.

Published by *Educational Connections*, Toronto, Ontario and *Professional Development Associates*, Bothell, Washington.
Designed and typeset by Jennifer Loates, (12) 467 Westney Road South, Ajax, ON, L1S 6V7.
Printed and bound in Canada by Versatel Corporate Services Limited.

ISBN 0-9695388-0-4

Distributed through *Educational Connections*, Station "P", 704 Spadina Ave., P.O. Box 249, Toronto, Ontario, M5S 2S8.

Additional copies of this publication are available by completing the Order Form at the end of the book.

Table of Contents

Dedicated to...

all the students and colleagues I have learned with over the years.

- B.B.-

my family, who taught me to challenge my mind while living from my heart.

- C.R.B. -

Donny... and my family, Mom, Dad, and Mike... whose love, support, and encouragement enrich my life beyond measure.

- L.S. -

Preface

We care about the implementation of cooperative learning and all those working together to make cooperative learning an ongoing reality in schools. *Cooperative Learning: Where Heart Meets Mind* collaboratively evolved out of that care.

The purpose of this resource book is to involve educators in critical inquiry, personal reflection, and supportive discussion about the concepts underlying cooperative strategies and effective classroom applications. Specifically, the book is designed to:

- promote understanding of elements basic to cooperative learning,
- stimulate critical and creative thinking about effective classroom use,
- raise and explore implementation issues and options, and
- encourage supportive interaction among educators experiencing and facilitating cooperative strategies.

Organized into three main sections, Part I of the book considers cooperative learning as a valuable strategy within a framework of other effective classroom practices. Part II deals with student interaction patterns and how to facilitate cooperative groups. Part III presents practical ideas for getting started, sample lessons, and activities for continued professional growth with cooperative learning.

The chapters that constitute each part of the book contain questions and activity sheets for discussion, making this book a resource to be used interactively among colleagues. For example, teachers working together in peer coaching or study groups may use this book to explore cooperative learning concepts, develop classroom applications, and design student materials. The sample lessons and student forms that appear throughout the book are readily adaptable to a variety of classroom situations. Staff developers may also use this resource to facilitate cooperative activities and discussions among educators studying cooperative learning in professional development programs.

In presenting this book, we wish to express our sincere thanks to all those who have contributed to our growth with cooperative learning and who have challenged our thinking about teacher development and school improvement. The students, teachers, administrators, staff developers, and researchers with whom we have interacted have taught us valuable lessons. Together, we continue to learn.

Barrie Bennett
Carol Rolheiser-Bennett
Laurie Stevahn

Part I

Cooperative Learning in Context

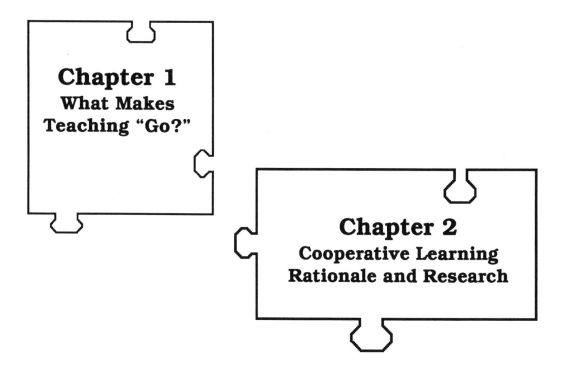

Chapter 1
What Makes Teaching "Go?"

Chapter 2
Cooperative Learning Rationale and Research

Part I

Cooperative Learning in Context

Overview

As an instructional strategy, cooperative learning exists within the domain of effective classroom practices. This section considers cooperative learning in that context. Specifically...

- **Chapter 1 – What Makes Teaching "Go?"** presents a framework for thinking about a variety of factors that, along with cooperative strategies, influence effective teaching and learning.

- **Chapter 2 – Cooperative Learning Rationale and Research** examines reasons for employing cooperative strategies in the classroom and highlights supporting research.

B. Bennett, C. Rolheiser-Bennett, L. Stevahn (1991)
Cooperative Learning: Where Heart Meets Mind

Chapter 1

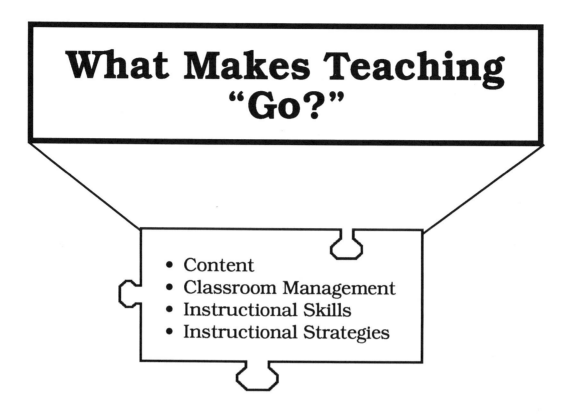

What Makes Teaching "Go?"

- Content
- Classroom Management
- Instructional Skills
- Instructional Strategies

Overview

This chapter presents a conceptual framework for thinking about factors that enhance teaching and learning. The questions that start the chapter focus attention on those factors. The diagram of interconnected cogs that follows provides one way to systematically organize the factors, as well as think about classroom improvement. Cooperative learning is considered within this classroom improvement framework.

What Makes Teaching "Go?"

What factors do you feel are important for making teaching "go?"

After recording your response, interview a colleague for another perspective. Compare, contrast, and extend your lists.

B. Bennett, C. Rolheiser-Bennett, L. Stevahn (1991)
Cooperative Learning: Where Heart Meets Mind

A Framework for Classroom Improvement

Factors that influence effective teaching and learning may be categorized into four main areas:

- **Knowledge of Content**
- **Classroom Management Skills**
- **Instructional Skills**
- **Instructional Strategies**

The diagram on the following page depicts these areas as interconnected cogs and lists some of the factors that comprise each. As the diagram suggests, a change in one cog impacts the others. For example, the *instructional skill* of modeling directions helps students to understand and carry out behavior expectations. This affects *classroom management* as well as student involvement with the *instructional strategy* employed. More specifically, suppose a teacher chooses to facilitate a cooperative lesson. By modeling procedures for moving to groups, appropriate social interactions skills, and steps to complete the assignment, the teacher will help ensure that students know how to act in self-managed ways and can successfully engage in the strategy. Similarly, *knowledge of content* affects one's ability to effectively employ *instructional skills* and *strategies* which, in turn, affects *classroom management.*

Although the cogs work in conjunction with one another, they do not work together in a mechanistic fashion. One cog does not necessarily start another, nor do the cogs simply move in one direction. Instead, they interact dynamically and in complex ways with one another, moving educators and students toward effective teaching and learning. With this in mind, the diagram serves as a framework for guiding classroom improvement.

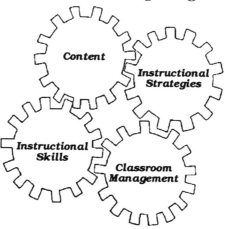

Where do the factors that you listed on the previous page fit in the framework?

B. Bennett, C. Rolheiser-Bennett, L. Stevahn (1991)
Cooperative Learning: Where Heart Meets Mind

What Makes Teaching "Go?"

- Art
- Second Language
- Business Studies
- Family Studies
- Design & Technology/Industrial Arts
- Language Arts
- Mathematics
- Music
- Physical Education & Health
- Science
- Social Sciences
- Other...

- Cooperative Learning
- Direct Instruction
- Concept Attainment
- Concept Formation
- Inquiry
- Advance Organizer
- Memory Models
- Synectics
- Simulations
- Mind Mapping
- 4 - Mat Planning
- Other...

Content

Instructional Strategies

Instructional Skills

Classroom Management

- Formulate Objectives
- Task Analyze
- Share Objective and Purpose
- Teach to the Objective
- Affirmatively Involve All Students
- Monitor and Adjust
- Frame Questions
- Encourage Thinking at Various Levels
- Provide Wait Time
- Give Clear Directions
- Model
- Provide Appropriate Practice
- Hold Students Accountable
- Give Knowledge of Results
- Stimulate Interest
- Make Learning Meaningful
- Structure Success
- Promote Retention
- Promote Transfer
- Provide a Set for Learning
- Facilitate Closure
- Accomodate/Stretch Learning Styles
- Dignify All Students
- Other...

- Win Students Over
- Teach Appropriate Behaviors
- Provide Clear Direction
- Establish Routines
- Low Key Responses
- Encouragement
- Provide Choices
- Informal and Formal Contracts
- Defuse Power Seeking Behaviors
- Teach students to resolve conflicts
- Other...

B. Bennett, C. Rolheiser-Bennett, L. Stevahn (1991)
Cooperative Learning: Where Heart Meets Mind

Remember:

Although the content, management, skills, and strategies of teaching are important technical dimensions, one's personal philosophy of teaching determines how these are implemented and integrated. Given we view teaching from a holistic paradigm, we place students and their needs and experiences at the heart of decision-making. In addition, our philosophy also includes the belief that the climate of the class is greatly influenced by the affective qualities of the teacher and students. Teachers who foster politeness, humor, concern, caring, enthusiasm, and consideration while integrating these with the technical dimensions, truly make teaching "GO."

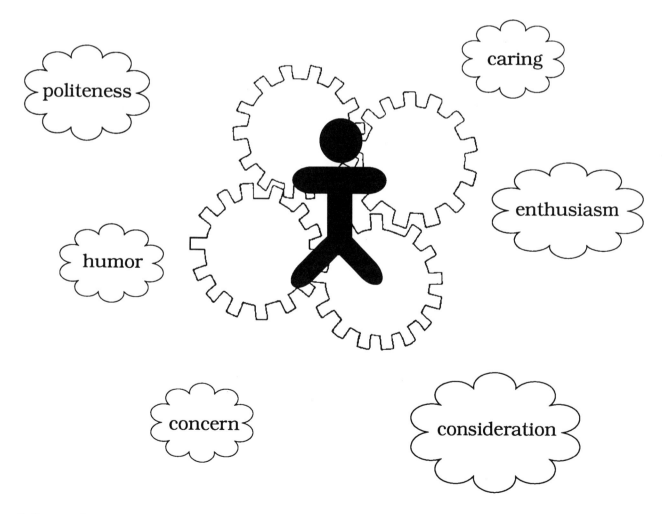

A Perspective On

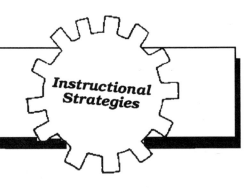

Instructional Strategies

Cooperative learning is one of many effective instructional strategies. Each of the strategies or models of teaching can be classified according to its theoretical base, intended purposes, and learning outcomes. The categorization developed by Joyce and Weil (1986), depicted on the following page, groups strategies into four main "families."

- Models in the **information processing family** enhance the learning of academic concepts and information, methods of inquiry, and logical thinking.

- Models in the **personal family** promote individual development by increasing self-awareness, self-worth, and self-responsibility for self-determination.

- Models in the **social family** capitalize on the energy and coordination of students working together in groups. Primary goals include problem-solving, the development of social interaction skills, and group mastery of academic material.

- Models in the **behavioral family** focus on learning information, skills, and behaviors through feedback or reinforcement of performance.

One aspect of classroom improvement could be the addition of some of the research-based instructional strategies to teachers' repertoires. Although mastery of those strategies is one small part of teaching, the effective use of a variety of strategies would provide educators with alternative approaches to meet the needs of students. We can no longer naively accept the long-standing belief that one model can "do it all." Given the varied learning styles that students and teachers possess and the amount of information students must learn, it remains important that we appropriately select and combine strategies. The power of an extensive repertoire including cooperative learning, will enable teachers to create rich and varied learning environments that move students toward desired learning outcomes.

B. Bennett, C. Rolheiser-Bennett, L. Stevahn (1991)
Cooperative Learning: Where Heart Meets Mind

The Models of Teaching Families

the information processing family	the personal family	the social family	the behavioral family
CONCEPT ATTAINMENT (Jerome Bruner)	NONDIRECTIVE TEACHING (Carl Rogers)	COOPERATIVE LEARNING (Elliot Aronson, David & Roger Johnson, Spencer Kagan, Shlomo Sharan, Robert Slavin)	CONTINGENCY MANAGEMENT
INDUCTIVE THINKING (Hilda Taba)	SYNECTICS (William Gordon)		SELF CONTROL THROUGH OPERANT METHODS
INQUIRY TRAINING (Richard Suchman)	AWARENESS TRAINING (William Schutz & George Brown)	ROLE PLAYING (Fannie & George Shaftel)	TRAINING MODEL
ADVANCE ORGANIZERS (David Ausubel)	CLASSROOM MEETING MODEL (William Glasser)		STRESS REDUCTION
MEMORY MODELS (Jerry Lucas)		JURISPRUDENTIAL INQUIRY (Donald Oliver)	DESENSITIZATION
COGNITIVE GROWTH (Lawrence Kohlberg & Irving Sigel)			ASSERTIVENESS TRAINING
BIOLOGICAL SCIENCE INQUIRY (Joseph Schwab)		LABORATORY TRAINING	
		SOCIAL SIMULATION	

Adapted from: Joyce, B., & Weil, M. (1986). *Models of Teaching* (3rd ed.). Englewood Cliffs, NJ: Prentice-Hall.

"The power of any given model of teaching is relative to any other model (and is affected by the style of the learner as well). Even when one model is clearly the most powerful with respect to the objective sought, one may not necessarily select that model at any given time because another model boosts other objectives deserving some priority or because a different model will reach the learner more clearly and effectively."

- Joyce & Weil (1986) -

For classroom improvement, we and others have found that teachers must work simultaneously (but not necessarily at the same pace) on all four dimensions - content, classroom management, instructional skills, and instructional strategies. For both teachers and students, the combined capacity to manage the classroom, the continuous acquisition of proven instructional strategies and skills, and the focus on desired educational goals and content are essential.

- Michael Fullan, Barrie Bennett,
& Carol Rolheiser-Bennett (1990) -

B. Bennett, C. Rolheiser-Bennett, L. Stevahn (1991)
Cooperative Learning: Where Heart Meets Mind

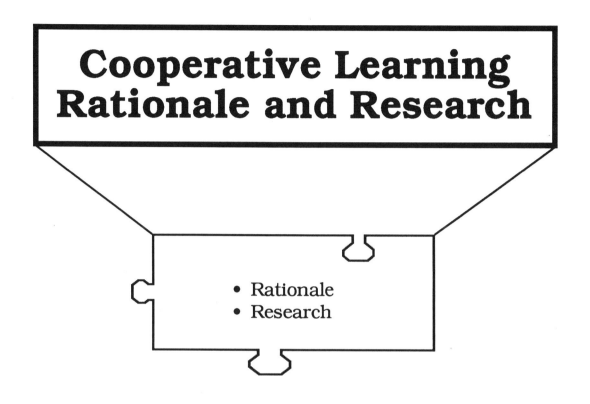

Chapter 2

Cooperative Learning Rationale and Research

- Rationale
- Research

Overview

This chapter considers purposes and supporting research for using cooperative learning in the classroom. The questions that start the chapter personalize thinking about desired learning outcomes for students and lead to a rationale for selecting cooperative learning as a possible teaching strategy to achieve those outcomes. A summary of the research on cooperative learning follows.

B. Bennett, C. Rolheiser-Bennett, L. Stevahn (1991)
Cooperative Learning: Where Heart Meets Mind

Learning Goals

September

I learned...

What would you like students to be able to say they've gained from being in your classroom?

I developed...

I experienced...

Now I can...

Discuss your goals for student learning with a colleague. What else might you add?

I felt...

June

B. Bennett, C. Rolheiser-Bennett, L. Stevahn (1991)
Cooperative Learning: Where Heart Meets Mind

What Goals will Cooperative Learning Help Students Achieve?

The page that follows summarizes the research on cooperative learning. Elaborations may be found in a variety of sources, including those resources listed in the reference section of this book.

After reviewing the research, consider:

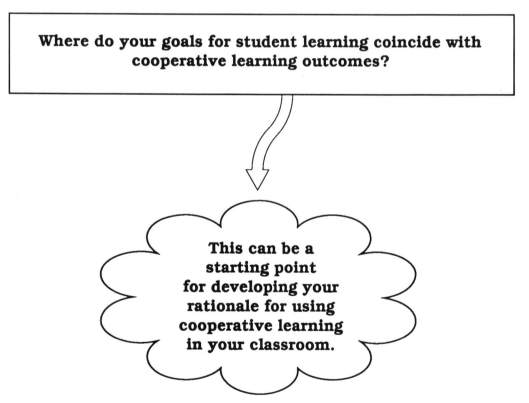

Where do your goals for student learning coincide with cooperative learning outcomes?

This can be a starting point for developing your rationale for using cooperative learning in your classroom.

Research

When Cooperative Learning is implemented effectively we can expect ...

- Higher Self-esteem
- Higher Achievement
- Increased Retention
- Greater Social Support
- More On-task behavior
- Greater Collaborative Skills
- Greater Intrinsic Motivation
- Increased Perspective Taking
- Better Attitudes Toward School
- Better Attitudes Toward Teachers
- Greater Use of Higher Level Reasoning
- More Positive Psychological Adjustment

- Johnson, Johnson, & Holubec (1990) -

There is nothing as practical as good theory ...

Certainly one of the hallmarks of the teaching profession is our inquiry into the theory and practice of teaching and learning and the decisions we make as a result of that inquiry.

B. Bennett, C. Rolheiser-Bennett, L. Stevahn (1991)
Cooperative Learning: Where Heart Meets Mind

Developing A Rationale

B. Bennett, C. Rolheiser-Bennett, L. Stevahn (1991)
Cooperative Learning: Where Heart Meets Mind

Part II

What Makes Cooperative Learning "Go?"

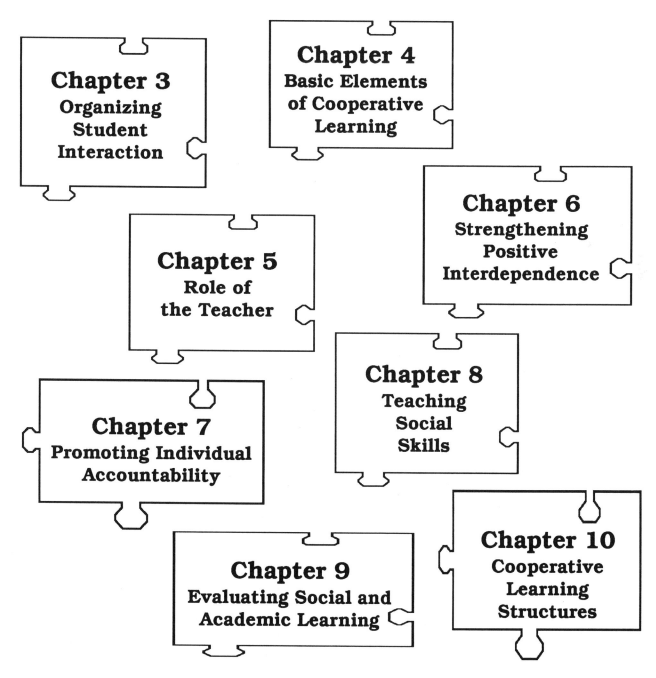

Chapter 3
Organizing Student Interaction

Chapter 4
Basic Elements of Cooperative Learning

Chapter 6
Strengthening Positive Interdependence

Chapter 5
Role of the Teacher

Chapter 8
Teaching Social Skills

Chapter 7
Promoting Individual Accountability

Chapter 9
Evaluating Social and Academic Learning

Chapter 10
Cooperative Learning Structures

B. Bennett, C. Rolheiser-Bennett, L. Stevahn (1991)
Cooperative Learning: Where Heart Meets Mind

Part II

What Makes Cooperative Learning "Go?"

Overview

Understanding how to effectively apply cooperative learning in the classroom begins with understanding and integrating the ideas developed in chapters 3-10.

- **Chapter 3 – Organizing Student Interaction** explores dimensions of cooperative, individualistic, and competitive interaction patterns.

- **Chapter 4 – Basic Elements of Cooperative Learning** identifies five elements basic to cooperative learning.

- **Chapter 5 – The Role of the Teacher** explores the teacher's role in planning and facilitating cooperative lessons.

- **Chapter 6 – Strengthening Positive Interdependence** considers ways to strengthen positive interdependence within and among groups.

- **Chapter 7 – Promoting Individual Accountability** considers ways to facilitate individual responsibility for learning.

- **Chapter 8 – Teaching Social Skills** presents ideas for teaching social interaction skills.

- **Chapter 9 – Evaluating Social and Academic Learning** examines the academic and social evaluation of cooperative learning.

- **Chapter 10 – Cooperative Learning Structures** summarizes a variety of ways to structure cooperative experiences.

B. Bennett, C. Rolheiser-Bennett, L. Stevahn (1991)
Cooperative Learning: Where Heart Meets Mind

Chapter 3

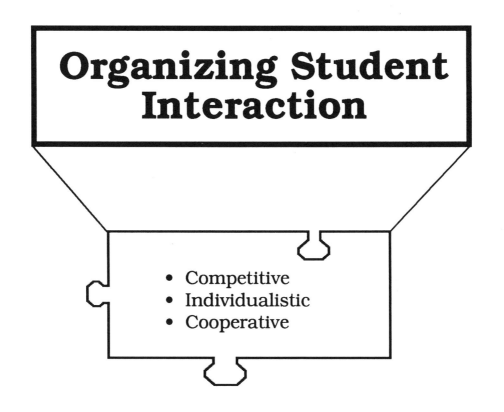

Organizing Student Interaction

- Competitive
- Individualistic
- Cooperative

Overview

This chapter explores differences between competitive, individualistic, and cooperative interaction patterns among students. The questions that start the chapter focus attention on the importance of all three interaction patterns for learning. Explanations of competitive, individualistic, and cooperative learning are followed by activity ideas that can be used with students in your class to explore and compare the different interaction patterns.

Opinion Poll

Do we need to educate students to be winners?
When are competitive skills beneficial?

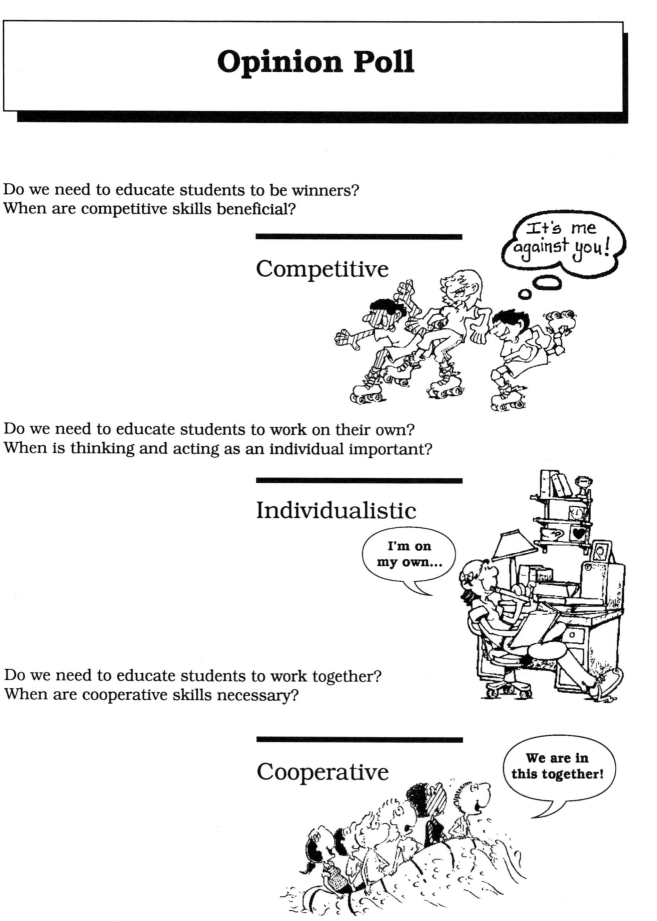

Competitive

Do we need to educate students to work on their own?
When is thinking and acting as an individual important?

Individualistic

Do we need to educate students to work together?
When are cooperative skills necessary?

Cooperative

B. Bennett, C. Rolheiser-Bennett, L. Stevahn (1991)
Cooperative Learning: Where Heart Meets Mind

Organizing Student Interaction

Learning activities or assignments can be organized in three ways. Each helps determine how students will interact with one another, the teacher, and the learning material.

Competitive

Individualistic

Cooperative

What activities in your life exemplify each interaction pattern?

Characteristics of Each Interaction Pattern

Competitive

Me instead of you

- If I achieve my goal you cannot achieve yours and vice versa.
- My success depends on doing better than you.
- I do not want competitors to do as well as me.
- Often my concern for self is greater than my concern for others.
- Interpersonal comparisons are made.
- Evaluation is norm-referenced.

Individualistic

Me alone

- My achieving my goal is unrelated to you achieving yours.
- My success is independent of the success or failure of others.
- I am accountable to myself.
- Evaluation is criterion-referenced.

Cooperative

We as well as me

- I can attain my goal only if you attain yours.
- Group success depends on the success of all members.
- We care about the success and effort of our group.
- We have greater concern for one another.
- Evaluation is criterion-referenced.

B. Bennett, C. Rolheiser-Bennett, L. Stevahn (1991)
Cooperative Learning: Where Heart Meets Mind

In the classroom, what might you say to organize different types of student interaction?

Consider the following example ...

"Today in class you will complete a set of math problems."

Competitive:
"You've got 30 minutes to work these math problems on your own. Your grade will be determined by comparing your score to the top score in the class." (Grades are distributed on a normal curve.)

Individualistic:
"You've got 30 minutes to work these math problems on your own. Your individual grade will be determined as follows:
A — 90 - 100%
B — 80 - 89%
C — 70 - 79%
D — 60 - 69%
F — Below 60%."

Cooperative:
"Your team has 30 minutes to complete the set of math problems. Your group will submit one answer sheet. Each person will sign the sheet to indicate that you all agree and can explain the answers if called upon to do so. Be sure to help one another understand as you work."
(Note: Assignment of grades for initial cooperative activities is avoided. For future grading options see Chapter 9.)

How might you utilize all three interaction patterns?

When deciding a balance for **competitive**, **individualistic**, and **cooperative** patterns in your classroom, the following considerations may guide your thinking:

- The goals of education and curriculum in your setting ...

- You and your philosophical beliefs about teaching and learning ...

- Your students and the skills they have developed and need to develop ...

- The cultures represented in your class ...

- Other ... (What additional considerations are important in your situation?) ...

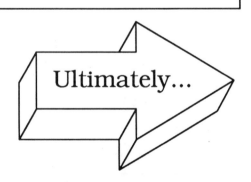

Ultimately...

B. Bennett, C. Rolheiser-Bennett, L. Stevahn (1991)
Cooperative Learning: Where Heart Meets Mind

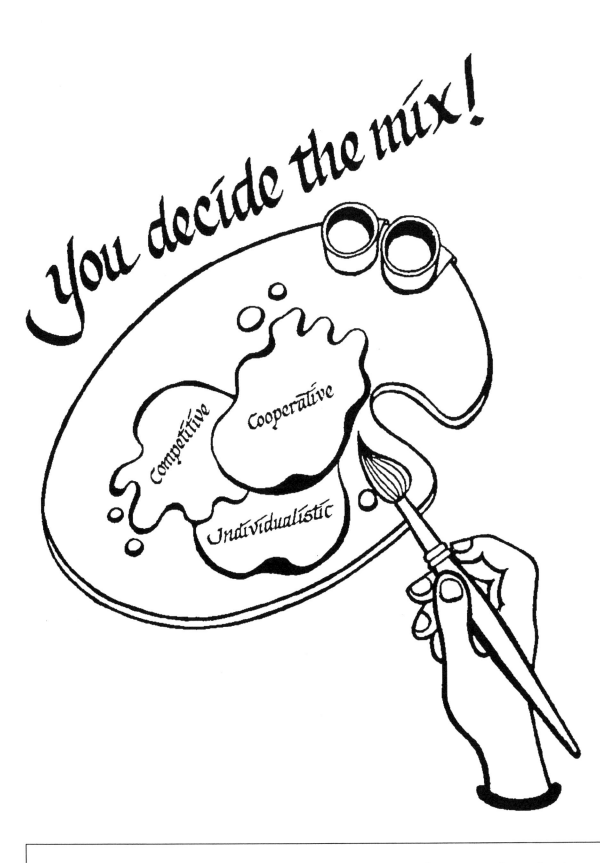

You decide the mix!

Competitive   Cooperative   Individualistic

"Teachers should use all three ... in an integrated way, and students should be taught the skills necessary to function in all three types of situations."

— Johnson, Johnson, & Holubec (1986) —

Helping Students Understand Interaction Patterns

Pages 27 and 28 provide ideas for introducing competitive, individualistic, and cooperative activities in a variety of classrooms. After experiencing each interaction pattern, students can debrief and compare what they noticed and how they felt about each experience (see pages 29 and 30, **Debriefing Interaction Patterns**). For example, competitive, individualistic, and cooperative activities could be designed using the **Thinking Creatively** page that follows.

⇩

To organize a **Competitive** experience...

Instruct students to complete the first question on their own (e.g., "List 10 objects that are blue and soft"). Tell students that the first person to finish will win. After the activity, ask students what they noticed and how they felt during the competition.

⇩

To organize an **Individualistic** experience...

Next, instruct students to complete the second question on their own (e.g., "Sometimes it is a good idea to be late. List 10 occasions when being late is good"). Set a reasonable time limit for completing the task (so that students will not feel rushed) and tell students that every individual who completes the task will be recognized. After the activity, ask students what they noticed and how they felt while they worked individualistically.

⇩

To organize a **Cooperative** experience...

Finally, arrange students in small groups (two or three students per group). Instruct students to work together to complete the third question (e.g., "Name 10 new jobs that will exist 20 years from now. Explain each job that you list"). Discuss the importance of encouraging and including every partner. Help students generate phrases they could use to encourage each other. At the end of the activity, have students assess how well they encouraged each other and worked together. Also, ask students what they could do next time to work together even better. Debrief the entire experience by asking students what they noticed and how they felt during the cooperative experience.

(Note: The activity you select to introduce cooperative interaction should be simple, enjoyable, and non-threatening. The purpose of this beginning activity is to build a sense of trust and communication in the group.)

B. Bennett, C. Rolheiser-Bennett, L. Stevahn (1991)
Cooperative Learning: Where Heart Meets Mind

Thinking Creatively

Students can answer the following questions competitively, individualistically, or cooperatively.

1. List 10 objects that are blue and soft.

2. Sometimes it is a good idea to be late. List 10 occasions when being late is good.

3. Name 10 new jobs that will exist 20 years from now. Explain each job that you list.

4. List 8 ways to help you remember a list of names or ideas.

5. List all the words you can make using the letters in CELEBRATION.

6. List as many group or individual viewpoints as possible on the use of steroids in sports.

7. You have been asked to design new and unusual school bells. Name and describe what 5 of these will look like.

8. Dogs hate to have baths. Think of 8 ways to persuade a dog to be washed.

9. Brainstorm ways to use a toothpick. List as many as possible in 5 minutes.

10. If there were no television, list 20 ways life would be different.

What else might you add?

In Your Curriculum...

What activities could you use to introduce students to competitive, individualistic, and cooperative interaction patterns?

Brainstorm possibilities with a colleague!
For example...

1. Find hidden shapes, objects, or numbers in a drawing.

2. Solve a mathematical problem or puzzle involving logic.

3. Solve a riddle or puzzling situation.

4.

5.

6.

7.

8.

B. Bennett, C. Rolheiser-Bennett, L. Stevahn (1991)
Cooperative Learning: Where Heart Meets Mind

Debriefing Interaction Patterns
(Sample Format)

After students experience each interaction pattern, ask:

- How did you feel?

- What did you notice?

Reproduce the form below (e.g., on a chalkboard, poster, or transparency) and have students record reactions in the appropriate columns. Typical responses include:

Competitive	Individualistic	Cooperative
• Anxious • Pressured • Why bother? • Can't win • Not my subject • Motivated • Challenged	• Not as pressured • Neutral • Don't care • Frustrated • Not my subject • O.K. • Like working on my own	• Supported • Successful • Fun ! • Encouraged • Responsible • Pressure (to follow through)

After all columns are complete, have students compare and contrast their reactions to the three experiences. The page that follows presents possible questions to guide discussion.

B. Bennett, C. Rolheiser-Bennett, L. Stevahn (1991)
Cooperative Learning: Where Heart Meets Mind

Discussion Questions
For Debriefing Interaction Patterns

1. **What conclusions can you draw about competitive, individualistic, and cooperative work?**
   (Sample answer: the number of positive reactions increased as students moved from a competitive to an individualistic to a cooperative experience)

2. **When is competition motivating?**
   (Sample answers: when you feel you have a chance to win, when you know you can be successful, when the content or task interests you, etc.)

3. **When is working on your own beneficial?**
   (Sample answers: when you understand and can successfully complete the task, when you are self-motivated, etc.)

4. **How is cooperative groupwork helpful?**
   (Sample answers: partners can explain material to one another and coach each other, you don't feel alone, many ideas aid problem-solving, more people are successful, etc.)

5. **How is "pressure" in cooperative groupwork different from "pressure" in competitive activities?**
   (Sample answer: "pressure" in cooperative groupwork often stems from feeling responsible to partners for "following through" with learning, "pressure" in competitive activities often stems from knowing you will be compared to opponents)

6. **What is difficult about working in groups?**
   (Sample answers: partners must listen to one another, share responsibility, pace groupwork, reach agreement, solve conflicts, etc.)

B. Bennett, C. Rolheiser-Bennett, L. Stevahn (1991)
Cooperative Learning: Where Heart Meets Mind

Chapter 4

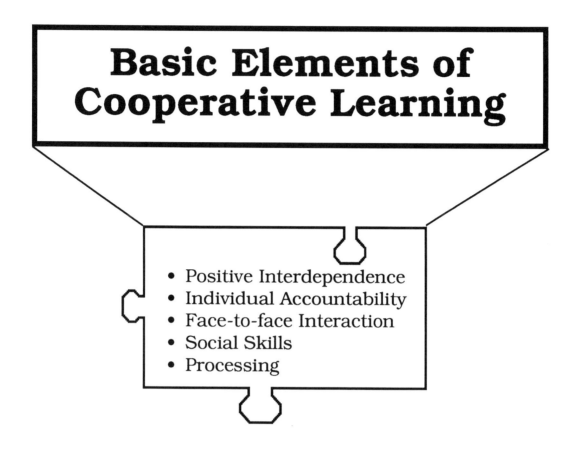

Basic Elements of Cooperative Learning

- Positive Interdependence
- Individual Accountability
- Face-to-face Interaction
- Social Skills
- Processing

Overview

This chapter outlines foundational concepts of cooperative learning. The questions that start the chapter focus attention on benefits and challenges you have experienced when using small groups. The chapter continues by identifying and explaining five elements fundamental to effective cooperative small group learning: (1) positive interdependence, (2) individual accountability, (3) face-to-face interaction, (4) social skills, and (5) processing. These elements assist us in distinguishing cooperative groups from traditional groups. The activity page that concludes the chapter fosters discussion on those distinguishing elements.

Examining Your Experiences

1. How have you used small groups in your teaching situation?

2. What are the benefits you've experienced?

3. What challenges/frustrations have you faced?

B. Bennett, C. Rolheiser-Bennett, L. Stevahn (1991)
Cooperative Learning: Where Heart Meets Mind

Five Basic Elements of Cooperative Learning *

Facilitating effective small group learning means helping group members perceive the importance of working together and interacting in helpful ways. This can be accomplished by incorporating five basic elements into small group experiences. Ultimately, these elements become tools for solving problems associated with groupwork.

Positive Interdependence
When all members of a group feel connected to each other in the accomplishment of a common goal. All individuals must succeed for the group to succeed. (Refer to Chapter 6 for further information.)

Individual Accountability
Holding every member of the group responsible to demonstrate accomplishment of the learning. (Refer to Chapter 7 for further information.)

Face-to-face Interaction
When group members are close in proximity to each other and dialogue with each other in ways that promote continued progress.

Social Skills
Human interaction skills that enable groups to function effectively (e.g., taking turns, encouraging, listening, giving help, clarifying, checking understanding, probing). Such skills enhance communication, trust, leadership, decision-making, and conflict management. (Refer to Chapter 8 for further information.)

Processing
When group members assess their collaborative efforts and target improvements. (Refer to Chapter 9 for further information.)

* See: Johnson, D.W., Johnson, R.T., & Holubec, E.J. (1990). *Cooperation in the Classroom* (rev. ed.). Edina, MN: Interaction Book Company.

Cooperative Learning

Cooperative Learning is Groupwork, but not ALL Groupwork is Cooperative Learning!

What is the Difference?

Cooperative Learning Groups	Traditional Learning Groups
Positive Interdependence is structured	Positive Interdependence is not structured
Individuals demonstrate accountability for self and teammates	Individuals are accountable to self, not teammates
Team membership is heterogeneous	Team membership is homogeneous
Teambuilding activities promote trust, commitment, and group cohesion	No teambuilding activities
Teammates share leadership responsibilities	One teammate is appointed leader
Social skills are taught, practiced, and processed	Social skills are assumed (but are often lacking)
The teacher continually monitors groupwork, documents observations, provides feedback on group functioning, and intervenes when necessary	The teacher does not monitor groupwork or provide feedback on group functioning

Adapted from: Johnson, D.W., Johnson, R.T., & Holubec, E.J. (1990). *Cooperation in the Classroom* (rev. ed.). Edina, MN: Interaction Book Company.

B. Bennett, C. Rolheiser-Bennett, L. Stevahn (1991)
Cooperative Learning: Where Heart Meets Mind

Basic Elements Activity

How are the basic elements of cooperative learning reflected in the following statements? With a colleague, take turns analyzing each statement and its relationship to the basic elements.

1. Cooperative learning groups are based on positive interdependence among group members. Goals are formulated so that teammates value one another and care about each other's academic performance and social performance.

2. Students are responsible to master the material and encourage the achievement of all teammates. Both individual and group progress are monitored and assessed.

4. Leadership is equally shared among group members.

5. Group members are expected to provide help and encouragement to one another in order to ensure that all members do the assigned work.

6. Students use purposeful talk as a vehicle for understanding. The talk aids idea clarification, promotes exploration, and encourages personalization of information.

7. Students' goals focus on maximizing each member's learning as well as maintaining effective working relationships among members.

8. The social skills students need to work cooperatively (such as leadership, communication, trust building, and conflict management) are taught and practiced.

9. The teacher and students analyze how well the groups are functioning. Goals for improvement are formulated.

10. Group members arrange themselves in close proximity and dialogue in ways that promote successful accomplishment of team goals.

"Jules Romains, the eminent French novelist and dramatist, began his career by working out a theory [Unanimism] which he later put into several excellent plays and stories. This is the idea that collections of people remain individuals until a single event or purpose or emotion molds them into groups, and that then the group lives, feels, and thinks in a way of its own, superior in energy and intensity to the activity of any one of its members."

- Gilbert Highet (1950) -

B. Bennett, C. Rolheiser-Bennett, L. Stevahn (1991)
Cooperative Learning: Where Heart Meets Mind

Chapter 5

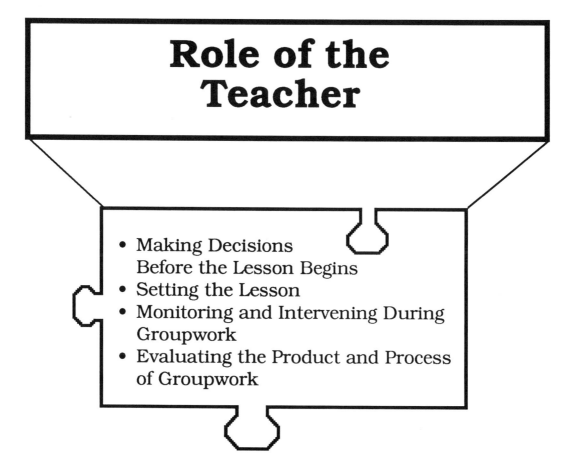

Role of the Teacher

- Making Decisions Before the Lesson Begins
- Setting the Lesson
- Monitoring and Intervening During Groupwork
- Evaluating the Product and Process of Groupwork

Overview

This chapter considers four main phases that comprise cooperative lessons and explores the teacher's role in each:

- Making Decisions Before the Lesson Begins
- Setting the Lesson
- Monitoring and Intervening During Groupwork
- Evaluating the Product and Process of Groupwork

The questions that start the chapter initiate thinking about important teacher behaviors within each phase, followed by a page for recording personal concerns. The chapter proceeds by summarizing key aspects of the teacher's role in each phase, then directs attention to a sample Lesson Planning Guide. The chapter concludes by prompting reflection on the implementation concerns targeted at the start and encouraging discussion of options for dealing with the concerns.

The Role of the Teacher

Envision yourself facilitating a cooperative lesson. Then, with a colleague, anticipate and discuss:

1. What will you have to consider before the students are involved in the lesson?

2. What needs to be considered when initiating the lesson? (i.e., What direction/instructions will students need to be successful?)

3. What will you do while students are working in their cooperative groups?

4. How will closure be accomplished to maximize student learning?

Use the following page to record any questions or concerns that surface during your discussion.

B. Bennett, C. Rolheiser-Bennett, L. Stevahn (1991)
Cooperative Learning: Where Heart Meets Mind

Questions and Concerns

I would like to know . . .

Directions: List questions and concerns you have regarding the teacher's role in planning and implementing cooperative lessons.

1. How do you set up the groups?

2. What is optimal group size?

3. How long do you keep groups together?

4.

5.

6.

7.

8.

9.

10.

Use these questions to guide your inquiry as you begin to explore the teacher's role in planning and implementing cooperative lessons.

The Role of the Teacher: Four Phases

Consider these four phases in both planning and implementing cooperative lessons:

I Making Organizational Decisions Before the Lesson Begins

II Setting the Lesson

III Monitoring and Intervening During Groupwork

IV Evaluating the Product and Process of Groupwork

Important aspects of each phase are briefly discussed in the pages that follow.

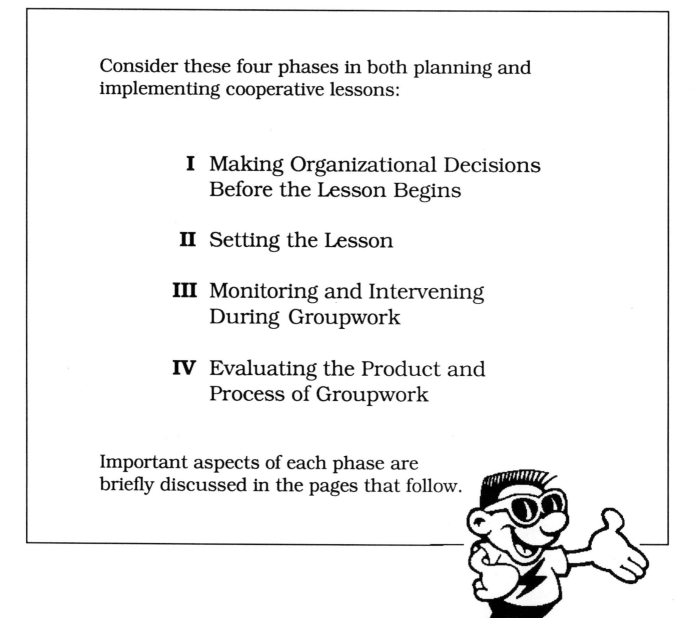

B. Bennett, C. Rolheiser-Bennett, L. Stevahn (1991)
Cooperative Learning: Where Heart Meets Mind

Role of the Teacher in Cooperative Learning *

Part I
Making Decisions Before the Lesson Begins

A. Determining the Academic and Social Objectives
Cooperative lessons always have two objectives: academic and social.
1. Academic objectives communicate the cognitive content and skills to be learned.
2. Social objectives communicate the interaction skills that are emphasized and practiced.

B. Determining the Appropriate Group Size
The size of the group facilitates the attainment of the academic and social objectives.
Consider the following when deciding group size:
1. Partner work tends to promote involvement. It's difficult to get left out of a pair. Start with pairs or groups of three.
2. Tasks that demand diversity in thinking or a wide range of skills and expertise are often most successfully accomplished in larger groups (e.g., 3 or 4).
3. The larger the group, the more skillful the group members must be in maintaining good working relations.
4. The nature of a task or materials available may dictate the group size.
5. The shorter the time periods the smaller the groups need to be in order to maximize involvement.

C. Assigning the Students to Groups
The mix of the groups is important in helping teams achieve the goals of cooperative learning. The following considerations will assist in deciding the most appropriate mix:
1. Heterogeneous groups are recommended for most tasks. The mix can be by ability, cultural background, gender, learning style, etc. For example, a math group may consist of a high, middle, and low ability student.
2. Teacher selected groups usually have the best mix. By assigning groups, teachers can carefully build supportive group situations for isolates or students with special needs.
3. Determining how long groups should stay together demands careful observation of teammates during cooperative activities. As a general rule, keep groups together long enough for them to be successful. Breaking up groups that are having difficulty is usually counterproductive as students learn to avoid dealing with problems. Teams that are struggling will need guidance in problem-solving, but persistence usually pays.

D. Arranging the Room
Consider clustering chairs or desks before students arrive, teaching a procedure for moving into groups quickly and quietly, and specifying group locations (e.g., with markers or diagrams). The room arrangement affects how the students will interact. Arranging teammates so they are "nose-to-nose, toes-to-toes" and providing paths between groups for easy teacher access increases the likelihood that group members will successfully interact.

E. Preparing the Materials
Prepare any necessary materials or incentives.

* See: Johnson, D.W., Johnson, R.T., & Holubec, E.J. (1990). *Cooperation in the Classroom* (rev. ed.). Edina, MN: Interaction Book Company.

When it Comes to Grouping Remember ...

B. Bennett, C. Rolheiser-Bennett, L. Stevahn (1991)
Cooperative Learning: Where Heart Meets Mind

Role of the Teacher in Cooperative Learning

Part II
Setting the Lesson

A. Structuring Positive Interdependence

Students are more likely to work together when they feel linked to one another and believe they need one another to accomplish the group's task. Carefully structuring positive interdependence into the lesson can enhance those feelings and beliefs. Fundamentally, this means formulating a mutual team goal as well as establishing shared responsibility among teammates to achieve the goal. For example, students are more likely to feel committed to working together toward a common goal when every teammate has a meaningful role, materials are shared, and group success is rewarded. Similarly, class-wide interdependence can be promoted by setting a class goal attainable only when all teams achieve success. Chapter 6 provides additional information on ways to build interdependent relationships within and among cooperative groups.

B. Explaining the Academic Task

To ensure students understand what their group is trying to accomplish, the teacher needs to clearly explain and, if required, provide a model for the academic task. In addition, the teacher can help the students see the purpose for the task by having them relate it to their past, present, or possibly future experiences. Also, to facilitate a smooth transition into the groups, the teacher might check to see if the students clearly understand their assignment before beginning.

C. Explaining the Criteria for Success

Groups should know how their success will be measured or evaluated. Students and the teacher can generate this criteria jointly. For example, are the teams or groups to:
1. Simply complete a task? (e.g., "Finish your team map within 30 minutes.")
2. Answer correctly? (e.g., "A score of 90 to 100 will be an "A" grade.")
3. Provide a minimum number of ideas or justifications? (e.g., "Give at least 10 reasons to support your position.")
4. Exhibit particular social skills? (e.g., "Be prepared to provide evidence that your group used positive comments while working together.")

D. Structuring Individual Accountability

Individual accountability is built into a lesson when students know beforehand that there will be individual follow-up to the task and/or social skills. Structuring individual accountability by the teacher raises the students' level of concern, and subsequently, their involvement. Ways to help ensure individual accountability include randomly calling on students to answer for their teams, having all teammates sign a statement verifying participation and mastery of the material, and 'spot checking' teammates during groupwork. See Chapter 7 for additional information.

E. Specifying Desired Social Behaviors

The teacher or students specify the behaviors that are both appropriate and expected during the lesson. The more specific the desirable behaviors are, the greater the likelihood that students will demonstrate those behaviors. Helping students understand why a social skill is important and what that skill "looks like and sounds like" ensures greater student success with the skill. Clearly and meaningfully defining a social skill also facilitates effective student processing of their use of that skill. Chapter 8 provides further information on the teaching of social skills.

Role of the Teacher in Cooperative Learning

Part III
Monitoring and Intervening During Groupwork

A. Monitoring Students' Behavior

While teams are working the teacher moves around the room to observe student progress. This promotes student accountability and enables the teacher to decide when intervention is appropriate. Recording observations is useful for providing feedback to groups during processing. Students can also assist in monitoring (e.g., by being the team "observer"), but should only do so after a clear understanding of the behavior being monitored has been attained.

B. Intervening During Group Work

Teacher intervention may be needed to provide task assistance or to teach collaborative skills.

1. **Providing Task Assistance** may include clarifying directions, reviewing procedures, teaching task skills, or asking and answering questions. When providing task assistance, try to draw upon the skills and expertise of the group members as much as possible. That helps guide teammates to use each other as resources first. For example, if a student asks a question, the teacher can redirect the question back to the team instead of responding.

2. **Teaching Collaborative Skills** may be necessary when a group is not functioning cooperatively. When that occurs, the need for learning helpful social interaction skills is immediate and therefore meaningful. For example, in a group where one person is not contributing, teammates need to learn the skill of "getting everyone involved."

When intervening, find ways to turn the problem-solving back to group members. This tends to increase individual commitment to the group as well as maximize learning.

Although intervention will be needed at times, intervene only when necessary. For example, in tasks where the group process or product is unpredictable or complex, teacher interference may result in reducing collaboration within the group, lowering the level of thinking, and increasing the probability that students will defer to the teacher (Cohen & Lotan, 1987).

B. Bennett, C. Rolheiser-Bennett, L. Stevahn (1991)
Cooperative Learning: Where Heart Meets Mind

Role of the Teacher in Cooperative Learning

Part IV
Evaluating the Product and Process of Groupwork

Providing Closure

Students need opportunities to summarize and reflect on their learning. The teacher's role is to facilitate those opportunities. Closure provides a chance for both teacher and students to highlight major points, ask questions, or generate insights. Closure includes both evaluating the academic work and processing the social skills.

1. **Evaluating the academic objectives** involves an assessment of how well the students carried out and completed the assigned task and provision of subsequent feedback. This can be accomplished by the teacher or the students. For example:

    a. the teacher may randomly select one group member to share the group's response to a question, or
    b. group members may get together after an individual quiz to discuss questions or rework problems with which they experienced difficulties.

2. **Evaluating the social objectives** involves processing how well the group functioned, and in particular, how successfully group members enacted the expected social skill. Processing involves two aspects:

    • reflecting on what went well in the group
    • determining what could be improved for next time

    For example, this can be accomplished by:

    a. individuals specifically sharing something they said that contributed to their group's success, and
    b. each team agreeing on one way to improve next time teammates work together.

Student reflection on group functioning is a critical element to successful cooperative learning.

A Teacher's Role ...
In Brief

1. Arrange Groups

2. Provide Warm-up / Community-building (especially if groups are new . . . see Chapter 11 for practical ideas)

3. Teach / Emphasize the

    Social Skill 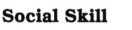 • Looks like . . .
    • Sounds like . . .

4. Give directions, consider roles, and check understanding

5. Monitor while groups work, and intervene if necessary

6. Facilitate feedback on the academic learning

7. Facilitate reflection on the

    Social Skill 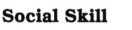 • How well was it used?
    • Ways to improve?

B. Bennett, C. Rolheiser-Bennett, L. Stevahn (1991)
Cooperative Learning: Where Heart Meets Mind

Sample Format
for Cooperative Lessons

The following Cooperative Learning Lesson Planning Guide outlines key aspects of the teacher's role in planning and facilitating cooperative lessons. Where do you see the basic elements of cooperative learning throughout the lesson?

COOPERATIVE LEARNING -- LESSON PLANNING GUIDE

DATE: _____   NAME: _____

ACADEMIC OBJECTIVE: _____   GRADE LEVEL: _____

SOCIAL OBJECTIVE: _____   SUBJECT: _____

I   ORGANIZATIONAL DECISIONS PRIOR TO TEACHING

GROUPS: SIZE: ASSIGNMENT: ☐ Heterogeneous   ARRANGING THE ROOM: ☐ Desk Clusters   MATERIALS: ☐ Shared

☐ Homogeneous   ☐ Chair Clusters   ☐ Individual

☐ Floor clusters

Method: _____   ☐ Tables   LIST:

☐ Other...

II   SETTING THE LESSON

POSITIVE INTERDEPENDENCE:	ACADEMIC TASK DIRECTIONS:	CRITERIA FOR SUCCESS:	INDIVIDUAL ACCOUNTABILITY:	INTRODUCING SOCIAL BEHAVIORS:
☐ GOAL ☐ INCENTIVE ☐ RESOURCE ☐ ROLE ☐ ENVIRONMENT ☐ SEQUENCE ☐ IDENTITY ☐ OUTSIDE FORCE ☐ SIMULATION				

III   MONITORING AND INTERVENING

WHO WILL MONITOR GROUP WORK?   HOW WILL MONITORING BE DONE?   WHAT BEHAVIORS WILL BE MONITORED?

TEACHER ☐   INFORMAL NOTES ☐   _____

TEACHER/STUDENTS ☐   FORMAL OBSERVATION SHEET ☐   _____

IV   EVALUATING THE PRODUCT AND PROCESS OF GROUPWORK

ACADEMIC FEEDBACK: SOCIAL SKILL PROCESSING:

(How will academic learning be evaluated?)   (How will students' reflect on social interactions?)

Self-evaluation, by: _____

In Small Group, by: _____

Whole Class, by: _____

Copies of this guide (along with directions for use) are provided in Chapter 13.

Cooperative Learning: An Overall Perspective

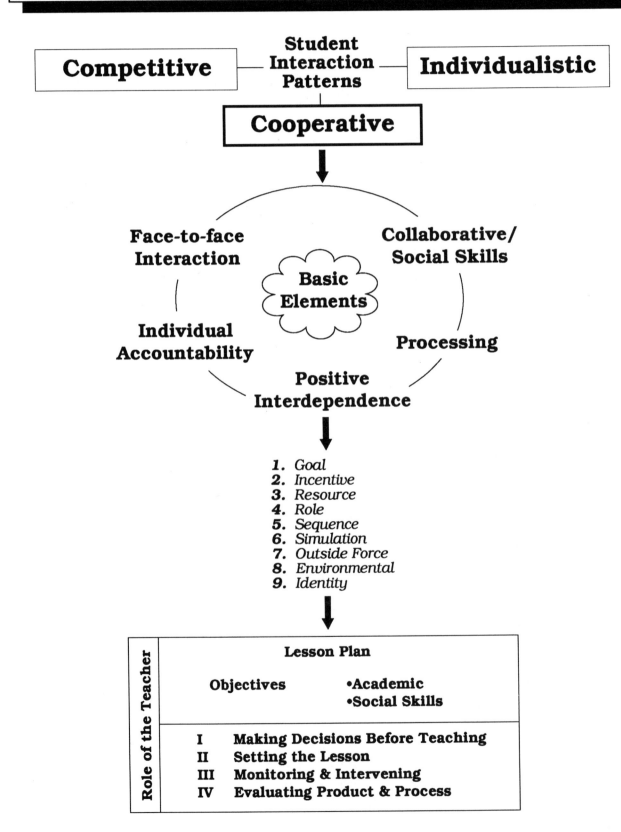

Competitive — Student Interaction Patterns — **Individualistic**

Cooperative

Face-to-face Interaction

Collaborative/ Social Skills

Basic Elements

Individual Accountability

Processing

Positive Interdependence

1. Goal
2. Incentive
3. Resource
4. Role
5. Sequence
6. Simulation
7. Outside Force
8. Environmental
9. Identity

Role of the Teacher	Lesson Plan		
	Objectives	•Academic	
		•Social Skills	
	I	Making Decisions Before Teaching	
	II	Setting the Lesson	
	III	Monitoring & Intervening	
	IV	Evaluating Product & Process	

B. Bennett, C. Rolheiser-Bennett, L. Stevahn (1991)
Cooperative Learning: Where Heart Meets Mind

Revisiting Your Initial Questions and Concerns

Return to the questions and concerns you listed on page 39. Given the information you've considered in this chapter, address each question or concern and discuss your options for action. For example:

1. How do you set up the groups?

   Teacher selection ensures that groups are heterogeneous. Criteria for mixed group membership may be academic ability, learning style, gender, cultural background, personal characteristics, etc. When establishing groups, arrange brief warm-up activities that enable teammates to become comfortable with one another. Warm-ups should help "break the ice," evoke safe self-disclosure, and promote team-building (especially when teammates are challenged to discover what they have in common).

2. What is optimal group size?

3. How long do you keep groups together?

4.

5.

6.

7.

8.

9.

10.

What do you know now that you did not know before? Continue to seek additional information related to each concern as you work your way through the chapters that follow.

"Groupwork changes a teacher's role dramatically. No longer are you a direct supervisor of students, responsible for insuring that they do their work exactly as you direct. No longer is it your responsibility to watch for every mistake and correct it on the spot. Instead, authority is delegated to students and to groups of students. They are in charge of insuring that the job gets done, and that classmates get the help they need. They are empowered to make mistakes, to find out what went wrong, and what might be done about it."

- Elizabeth G. Cohen (1986) -

B. Bennett, C. Rolheiser-Bennett, L. Stevahn (1991)
Cooperative Learning: Where Heart Meets Mind

Chapter 6

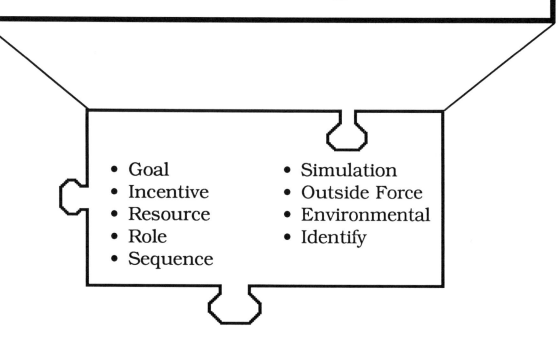

Strengthening Positive Interdependence

- Goal
- Incentive
- Resource
- Role
- Sequence
- Simulation
- Outside Force
- Environmental
- Identify

Overview

This chapter considers ways to strengthen positive interdependence within and among cooperative groups. The questions that start the chapter focus attention on the effect that positive interdependence has on fostering a commitment to work together to accomplish a common goal. The chapter continues by identifying, describing, and illustrating nine types of positive interdependence: Goal, Incentive, Resource, Role, Sequence, Simulation, Outside Force, Environmental, and Identity. Activity pages that follow provide opportunities to test thinking about the various types of positive interdependence by analyzing classroom applications. Ideas for building class interdependence are also considered. The chapter concludes by emphasizing important aspects of positive interdependence, including its use as an effective tool for problem-solving.

Positive Interdependence

Working Toward A Common Goal

Each of the following situations describes a cooperative group effort. With a colleague, review each situation and discuss:

- What factors motivate those involved to contribute to the group effort?
- What roles are necessary for successful accomplishment of the goal?
- What might happen if a group member refuses to work toward the common goal?

1. An airline crew flying a commercial jet . . .

2. A medical staff performing surgery . . .

3. A neighborhood citizens' group organized to lobby for environmental protection . . .

4. A professional baseball team playing for the pennant . . .

5. A school drama club producing a performance . . .

6. A cooperative effort in which you recently participated (describe and analyze) . . .

Positive interdependence exists when all members of a group feel committed to work together to accomplish a shared goal. The following pages explore ways to build positive interdependence within and among groups in classroom situations.

B. Bennett, C. Rolheiser-Bennett, L. Stevahn (1991)
Cooperative Learning: Where Heart Meets Mind

Positive Interdependence

Positive interdependence exists when all group members perceive the need to work together toward the accomplishment of a common task. Simply assigning students to groups does not ensure that students will perceive that need. However, teachers can help teammates feel connected and committed to learn cooperatively by structuring positive interdependence into the group activity. There are a number of ways to do this.

Ways to Structure Positive Interdependence *

1. Goal _____ Common purpose is established. One achieves if all achieve.

2. Incentive _____ All teammates receive the same reward if every teammate succeeds.

3. Resource _____ One set of shared materials per group.

4. Role _____ Each member is assigned a complementary and interconnected role.

5. Sequence _____ Overall task is divided into sub-units and usually performed in a set order.

6. Simulation _____ Teammates work through a hypothetical situation to succeed or survive.

7. Outside Force _____ Groups compete against an outside force.

8. Environmental ___ Group members are bound together by the physical environment.

9. Identity _____ Teammates establish a mutual identity through a group name, flag, motto, song, etc.

---

* See: Johnson, D.W., Johnson, R.T., & Holubec, E.J. (1990). *Cooperation in the Classroom* (rev. ed.). Edina, MN: Interaction Book Company.

B. Bennett, C. Rolheiser-Bennett, L. Stevahn (1991)
Cooperative Learning: Where Heart Meets Mind

Directions

Pages 56 through 78 elaborate ways to structure positive interdependence. For each of the nine types of positive interdependence there is an explanation page followed by an activity page. The activity page provides examples and non-examples designed to clarify thinking about the specified type of positive interdependence. To use each activity page:

- Compare all the **examples** on the page (in the left column) and determine common characteristics.

- Contrast the **examples** to the **non-examples** (in the right column). The **non-examples** do not exhibit the characteristics common to the **examples**.

- Use the common characteristics to write a definition for the type of positive interdependence that the examples illustrate.

- Challenge Activity:
  How could you change each **non-example** into an **example**?

Just follow this plan

Goal Positive Interdependence

. . . exists when teammates perceive they have a mutual goal or outcome to achieve. Striving to reach that outcome is what makes them interdependent. Success depends on all team members reaching that goal. Cooperative goals, activities, or tasks enable students to achieve learning objectives. Goals as well as objectives can be determined by teachers and students. The following examples illustrate the types of goals that may be set:

- creating a product

- completing an assignment

- analyzing information

- scoring above a minimum criterion

- improving a previous score

- using appropriate social skills

Ways to structure goal interdependence:

1. Request one paper or product from the group.

2. Set a minimum criterion for the number of correct answers from the group or number of times learners are to exhibit a targeted social skill while working together.

3. Accept individualized assignments only when all teammates have completed their homework (e.g., Mary's math problems and Paulo's science questions). This makes partners responsible for checking and helping each other to achieve their team goal.

Extend your thinking about **Goal Positive Interdependence** by analyzing the examples on the next page.

B. Bennett, C. Rolheiser-Bennett, L. Stevahn (1991)
Cooperative Learning: Where Heart Meets Mind

Goal Interdependence

Examples

1. Your team goal is to make sure everyone in your group understands the material related to the three major types of foreign aid.

2. Each team is to produce one diagram, with every member contributing.

3. To achieve success on the assignment, everyone in your group must contribute at least five ideas to promote world peace.

4. Your team will be finished when all members of your group have contributed their part of the experiment and can explain all parts of the experiment.

Non-Examples

1. You may use this study period to work individually on any assignment of your choice.

2. Every individual is to complete and submit the assignment by tomorrow. Late papers will not be accepted.

3. Work at your own pace and in 30 minutes be ready to submit whatever you have completed. Your individual grade will be based on the originality of your thinking.

4. Your assignment will be graded on the normal curve.

What characteristics do all the **Examples** have in common?

Definition: Goal interdependence exists when . . .

Incentive Positive Interdependence

. . . exists when each member of the team works to achieve an incentive that will be realized only when the cooperative goal has been met. Either everyone in the group is rewarded or no one in the group is rewarded. **For example,** incentive interdependence occurs when all group members earn bonus points to be added to their individual scores because every score in the group was above 80%.

Ways to structure incentive interdependence:

1. Display a group's completed project.
2. Team members get their names printed in the school newspaper when all group members improve individual baseline scores on a given task (e.g., the criterion for Susie on the science quiz is 6/10, for Rajiv 8/10, and for Erika 10/10).
3. The group receives teacher encouragement for accomplishing their task.
4. A group grade is given for the combined efforts of the teammates.

Note: Giving group grades should be approached cautiously. Until all students and parents are familiar with the concept of cooperative learning this type of incentive can be problematic.

Helpful Tips:

- The use of incentives should be consistent with an individual teacher's philosophy and the needs of the students.

- Extrinsic rewards can be powerful motivators when introducing cooperative learning. Nonetheless, as intrinsic motivation becomes apparent (e.g., just wanting to work with their group), there is less of a need for the teacher to structure extrinsic rewards.

- Incentives need to be appealing to students or they don't serve the purpose for which they were intended. Lists of possible incentives can be generated by the students.

Extend your thinking about **Incentive Positive Interdependence** by anlayzing the examples on the next page.

B. Bennett, C. Rolheiser-Bennett, L. Stevahn (1991)
Cooperative Learning: Where Heart Meets Mind

Incentive Interdependence

Examples

1. When all members of your group have completed the assignment you can have free time at one of the learning centers.

2. Once your group finishes editing each other's rough draft, you can brainstorm activities for the class field trip.

3. Everyone in your team will earn bonus points if every member of your group accurately explains at least 9 of the 10 concepts on the quiz.

4. If all group members have shared how they factored their equations and can explain any of the ways when asked, you each can eliminate any five of the homework problems.

Non-Examples

1. The teacher will shake hands with the first person in the class who successfully finishes the assignment.

2. Each person in the class will earn an individual grade.

3. Any individual in the class has a chance to earn bonus points by correctly answering the "Challenge Question."

4. Any person in the class who scores 90% or better will earn an 'A' grade and can add a gold star to the achievement chart.

What characteristics do all of the **Examples** have in common?

Definition: Incentive interdependence exists when . . .

Use of Incentives

An issue regarding the use of tangible incentives is whether or not they are necessary or desirable. If tangible rewards are used, ensure they are earned as a team for joint accomplishment of academic or social goals. As you consider the use of tangible incentives, be creatively cautious as to when, how often, and for whom you use them. They can open or close the doors to intrinsic motivation. Try to use incentives that have a relationship to the learning or are a natural outcome of the learning.

For example, in a grade one classroom, the incentive for groups who successfully completed a task was to make a guess at how many pennies were in a penny jar. They placed their guess in the "guess box." No prize was given to the group whose guess was closest to the correct number. Rather, the teacher used student curiosity about how close the guesses were as a way to open the door of interest into the next unit designed around the concept of estimation. The opportunity to make a guess was an incentive that related to the learning objectives and was a factor in motivating the group to work together to complete the task.

B. Bennett, C. Rolheiser-Bennett, L. Stevahn (1991)
Cooperative Learning: Where Heart Meets Mind

Possible Incentives

Note: Consider incentives that have a relationship to the learning. More importantly, consider incentives that are a natural extension of the activity.

Active Incentives
- read with a friend/study with a classmate
- computer time
- extra time in learning centers
- work on school newspaper/yearbook
- plan class project
- open discussion
- work again with cooperative team

Incentives of Choice
- decide how or when to use free time
- select a topic for discussion, or select the next experiment
- select activities for the class field trip
- bring something special to show the class
- decide where to post work/project
- eliminate part of an assignment
- decide what story the teacher will read to students

Incentives from the Heart
- release time to do volunteer work
- notes of recognition
- pats on the back/handshakes
- take a special note home
- display work in a special place for others in the school to view

Tangible Incentives
- picture taken
- watch selves on video after completion of a presentation
- stars/stickers/bonus points/library pass
- redeemable coupons (e.g., for points, prizes, free time, skip test)
- get a fortune cookie

Fun and Crazy Incentives
- teacher tells a joke or shares a humorous personal experience
- students get to select the color of the teacher's socks for the next day
- teacher writes a funny paragraph (e.g., "My Life as a Banana")

What can you add that reflects your philosophy and would motivate your students to more effectively work together?

B. Bennett, C. Rolheiser-Bennett, L. Stevahn (1991)
Cooperative Learning: Where Heart Meets Mind

Resource Positive Interdependence

... exists when one set of materials or information must be **shared by group members** as a means or way to bring the group together. For example, resources could be materials such as pens, scissors and glue, or sources of information such as articles to read or problems to solve.

Ways to structure resource interdependence:

1. Limit the number of resources among teammates. For example, give a group one textbook, one pencil, and one answer sheet.

2. Provide each group member with a different math problem. Each member must share how they solved their question with the group in order to prepare for a quiz.

3. Jigsaw the materials by making each teammate responsible for utilizing and/or contributing a specific (and often different) resource needed to complete the team task. With younger students, for example, one partner has an address, another has a return address, and the third has a postage stamp to be used in preparing an envelope for mailing. All partners must contribute their resource for the team to succeed. Information can also be jigsawed. With older students who are studying a culture, for example, one teammate might have information on folklore, another on communication, another on economy, and another on sustenance.

Extend your thinking about **Resource Positive Interdependence** by analyzing the examples on the next page.

B. Bennett, C. Rolheiser-Bennett, L. Stevahn (1991)
Cooperative Learning: Where Heart Meets Mind

Resource Interdependence

Examples	**Non-Examples**
1. I will distribute one Activity Sheet per group.	1. All individuals will work on their own Activity Sheet.
2. Your team will be using one book, one answer sheet, and one pencil.	2. Everybody will need their own materials.
3. Teammates will share one computer.	3. Every individual in this class will need a calculator.
4. You and your "Study Buddy" will each get half of the deck of flash cards.	4. All students in the class need to look at their own textbooks.

What characteristics do all of the **Examples** have in common?

Definition: Resource interdependence exists when . . .

Role Positive Interdependence

... exists when each member is assigned a complementary and interconnected role. The roles relate to the task and act as a means to help the group function more effectively. By having each group member perform a role, an emphasis is placed on the value of that person to the group.

There are two types of roles:

Working Roles

Reader
Writer
Summarizer
Time-keeper
etc.

Social Roles

Encourager
Observer
Noise monitor
Energizer
etc.

Helpful Tips:

- Rather than getting caught up in whether to assign social or working roles, focus on what the task and/or student needs dictate are appropriate.

- Each student should experience a variety of roles, allowing them to strengthen weaker skills, reinforce stronger skills, and learn new skills.

- Students will learn new roles more readily when roles are explained or modeled, observed, and acknowledged (e.g., discussed or rewarded).

- Some roles pertain to both social and working categories. For example, a "checker" (the person who checks on the comprehension or learning of group members by asking them to explain, paraphrase, etc.), may be necessary for the group to successfully complete their academic tasks, while at the same time contributing to the involvement of all team members.

Extend your thinking about **Role Positive Interdependence** by analyzing the examples on the next page.

B. Bennett, C. Rolheiser-Bennett, L. Stevahn (1991)
Cooperative Learning: Where Heart Meets Mind

Role Interdependence

Examples

1. In your group of three, one of you will be the **reader**, one of you will be the **card mover**, and one of you will be the **recorder**.

2. There will be a **reader**, **checker**, **coach**, and **summarizer** in your group of four.

3. You will be working with your partner. Brainstorm the jobs that will be needed to complete the task. Ensure each partner has a job.

4. With your partner, decide who will be the **cutter** and who will be the **gluer**.

Non-Examples

1. In your team of three, decide who will be the team leader.

2. There will be a **quizzer** and a **timekeeper** in your group of four.

3. In your team of five, one of you will be the **direction giver**.

4. Appoint a team captain.

What characteristics do all of the **Examples** have in common?

Definition: Role interdependence exists when . . .

Thoughts About Assigning Roles

Be careful that roles do not get in the way of the learning. When students are first learning to work with other students in a cooperative learning environment, you might consider:

- deciding whether or not roles are appropriate for the task or students

- spending time clarifying the reasons for roles and the responsibilities involved in each role (modeling may be useful)

- keeping the academic task simple and enjoyable as students learn appropriate roles.

One problem you may encounter is, "What do I do if the student who is assigned the reader is not a good reader or does not want to be the reader?" or, "What if the student who was assigned to draw would rather read and the person who is assigned to read would rather draw? Should I allow them to switch?"

There exist a number of solutions to the first problem. There is no one best answer.

- We know that we get better by practice and when we receive supportive feedback. Encourage the group to support and help the student learn to read.

- Ensure that the item to be read is at the appropriate level of difficulty for the reader.

- If students who struggle with reading are aware of their task ahead of time, they can practice before the activity.

Second, there are also a variety of solutions regarding the switching of roles.

- One response is to allow students to take the responsibility of assigning roles to each group member. Nonetheless, that does not guarantee they will be stretched to work in areas that are not their strengths.

- Rotating roles is one way to make sure each group member works in all assigned areas.

- A discussion of why roles are appropriate and making that link to the world outside the classroom helps students to see that learning the responsibilities of particular roles is worth the effort.

Remember, don't assign roles for the sake of assigning roles. If you need them, use them; if you don't need them, don't use them.

B. Bennett, C. Rolheiser-Bennett, L. Stevahn (1991)
Cooperative Learning: Where Heart Meets Mind

Sample Roles & Possible Descriptions of Those Roles

Checker ensures that everybody understands the work in progress

Scout seeks additional information from other groups

Timekeeper keeps the group focused on the task and monitors the time

Active Listener repeats or paraphrases what has been said

Questioner seeks information and opinions from other members of the group

Summarizer pulls together the conclusions of the group so that they can be presented coherently

Encourager provides support to members of the group so that they are more enthused about their participation

Materials Manager collects all necessary material for the group

Reader reads material to the group

Pacer keeps the group moving toward the accomplishment of the goal

Observer completes a check list of social skills for the group

This is a basic list. You may wish to include others (painter, cutter, assembler, quality controller, etc.).

Role Reminders

Listing roles can help students remember, as well as carry out their roles. This can be accomplished by distributing role sheets, tickets, cards, buttons, etc. Symbols or illustrations may help younger pupils or non-readers to remember their responsibilities (e.g., a ♡ for encourager, a ✔ for checker).

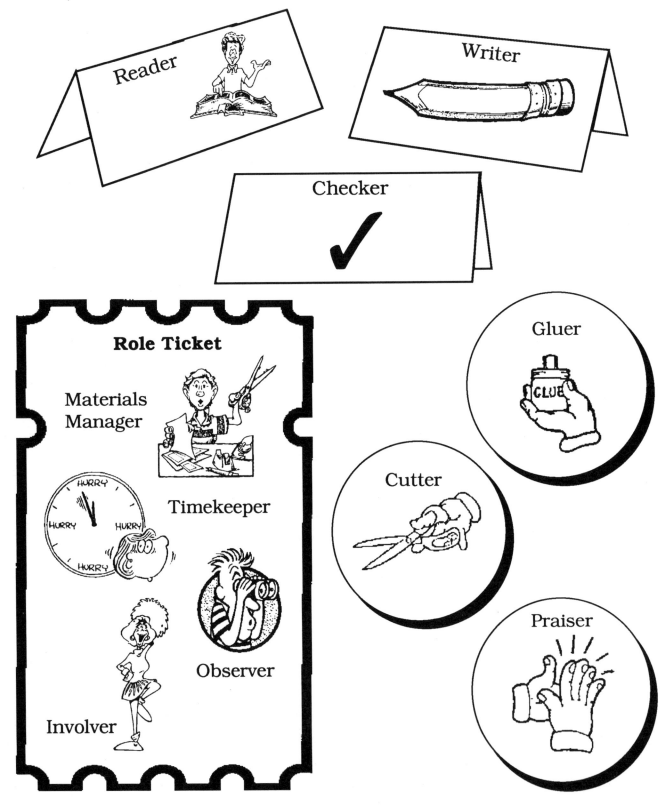

B. Bennett, C. Rolheiser-Bennett, L. Stevahn (1991)
Cooperative Learning: Where Heart Meets Mind

Sequence Positive Interdependence

... exists when an overall team task is accomplished by completing a series of sub-tasks in an established step-by-step order. For example, baking a cake requires that ingredients be gathered, then measured, and then mixed. Each group member can be responsible for completing one step in the sequence. Through sequencing, group members feel more interdependent.

Ways to structure interdependence:

1. Teams produce products in an "assembly line" or "chain reaction" fashion. For example, in designing a class report, one person will research ideas in the library, one person will illustrate, one person will write, and one person will edit the writing.

2. Teammates switch or rotate roles to complete the overall group task. For example, to solve a set of story problems, the first partner will read the problem aloud, then the second partner will write the equation, and the third partner will solve the equation. On the next problem, roles will rotate so that the second partner will read, the third partner will write, and the first partner will solve.

Helpful tips:

- Any task that inherently contains steps or procedures (e.g., conducting a science laboratory experiment, checking out a library book, constructing a bird house, swimming a relay, etc.) lends itself to sequence interdependence.

- In a task that does not have a built-in sequence, rotating the roles can invoke a type of sequencing which, in turn, increases the positive interdependence of the group.

Extend your thinking about **Sequence Positive Interdependence** by analyzing the examples on the next page.

Sequence Interdependence

Examples

1. In your group of four, one of you will complete the first step to solve the equation, one of you will complete the second step, one of you will complete the third step, and one of you will write the answer on the answer sheet. Then, rotate responsibilities.

2. In your group one person traces the object, then the next person cuts it out.

3. In your laboratory groups one person will collect the materials, then the next will prepare the slide, and then the last person will record the observations.

4. In teams of three, students target an issue and decide on three sub-topics to research. Each student explores one of the sub-topics, then the group decides on an appropriate sequence for presentation.

Non-Examples

1. With your teammates, brainstorm as many ideas as possible.

2. Work together to solve the ten equations assigned to your group. Help and check each other as you work.

3. Everyone in your team of four will cut out pictures for your team collage.

4. One partner will write the letter while the other partner prepares the envelope.

What characteristics do all of the **Examples** have in common?

Definition: Sequence interdependence exists when . . .

B. Bennett, C. Rolheiser-Bennett, L. Stevahn (1991)
Cooperative Learning: Where Heart Meets Mind

Simulation Positive Interdependence

... exists when teammates work through a hypothetical situation to succeed and/or survive as a group. The simulation they participate in is a means of binding them to each other. Some examples of "survival" activities are exercises such as Desert Survival, Winter Survival, and Nuclear Attack Survival. Or, the simulation can involve students in milder forms of fantasy such as pretending they are part of a "restaurant team" and they must submit correct bills (math addition problems) in order to keep their "jobs."

Some other examples might be:

- "Pretend you are a group of scientists attempting to find a cure for a deadly disease. As a team, what are the first 3 steps you will take?"

- "You are a group of diplomats planning for world peace. Together, develop a plan."

- "You are a team of dieticians who together must plan a menu that will reduce cholesterol in order to save a person's life."

- "You are a group of English speaking tourists who have spent all your money. Pool your talents and resources to ensure that all of you get home from Tokyo."

Extend your thinking about **Simulation Positive Interdependence** by analyzing the examples on the next page.

Simulation Interdependence

Examples

1. Suppose you and your partners got "snowed in" during a skiing vacation. What steps would you take to ensure your group's survival? Prepare a news broadcast on how your team resolved the situation.

2. Suppose you and your partner are shopping in a large department store, when all of a sudden power is lost and the lights go out. It becomes pitch black inside. What will you do to make sure you both get out of the store safely? Dramatize your plan.

3. Suppose you and your teammates are going on a canoe trip. You can only take a total of 30 kilograms of equipment. As a team, reach agreement on what you should take and compile a list.

4. Imagine you and your teammates are shipwrecked on a deserted island. Develop a plan that would enable all of you to survive.

Non-Examples

1. Pretend you are the last living human being on earth. How will you survive?

2. Suppose you are the fastest runner on earth. Develop a plan to ensure that you are still the fastest runner when you reach the age of 60.

3. How would your life change if you could fly?

4. You have just read *Little Red Riding Hood.* Pretend you are the wolf. Rewrite the story ending to ensure your own survival. Be prepared to dramatize.

What characteristics do all of the **Examples** have in common?

Definition: Simulation interdependence exists when . . .

B. Bennett, C. Rolheiser-Bennett, L. Stevahn (1991)
Cooperative Learning: Where Heart Meets Mind

Outside Force Positive Interdependence

... exists when the group is placed in competition with some outside force. Group members work together, striving to "beat" that outside force. Outside force is a means or way to bring students together. Some examples of outside forces could be:

- other groups

- the group's previous score

- time

- a national standard

- the total score of last year's class.

Helpful Tips:

- Students need to perceive the amount of time given (or any other outside force) as a "challenge to beat" for it to work as a means of strengthening positive interdependence.

- When introducing cooperative learning to students, competition against outside forces can strengthen interdependence within teams. In order to prevent possible negative effects between teams we initially recommend that groups in the same class not compete against each other. A better approach is to use outside forces such as "beating your best time," "last year's average," etc.

- *Teams-Games-Tournaments* (see Robert Slavin, 1986) is a constructive cooperative learning model that provides a structure to effectively manage competition.

Extend your thinking about **Outside Force Positive Interdependence** by analyzing the examples on the next page.

Outside Force Interdependence

Examples

1. Let's see how many groups can beat our last year's record of ten community initiatives.

2. The first team to solve the puzzle will win a prize.

3. Let's see how many teams can be finished before the sand falls through this ten minute hourglass.

4. As a group, try to beat your previous team score.

Non-Examples

1. The student with the highest score will be exempt from the homework assignment.

2. If your team needs more time to finish, you may continue to work on your project together tomorrow.

3. Be sure to help and check each other so that everyone will succeed.

4. When your group is finished, your team may compare and check answers with other teams, helping everyone in the class to achieve 100%.

What characteristics do all of the **Examples** have in common?

Definition: Outside force interdependence exists when . . .

B. Bennett, C. Rolheiser-Bennett, L. Stevahn (1991)
Cooperative Learning: Where Heart Meets Mind

Environmental Positive Interdependence

... exists when the physical environment facilitates the group members being bound together. For example, mountain climbers are environmentally interdependent in that all team members are physically connected via their ropes. The rope is the means or way the group is brought together.

Ways to structure environmental interdependence:

1. Each group has a special meeting area.

2. Putting tables, desks, chairs, or pillows together as a meeting spot.

3. Requiring all group members to be within an area marked out by tape.

4. Have legs of chairs touching in a circle for a group discussion.

Extend your thinking about **Environmental Positive Interdependence** by analyzing the examples on the next page.

Environmental
Interdependence

Examples	Non-Examples

Examples

1. You and your teammates are to stay within the small circle outlined on the floor as you work on your task.

2. A table will be designated as "home base" for your team. Your group must stick to home base during the group activity.

3. Face your partner when you discuss the question.

4. Get close enough to your teammates so that everyone in your group can easily see the material and participate.

Non-Examples

1. Keep your desks in straight rows facing the front of the classroom.

2. If you need to sharpen your pencil, just tell your partners that you will be back soon.

3. It doesn't matter where you sit to do your assignment.

4. After your team has finished its task, you may individually walk through the stacks and select a library book to read.

What characteristics do all of the **Examples** have in common?

Definition: Environmental interdependence exists when . . .

B. Bennett, C. Rolheiser-Bennett, L. Stevahn (1991)
Cooperative Learning: Where Heart Meets Mind

Identity Positive Interdependence

... exists when group members establish a shared identity which facilitates joint pride. The sense of belonging to a group is strengthened through a name, motto, logo, flag, song, secret handshake, etc. This joint identity can be facilitated by the teacher (e.g., assigning famous explorers names to Social Studies groups) or can be established by the students (e.g., they create a symbol for their group). The outcome is a group that functions more cohesively.

Think of your own involvement in various groups or teams. Reflect on the sense of identification you feel when seeing your group emblem, exclaiming your team cheer, or earning your team colors. We all have a need to belong. Identity interdependence facilitates that need.

Extend your thinking about **Identity Positive Interdependence** by analyzing the examples on the next page.

Identity Interdependence

Examples

1. With your partners, decide on a name for your team.

2. You and your partners are to design and make a coat of arms for your group.

3. With your teammates, create and sing a group jingle that captures what you as teammates have in common.

4. Together, decide upon and make a group flag.

Non-Examples

1. As an individual, think of a nickname for yourself.

2. Present your own family history to the class.

3. What makes you a unique person? Make a list of your special characteristics!

4. I will assign you a personal identification number.

What characteristics do all of the **Examples** have in common?

Definition: Identity interdependence exists when . . .

B. Bennett, C. Rolheiser-Bennett, L. Stevahn (1991)
Cooperative Learning: Where Heart Meets Mind

Test Your Knowledge
of Positive Interdependence

The following activities (pages 80 to 86) provide opportunities to apply understanding of positive interdependence by analyzing classroom situations.

Test Your Thinking

Types of Positive Interdependence

As a group, identify the type of positive interdependence represented by each example. Each person initial the page when you have reached agreement.

1. _____

   Between the four of you, you have one piece of paper on which the paragraph must be written.

2. _____

   Ten points will be added to your score if the average for your group is above 90%.

3. _____

   One person will cut, one person will paste, and one person will draw in the connections.

4. _____

   As a group, complete ten of the problems on page 73.

5. _____

   Pretend you are members of The Clothing Company's marketing department. Develop a plan that will increase company profits.

6. _____

   Devise a hand signal for your group to use when you are successful at completing a task.

7. _____

   One person will be the reader and the other the writer. Switch roles for each question to be answered.

8. _____

   Last year's winners ran the relay in 25 seconds. See if you can better their time.

9. _____

   Sit inside the green circle with your partner.

10. _____

    Envision you are a pioneer family. Plan the first three things you will do if you get snowed in this winter.

B. Bennett, C. Rolheiser-Bennett, L. Stevahn (1991)
Cooperative Learning: Where Heart Meets Mind

Rally-Round

Reviewing Types of Positive Interdependence

In your group, please do the following:

- Start with one group member. That person chooses one of the nine types of positive interdependence and writes a short explanation and/or provides an example.

- Pass the sheet to the left. The next partner chooses another type and writes an explanation and/or provides an example.

- Continue until all types are explained and/or have examples.

Types	Explanation/Example
1. Goal Interdependence	
2. Incentive Interdependence	
3. Resource Interdependence	
4. Role Interdependence	
5. Sequence Interdependence	
6. Simulation Interdependence	
7. Outside Force Interdependence	
8. Environmental Interdependence	
9. Identity Interdependence	

Test your understanding of positive interdependence by discussing each question...

1. Predict what would happen if the goal, in **Goal Interdependence**, is not clear, meaningful, or interesting.

2. What is the main difference between **Role** and **Sequence Interdependence**?

3. Predict what would happen if only one person in the group had a role. For example: "Angelo will be the leader of Group A."

4. Think of a synonym or brief phrase that captures the essence of each type of Positive Interdependence.

B. Bennett, C. Rolheiser-Bennett, L. Stevahn (1991)
Cooperative Learning: Where Heart Meets Mind

Examples of
Positive Interdependence

With a colleague identify the type of positive interdependence each example represents. Justify your thinking.

1 | "I will distribute one activity sheet per group."

2 | "Your team goal is to make sure everyone in your group learns the material."

3 | "You and your teammates are to stay within the small circle outlined on the floor as you work on your task."

4 | "Each group is to produce one diagram, with every member contributing."

5 | "In your group of three, one of you will be the READER, one of you will be the CARD MOVER, and one of you will be the RECORDER."

6 | "With your partners, decide on a name for your team."

7 | "The group with the most items listed will win."

8 | "I will shake hands with each member of your group only after every member of your group achieves the criteria for success."

9 | "You and your partners are to design and make a coat of arms for your group."

10 "Imagine you and your teammates are a new crew on a space station. Develop a list of possible interpersonal difficulties that might arise. Devise a plan to deal with the three most important ones."

11 "A table will be designated as 'home base' for your team. Your group must stick to home base during the group activity."

12 "All members of your group will earn the same grade on the collage."

13 "The first team to solve the puzzle will earn a prize."

14 "There will be a READER, CHECKER, ENCOURAGER, and SUMMARIZER in your group of four."

15 "To achieve success on the assignment, everyone in your group must agree with answers and be able to defend the answers."

16 "With your teammates, create a logo for your group."

17 "Your team will be using one book, one answer sheet, and one pencil."

18 "Face your partner when you discuss the questions."

B. Bennett, C. Rolheiser-Bennett, L. Stevahn (1991)
Cooperative Learning: Where Heart Meets Mind

19 "Everyone in your team will earn bonus points if every member of the group accurately explains each concept on the quiz."

20 "Let's see which team can be first to finish."

21 "I will give each team one pencil and one sheet of paper."

22 "One person in your group of three will locate the word in the dictionary, the second person will read the definition aloud, and the third person will think of a synonym for the word."

23 "Suppose you and your partners got 'snowed in' during a skiing vacation. What steps would you take to ensure your group's survival?"

24 "Together, decide upon and make a group flag."

25 "You and your 'study buddy' will each get half of the deck of flashcards."

26 "Get close enough to your teammates so that everyone in your group can easily see the material and participate."

27 "Your team will be finished when everyone in your group has contributed at least five ideas."

28 "The group with the greatest number of correct answers will earn a special treat."

29 "Each member of your group will get a button that says, 'We did it!' when everyone in your group achieves the criteria for success."

30 "In your group of four, one of you will complete the first step to solve the equation, one of you will complete the second step, one of you will complete the third step, and one of you will write the answer on the answer sheet."

31 "Your team objective is to complete the assignment and have everyone understand the concepts."

32 "You will be working with your partner. One of you will be the STENCIL HOLDER and one of you will be the TRACER."

33 "Arrange your chairs in a small circle ensuring that all group members' chairs touch."

34 "In your group of three, one of you will cut out circles, one of you will write homonyms on the circles, and one of you will staple the circles together to make a worm."

35 "With your partner, decide who will be the CUTTER and who will be the GLUER."

36 "One partner will fold the letter, then the other partner will place the letter in the envelope."

B. Bennett, C. Rolheiser-Bennett, L. Stevahn (1991)
Cooperative Learning: Where Heart Meets Mind

Build Class Interdependence with...

Cooperative teams contribute to a class product!

Set a class goal (e.g., see the list below), then have each team assume responsibility to complete one segment that contributes toward accomplishing the goal. Just as teammates will work together to ensure the success of the team, groups will work to ensure the success of the class.

**Make a BIG BOOK, a mobile,
a time capsule, a poem,
a mural, a song, a quilt,
raise money for a worthy cause,
produce a class newspaper,
design a futuristic city or community,
plan and prepare a balanced meal,
organize a bake sale,
a class party, a field trip . . .**

Positive Interdependence:

- Goal Positive Interdependence is a must! It defines the cooperative relationship among teammates. Without it, we don't have cooperative learning. The goal should be meaningful, interesting, and clearly understood.

- Appropriately structuring various types of positive interdependence means we consider the nature and purpose of the lesson, as well as the students' needs and social skills.

- The effectiveness of positive interdependence will be enhanced when students are working in an environment built on trust and respect... where they can safely experiment and share their views.

- Positive Interdependence is a perception about how and why people interact. With practice, that perception strengthens.

- Positive Interdependence is also a tool for problem solving (see the next page for an example). When groups are not functioning, it guides students and teachers in thinking about what could be done differently to increase the chances of improving the situation.

B. Bennett, C. Rolheiser-Bennett, L. Stevahn (1991)
Cooperative Learning: Where Heart Meets Mind

Problem: Social Loafing

In *Cooperation and Competition: Theory and Research* (1989), David and Roger Johnson note:

> "One potential problem with cooperative efforts is that the responsibility for completing the work may be diffused and members may loaf and let others do the majority of the work... social loafing has been shown to occur especially when group members lack identifiable contributions... when there is an increased likelihood of redundant efforts... when there is a lack of cohesiveness among group members... and when there is lessened responsibility for the final outcome...."

Discuss how positive interdependence could be used to prevent or eliminate the factors associated with social loafing.

We

as well as ME!

B. Bennett, C. Rolheiser-Bennett, L. Stevahn (1991)
Cooperative Learning: Where Heart Meets Mind

Chapter 7

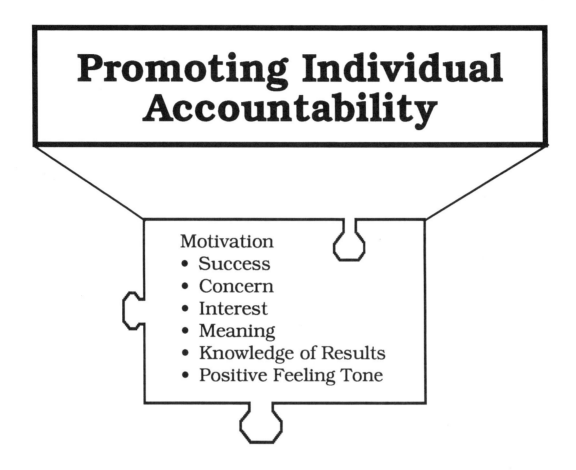

Promoting Individual Accountability

Motivation
- Success
- Concern
- Interest
- Meaning
- Knowledge of Results
- Positive Feeling Tone

Overview

This chapter explores ways to promote individual accountability for learning within cooperative groups. The chapter begins by defining individual accountability in a cooperative context, then focuses attention on the importance of helping students to become self-responsible learners in cooperative teams. The chapter continues by examining relationships between individual accountability and motivation, specifically noting how teachers can utilize six variables of motivation to help students accept and carry out personal learning responsibilities. The six variables are: Success, Concern, Interest, Meaning, Knowledge of Results, and Positive Feeling Tone. The chapter concludes by revisiting the concept of positive interdependence, exploring its relationship to motivation, and reconsidering its impact on individual accountability.

Individual Accountability

In cooperative groupwork, individual accountability is realized when every group member responsibly contributes to the accomplishment of group goals, can individually demonstrate what was learned from the cooperative endeavor, and supportively helps all members of the group learn successfully. In other words, individual accountability in a cooperative context means that teammates interact in ways that maximize the learning of every group member.

Ineffective group experiences frequently lack individual accountability. Consider the following situations:

- Predict what will happen in a group if one student takes control and does most of the work. How are teammates likely to react? What might they say? What reactions would you expect from parents?

- Predict what will happen if one or more students "buy out" of the group task and let the other group members do all of the work. How will attitudes be affected? What comments might you hear from students? What would you expect the effects to be on learning?

Not surprisingly, student complaints and parent apprehensions about groupwork echo many of the concerns that teachers raise. A team that is dominated by one student or gives a "hitch-hiker" a free ride is not truly cooperative, which points to the need for promoting individual accountability in teamwork.

As teachers, we increase the likelihood that all students will take responsibility for productively participating and learning in cooperative teams by encouraging student motivation to learn. The pages that follow examine motivation and its relationship to individual accountability, suggesting a variety of practical ways that teachers can affect student motivation to learn.

B. Bennett, C. Rolheiser-Bennett, L. Stevahn (1991)
Cooperative Learning: Where Heart Meets Mind

Motivation and Individual Accountability

If motivation is one's desire to exert effort toward a given outcome, then the connection between motivation and individual accountability for learning seems clear. Students motivated to learn will most likely take steps toward that purpose. Therefore, by attending to variables of motivation, teachers can increase the likelihood that students will participate appropriately in cooperative teams and exercise responsibility for learning.

Motivation itself has a long, rather constant history in education. For example, in 1897, John Millar (Deputy Minister of Education for the Province of Ontario) wrote about types of incentives that affect whether or not students would be responsibly involved in a task. He identified incentives as being either "Natural" or "Artificial," which today we label as "Intrinsic" and "Extrinsic," respectively. Miller argued that natural incentives provide the best results for motivating learning; whereas artificial incentives are at best merely temporary expedients. Miller contended that, if subjected to the light of pedagogical research, artificial incentives would be found as unsound as the rote system of teaching history or the rule method of solving arithmetical problems. Similar concerns continue to be raised today, as researchers debate the proper role of rewards in cooperative learning (Graves, 1991; Johnson & Johnson, 1989; Kohn, 1990, 1991a, 1991b, 1991c; Schaps & Lewis, 1991; Slavin, 1991b).

However, regardless of one's stance toward incentives for learning, most educators would agree that an ideal state would be students slipping through the classroom door, waiting with baited breath and palpitating hearts to begin the learning process— better still— not waiting! Unfortunately, not all of our students are so inclined.

Although effective teachers design learning environments that invite students to be intrinsically motivated, they may also weave extrinsic incentives into the lesson to motivate learners. For example, when first introduced to cooperative groupwork, students may be more interested in learning alone than learning with others. In this case, appropriately applying extrinsic incentives while reinforcing the value (and sometimes absolute necessity) of collaboration may be important steps in helping students to intrinsically appreciate groupwork.

Six variables that affect motivation include: Success, Concern, Interest, Meaning, Knowledge of Results, and Positive Feeling Tone. Understanding the impact of each variable can guide a teacher's actions in ways that will increase the likelihood of individual student accountability in cooperative learning. A brief examination of each motivational variable follows.

Success

Nothing succeeds like success. Success indicates that the approach a student is using to solve a problem is appropriate. Most students need to experience success — even when they start something new. Moreover, a student's self-concept is affected by the extent to which he or she experiences frequent success. The message is clear — learning tasks need to be structured to maximize success for all students.

Steps teachers can take to help students be successful include:

- Selecting (or having students select) appropriate instructional goals and relevant activities that allow students to learn at appropriate levels of difficulty

- Actively involving all students in meaningful learning

- Monitoring student learning and making appropriate adjustments in teaching

- Sequencing learning from easiest to most difficult, from simplest to most complex

Personal Reflection...

With a colleague, discuss steps you could take to increase student success in cooperative learning:

... with respect to formulating teams (e.g., start with pairs, consider personalities)

... with respect to tasks (e.g., start with familiar procedures, short tasks)

... with respect to role assignments (e.g., consider individual strengths, talents, interests)

B. Bennett, C. Rolheiser-Bennett, L. Stevahn (1991)
Cooperative Learning: Where Heart Meets Mind

Concern

If zero concern exists, there will probably be zero learning. On the other hand, too much concern and some students become frustrated; too little and some become bored. The teacher's challenge is to create an environment in which students are appropriately concerned for optimal learning. This can be accomplished by carefully attending to a number of factors described below.

(1) Framing Questions:

Framing questions is perhaps the most powerful instructional skill related to individual accountability. This skill involves asking questions in ways that hold all students on the alert. After everyone has had time to individually think through a response, then students most in need of answering aloud are selected to respond. Typically, questions start with a covert invitation like, "Think to yourself..."or "Picture in your mind ...." Then, individual "think time" (often referred to as "wait time") is provided. Factors such as the complexity of the question, the students' familiarity with the topic, and the content of the question influence the length of time provided. For example; if you were in a cooperative learning workshop the instructor might say:

> "We have just finished discussing individual accountability. Think to yourself for 10 seconds about how you would define that concept. Be ready to share your answer with a partner." (Note that your level of concern would likely dramatically increase if you were told to be ready to share your thinking with the entire workshop group!)

(2) Encouraging Student Responses:

Closely related to framing questions is the skill of distributing student responses. Our experience informs us that if students are allowed to volunteer answers, three or four students will answer more than 90 percent of the questions. However, remember that selecting volunteers to respond is not necessarily "bad." For example, allowing students to volunteer is a "low stress" way of starting to get students involved. As teachers, we must consider the relationship between framing questions and equitably distributing responses in our efforts to encourage students to be responsible and not hitch-hike off the efforts of others.

(3) Visibility:

When a teacher moves around the room, the students will more likely be concerned about participating in the lesson. The effect is similar to the increased concern you likely feel when you see a police car in your rear-view mirror. Additionally, if students' work will be shared with the class or displayed in the school, then those students will likely be more concerned about participating in the learning task.

(4) Consequences:

When students anticipate something enjoyable upon successful accomplishment of a goal (or missing something desired if the goal is not accomplished), students are more inclined to participate and complete the learning task. Of course, the more the consequence is viewed as intrinsically rewarding, the more likely students will participate with meaning and a sense of caring to both the learning process and their cooperative group.

(5) Time:

When students know how much time they have to complete a task, they are more likely to be concerned about the intensity of their effort. Have you noticed how people are affected by time on examinations? For some people, the more time, the lower the level of concern. For others, time restrictions negatively affect creative and divergent thinking. Certainly, time affects the breadth and depth of discussion. As teachers, we have to be sensitive to the varied effect time has on students in cooperative learning experiences.

(6) Assistance:

If students know that avenues for help exist, their level of concern is typically reduced. Nonetheless, we must be careful because students can become dependent on a helper. Whether the teacher or another student is offering assistance to a learner, there is quite a difference between "giving answers" or "doing work for" the learner versus supportively providing "cues," "clues," and "coaching" to encourage individual thinking.

B. Bennett, C. Rolheiser-Bennett, L. Stevahn (1991)
Cooperative Learning: Where Heart Meets Mind

Ways to Affect Student Concern... Personal Reflections

- With a colleague, predict the effects that each of the following might have on student concern.
- Rank order the techniques from "most likely" to increase level of concern to "least likely."
- Which techniques have you used in your teaching? Which techniques would you like to try? After you experiment, discuss your experiences with supportive staff members.

A. _____ All teammates stand in front of the class and take part in presenting their group collage.

B. _____ The teacher roams the room with a clipboard, pausing near cooperative groups and recording observations.

C. _____ When communicating the purpose of the group activity the teacher conveys a sense of importance by speaking carefully and deliberately, using a serious tone of voice, appropriately selecting words, and making eye contact with every student.

D. _____ Teammates discuss what the group did well and determine steps for improvement. The group assessment is written, signed by all teammates, and submitted to the teacher.

E. _____ Each group member uses a different colored pen to write ideas on the team brainstorming sheet.

F. _____ The teacher intervenes during groupwork to "spot-check" progress by randomly quizzing partners.

G. _____ The teacher looks around the classroom and randomly calls on individual students to share the team answer.

H. _____ The teacher randomly calls on teams to respond. For example, "Let's hear from the Rough Riders."

I. _____ Every team is numbered and teammates letter off A, B, C. The teacher randomly calls on individuals to respond by selecting a number and letter. For example, "Let's hear from team 9, person C."

J. _____ Every group member must "sign-off" on the team assignment sheet to indicate individual participation and understanding of the material, as well as certainty that all partners can demonstrate mastery of the material.

K. _____ Every student will individually demonstrate learning after a cooperative study session (e.g., by completing an exam or skill practicum). The team will earn something perceived as a "bonus" or "reward" if every teammate scores above a set criterion.

L. _____ After studying cooperatively, every teammate will individually complete a quiz on the material studied. One quiz will be randomly selected and scored for the team grade.

M. _____ The teacher intervenes during groupwork to discuss what teammates are doing to check one another and encourages them to generate at least one new idea. The teacher returns to follow-up on their progress with the idea.

N. _____ The teacher tells teammates to spend the first two minutes in silence, individually thinking about the question. After the "think time," all teammates should be ready to present ideas to one another.

Interest

We are motivated to do those things that we find interesting. Something novel, varied, or vivid will likely peak curiosity, stimulate imagination, and hold attention. Also, we are interested in those things that are personally meaningful (e.g., personal experiences, stories, concerns, aspirations). Interviewing and personal storytelling in cooperative teams can be powerful ways to spark interest and meaningfully involve all students in teamwork (see Chapter 11 for specific examples). In addition, humor and enthusiasm also create student interest. Obviously, students involved in an interesting task will more likely "stick with it," while enjoying it at the same time.

Personal Reflection...

With a colleague, discuss how you might use:

... interviewing as a strategy within cooperative teams. What interview topics would spark student interest as well as relate to the content of the lesson? Explore possibilities in your subject areas.

... cartoons in cooperative group learning tasks (e.g., relating cartoons to personal experiences, interpreting cartoons, creating new captions for cartoons). Predict the impact on student interest, participation, and accountability.

B. Bennett, C. Rolheiser-Bennett, L. Stevahn (1991)
Cooperative Learning: Where Heart Meets Mind

Meaning

The more the learning relates to the students' past, present, or future knowledge and experience, the greater the likelihood that students will be involved in the learning. Certainly, sharing or discussing the purpose of the learning with students increases the chances that students will be motivated to participate. As well, making sure that the activities in the cooperative lesson are age or developmentally appropriate increases the probability that students will perceive the learning as meaningful. Regardless of whether a student works alone or in cooperative groups, if the lesson lacks meaning, the teacher increases the chance the lesson will not be successful.

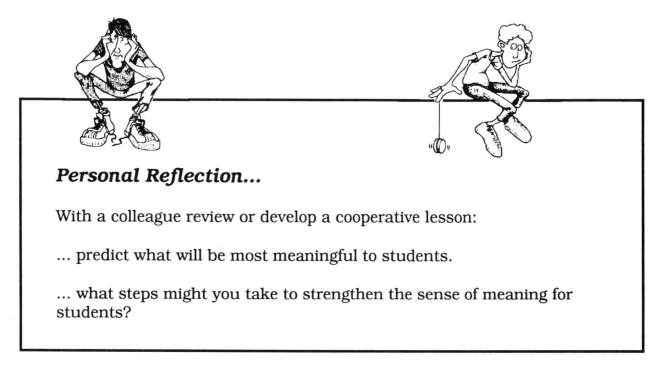

Personal Reflection...

With a colleague review or develop a cooperative lesson:

... predict what will be most meaningful to students.

... what steps might you take to strengthen the sense of meaning for students?

Knowledge of Results

When we know that what we are doing is being done well or we feel and believe we can be successful, we are motivated to continue. How teachers react to students' responses (and how peers react to the responses of one another in group situations) can influence whether a line of thinking stops or continues. Feedback that is immediate, specific, and supportive will most likely motivate students to take personal responsibility for continued involvement in learning activities.

Personal Reflection...

"Checking for understanding" is an important social interaction skill that directly relates to "knowledge of results" in cooperative group situations. At first, students in cooperative teams may check by asking one another, "Do you understand this?," only to hear the response, "Yes." However, without asking partners to demonstrate the learning, or explain in one's own words, or identify new examples, etc., no one knows for sure exactly what is understood. For this reason, students need to learn how to effectively check for understanding. How could you help students learn to effectively check one another and give specific, supportive feedback that will lead to continued involvement and improvement in learning?

B. Bennett, C. Rolheiser-Bennett, L. Stevahn (1991)
Cooperative Learning: Where Heart Meets Mind

Positive Feeling Tone

When learning is a pleasant experience, chances are students will want to continue. Although an unpleasant atmosphere can also motivate students to participate, if sustained, students will likely withdraw or move to power. Teachers can help create positive feeling tone in the classroom by:

- Demonstrating warmth, liking, acceptance, and respect
- Dignifying student responses
- Positively reinforcing learning efforts
- Establishing rules and expectations that help create a safe classroom environment
- Teaching social skills that enable students to interact with one another in positive, supportive ways

Linked to positive feeling tone is the idea of "Public versus Private Failure." We will fall off our bicycles in private and get back up and try again --- but how many times will we continue to try if we fall off in public? Remember, by placing students in groups, we are in fact asking them to possibly fail in front of their peers without having a say in whether or not they wish to respond in a group environment. Although teachers might not consider it a failure when students respond incorrectly in small group situations, students might, unless a safe environment for failing has been created. That is why teambuilding to create trust among partners is so important (see Chapter 11), as well as teaching students how to support, encourage, and help one another while working in groups (see Chapter 8). Structuring cooperative small group learning into our classroom program increases the likelihood that students who are afraid to fail will be more actively involved in the lesson, thereby taking on responsibility for learning.

Personal Reflection...

• Predict what would happen if you held a student accountable in an environment that lacks a sense of safeness.

• With a colleague, discuss and list the things you do that contribute to positive feeling tone in your classroom (e.g., What ground rules do you establish with your students?). As a result of the discussion note new ideas that you would like to try.

• What steps can you take to help students develop positive feeling within their cooperative groups? Make a list (e.g., determine which social skills are most related to positive feeling tone and how you might teach those skills).

Some Final Thoughts About Motivation & Individual Accountability

(1) Attribution Theory (Glasser, 1986) hypothesizes that unless students attribute success and failure to their own efforts, there will be no long term transfer of the motivation to learn. The implication is that we must find ways to help students understand the causal link between their efforts and their successes.

(2) If students receive encouragement on tasks that are easy or tasks where outcomes are primarily linked to luck, innate ability, or other factors over which students have little control, the encouragement will not usually sustain their motivation to learn.

(3) If students who work hard do not achieve success, alternate instructional approaches must be employed to enable success.

(4) In the student's defense, if the lesson being completed is boring, too difficult or too easy, or not appropriate to a cooperative learning activity, the "best thing" a student could do is "buy out!" After all, as adult learners, we do not tolerate those conditions when we attend workshops, so why should our students?

(5) The essence of individual accountability is moving students toward valuing personal learning in the context of cooperative groupwork. To achieve this aim, teambuilding is critical (see Chapter 11).

I Sure Can Positively Motivate Kids!!

Interest

Success

Concern

Positive Feeling Tone

Meaning

Knowledge of Results

B. Bennett, C. Rolheiser-Bennett, L. Stevahn (1991)
Cooperative Learning: Where Heart Meets Mind

Revisiting Positive Interdependence to Promote Individual Accountability

Reflect, for a moment, on what you know about structuring positive interdependence in cooperative groupwork. Revisit Chapter 6, review the nine types of positive interdependence, and recall some of the specific techniques you might use to structure each.

Thinking about promoting individual accountability in cooperative learning leads us back to positive interdependence. Essentially, the two concepts go "hand-in-hand." For example, when every teammate has a meaningful, interconnected role to carry out (i.e., role interdependence exists) in accomplishing the team goal, all teammates are more likely to be responsibly involved. In addition, when roles are determined in ways that tap students' interests, match learning style strengths, and ensure student success, motivation to be accountable will likely increase.

Personal Reflection...

With a colleague, discuss...

- specific ways that each type of positive interdependence promotes individual accountability.

- how each type of positive interdependence is connected to the variables of motivation described in this chapter.

Jot down insights from your discussion.

If learners can be "confident in their individuality, yet enriched by their collaborations with colleagues, then the result may be truly empowered individuals." As one student wrote, "The supportive environment helps us become more outgoing, encouraging, and sociable - helps us become more of who we want to be. We are all very different, with individual needs, strengths, and weaknesses. Yet, we have been able to find common ground, appreciate each other, and find a place for all our voices."

- Carol Rolheiser-Bennett, Ian Hundey,
& June Gooding (1991) -

B. Bennett, C. Rolheiser-Bennett, L. Stevahn (1991)
Cooperative Learning: Where Heart Meets Mind

Chapter 8

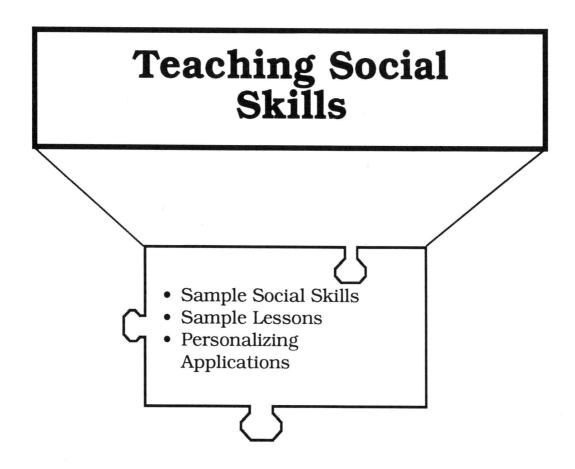

Teaching Social Skills

- Sample Social Skills
- Sample Lessons
- Personalizing Applications

Overview

This chapter presents ideas important to the teaching of social interaction skills. The chapter begins by focusing attention on the variety of social skills that can be taught, then challenges thinking about skill selection. The chapter continues by noting four concerns that are fundamental to teaching social skills. Five sample lessons follow, each illustrating different ways the concerns can be addressed. The chapter concludes by encouraging teachers to develop applications pertinent to their classroom situations.

"You know where self-esteem comes from?

It comes from peers, from being liked, accepted, connected."

- Roger Johnson (1987) -

B. Bennett, C. Rolheiser-Bennett, L. Stevahn (1991)
Cooperative Learning: Where Heart Meets Mind

Social Interaction Skills

This list provides a sample of possible social skills to teach.
What can you add?

- taking turns (equally)
- sharing materials
- asking for help
- asking for clarification
- praising
- using quiet voices
- everyone participating (equally)
- moving quietly to groups
- expressing support/no "put-downs"
- staying on task
- being gentle
- saying kind things
- checking for understanding
- using names
- encouraging
- criticizing ideas, not people
- disagreeing in "non-hurtful" ways
- saying please/thank-you
- occupying the same space cooperatively
- pacing group work
- extending another's answer
- asking for justification
- integrating ideas into single positions
- probing/asking in-depth questions
- controlling anger
- ignoring distractions

- negotiating
- being responsible
- accepting differences
- being assertive in acceptable ways
- listening (actively)
- being a good sport
- resolving conflicts
- reaching agreement/consensus
- acknowledging worth of others
- following through
- following directions
- asking questions
- summarizing
- paraphrasing
- including everyone
- managing materials
- expressing nonverbal encouragement/ support
- celebrating success
- sitting in the group
- staying with the group
- being self-controlled (keeping hands and feet to yourself)
- looking at each other within the group
- clarifying ideas
- contributing ideas
- brainstorming
- elaborating
- disagreeing without criticizing people
- describing feelings when appropriate
- energizing the group

Making Decisions About Teaching Social Skills

Consider these questions as you scan the list on the previous page:

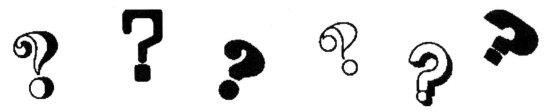

1. Which skills are most important for start-up given your particular context?

2. Which skills are most important for maintaining effective interactions among group members?

3. Which skills are most likely to promote higher level thinking processes?

4. Which skills are most likely to promote the development of trust among teammates?

5. Which skills increase the chances of resolving conflicts?

6. Which skills promote and clarify communication?

7. Which skills do your students already utilize?

8. Which skills would your students choose to concentrate on?

9. Select and prioritize the five most important social skills for your students to learn. How will you teach those skills?

B. Bennett, C. Rolheiser-Bennett, L. Stevahn (1991)
Cooperative Learning: Where Heart Meets Mind

Teaching Social Skills Means Helping Students Understand ...

1. why they are learning the skill;

2. what the skill is;

3. ways the skill will be practiced;

4. how well they used the skill and how they can improve their use of the skill.

What techniques or teaching strategies might you use to address each of the above concerns? Discuss your ideas with a colleague.

Some examples to get you started:

- simulation
- puppets
- literature
- anecdotes as catalysts for discussion
-
-
-
-
-
-
-
-
-

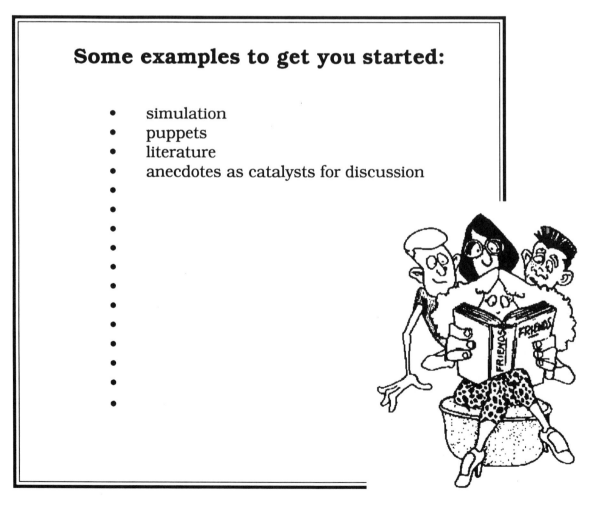

Social Skills Sample Lessons:

The following lessons show a variety of ways to teach social skills. Examine and compare each lesson. How does each address the four concerns on the previous page?

How might you adapt each lesson to your teaching situation?

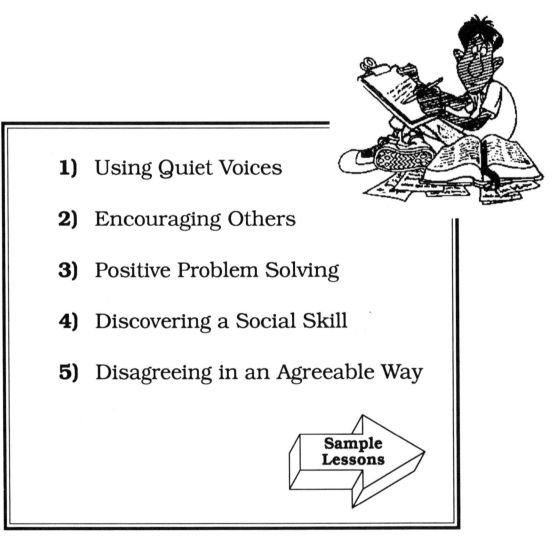

1) Using Quiet Voices

2) Encouraging Others

3) Positive Problem Solving

4) Discovering a Social Skill

5) Disagreeing in an Agreeable Way

Sample Lessons

B. Bennett, C. Rolheiser-Bennett, L. Stevahn (1991)
Cooperative Learning: Where Heart Meets Mind

Using Quiet Voices
A Sample Lesson on Teaching a Cooperative Skill

Step I: Help students understand why the skill is important by . . .

- Playing an audio or video recording of students working quietly versus students working with loud voices. Compare the two situations, discussing the advantages and disadvantages.

- Have the students prepare a bulletin board display emphasizing the importance of using quiet voices. For example:

continued...

B. Bennett, C. Rolheiser-Bennett, L. Stevahn (1991)
Cooperative Learning: Where Heart Meets Mind

Step II: Ensure that students understand what the skill is by . . .

- Generating and demonstrating specific ways to enact the skill. For example, develop and model a T-Chart:

T-Chart

Skill: Using Quiet Voices

What students can do	What students can say
• whisper • sit close together • lean into the group • put finger-to-lips to indicate "quieter please"	• "Let's remember to speak softly." • "Let's use our indoor (versus outdoor) voices." • "Let's turn down the volume." • "We're doing a good job discussing quietly!"

- Utilizing techniques that make the skill "tangible." For example:

1) Give "quiet voices" a name. For example, a "12 inch or 30 centimeter voice" indicates the distance within which your voice should be heard.

2) Assign the role of "voice checker."

3) Measure noise level with a volume indicator.

4) Warn a team that becomes loud by dropping a yellow card on their table (analogous to yellow warning flag used in athletics).

5) Reward quiet groups (e.g., verbal compliments, tokens, stickers).

continued...

B. Bennett, C. Rolheiser-Bennett, L. Stevahn (1991)
Cooperative Learning: Where Heart Meets Mind

Step III: Provide practice by . . .

- arranging cooperative activities that demand use of the skill. For example, partners can practice using quiet voices while . . .

    1) brainstorming ideas for a team name and logo,

    2) reaching consensus on a set of problems or questions, or

    3) drilling each other on a set of spelling words or math facts.

Step IV: Ensure that students evaluate their use of the skill by . . .

- discussing how effectively they used the skill and ways to improve using the skill.

- having teammates complete an evaluation sheet. For example:

---

1. **How well did you use your Quiet Voices?**

    Discuss as a team and mark your group answer. Explain your answer below.

    ☐ mostly quiet
    ☐ mostly medium
    ☐ mostly loud

2. **What could you do to improve? List one idea.**

Encouraging Others
A Sample Lesson on Teaching a Cooperative Skill

Objective

Students will demonstrate their understanding of what is meant by "encouraging others" by explaining what encouraging others looks like and sounds like, and then by applying that understanding to specific situations.

Task Analysis

1. Does the student understand what the word "encouraging" means?
2. Does the student understand the effect encouraging others has on groupwork?
3. Does the student understand the effect that not encouraging others has on groupwork?
4. Can the student generate examples of what encouraging others looks like and sounds like?
5. Can the student apply an understanding of encouragement to specific situations?

Set

Teacher says: "Take 15 seconds and think of the difference between these two statements: "Great idea!" versus "That's a stupid idea!" (Wait 15 seconds and then have the students partner up and share their ideas.)

Objective and Purpose

Teacher says: "Today, before we go into groups I want to make sure you understand the effect encouraging others can have on group dynamics. Obviously, if groups work together effectively more work can be accomplished and accomplished quickly. Also, it feels good to be around others who are encouraging."

continued...

B. Bennett, C. Rolheiser-Bennett, L. Stevahn (1991)
Cooperative Learning: Where Heart Meets Mind

Input

1. Have the students try to define what is meant by "encouraging." (For example, actions a person takes to increase the chances that other people will feel good about their effort. Encouragement motivates continued effort, building self-confidence and the courage to be imperfect. Encouragement focuses on assets and strengths, it recognizes the effort and the process, not just the final product.)

2. Have the students generate a list of how encouraging group members affects what happens in a group. Discuss.

3. Have the students generate how not encouraging others affects group work.

4. Have students brainstorm examples of what encouragement looks like and sounds like so they can recognize it in their groupwork. (Note: Pages 117-118 illustrate verbal examples students might generate.)

Modeling

This will occur when the students generate examples.

Check for Understanding

Have students share their explanation with a neighbor of what encouraging others means. Select several students to give that explanation to the rest of the class. Give several "testers" and have students identify them as positive or negative examples of encouragement.

Practice

In partners, students complete the "Situation Activity Sheet" on the following page, using encouragement as they work with one another.

Closure

At the end of the activity, partners process how effectively they encouraged one another.

Encouragement
Situation Activity Sheet

Directions: Together think of encouraging things to say in the following situations.
Take turns writing your ideas in the balloon next to each number.
Remember to practice encouragement as you work together.

1. Your partner has the wrong answer to a math problem.

3. A partner is being bossy and won't let anyone have a turn.

5. You are working on the computer and your partner pushes the wrong button.

7. Your partner needs more practice.

2. Your partner is not participating.

4. Your partners help you understand a problem.

6. Your partner doesn't understand the answer.

8. Your partner gave a creative idea.

(Adapted from: Colleen Windell, 1989, Marysville School District, Marysville, Washington)

B. Bennett, C. Rolheiser-Bennett, L. Stevahn (1991)
Cooperative Learning: Where Heart Meets Mind

Encouraging Starters

Challenge: How can you make each more specific?

Motivators
Key Phrases For Primary Pupils

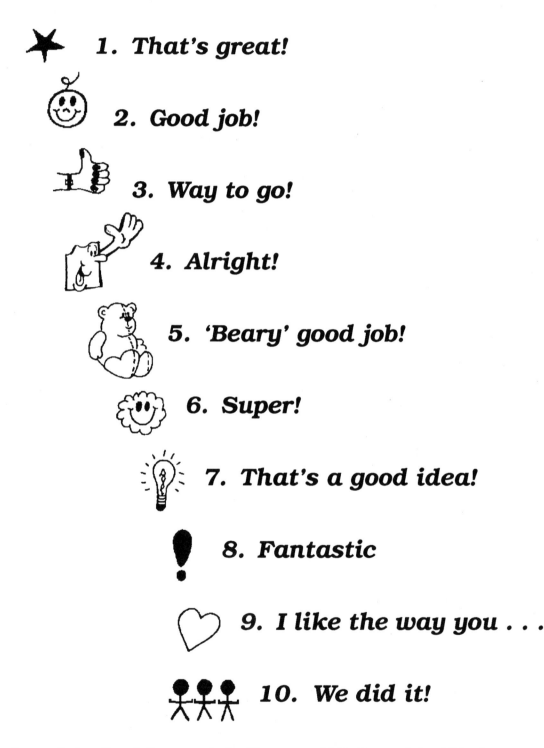

1. That's great!

2. Good job!

3. Way to go!

4. Alright!

5. 'Beary' good job!

6. Super!

7. That's a good idea!

8. Fantastic

9. I like the way you . . .

10. We did it!

(Adapted from: Joanne Ewing, Bonnie Pomeroy, & Jim Thompson, 1988, Renton School District, Renton, Washington)

B. Bennett, C. Rolheiser-Bennett, L. Stevahn (1991)
Cooperative Learning: Where Heart Meets Mind

Positive Problem-Solving
A Sample Lesson on Teaching A Cooperative Skill

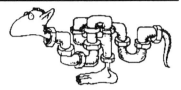

Objective:

Students will demonstrate their understanding of positive problem-solving by creating positive solutions to a problem they have encountered.

Task Analysis

1. Does the student understand what "problem-solving" means?
2. Does the student understand the effect that "put-downs" have on solving problems?
3. Can the student generate examples of solving problems in positive ways?

Set

Teacher A says to the class: "Oops! I forgot to return this book to (Teacher B). I promised to give it back first thing this morning because she said she needed it right away."

(Anticipate that a student might volunteer to take the book back to Teacher B.)

Teacher A says: "We have to get started on our lesson. I'll return it as soon as we're done."

Input

Teachers A and B role play a confrontational, negative, problem-solving situation.

1. Teacher B: (storming into Teacher A's class) "Where's my book? You promised me I'd have it first thing this morning."

2. Teacher A: "I was going to return it to you as soon as I had finished with this lesson."

3. Teacher B: "What's the matter with you? You knew I needed it right now during my prep period. How could you be so thoughtless?" (Teacher B grabs the book from Teacher A's desk and storms out.)

Input (*continued*)

With the students, teacher A discusses what just happened.

1. What do you think about the way Teacher B talked to Teacher A?

2. How did it make Teacher A feel?

3. How did you feel?

4. What "put-downs" did Teacher B use?

5. Was the problem solved?

6. What new problem might occur as a result of how the situation was handled?

Modeling

Teacher B returns to Teacher A's classroom, and the two teachers reenact the situation in a socially appropriate manner with "put-ups" instead of "put-downs."

Check for Understanding

Have students generate reasons why the last role play was a more positive problem-solving situation.

Practice

Group students randomly and have them generate a problem they have encountered, along with specific suggestions as to how this problem could be solved in a positive manner.

Closure

Groups share their problem and respective suggestions with the class.

(Adapted from: T. Bartlett, S. Fruetel, D. Libkin, E. Monica, K. Shaefer, and S. Vanderpool, 1989, Marysville School District, Marysville, Washington)

B. Bennett, C. Rolheiser-Bennett, L. Stevahn (1991)
Cooperative Learning: Where Heart Meets Mind

Discovering A Social Skill
A Sample Lesson on Teaching a Cooperative Skill

Strategy Used for this Lesson:
Concept Attainment

 ## Cooperative Team Directions:

Using the activity sheet that follows, your task is to identify the social skill that the positive examples illustrate. Work as a team! You must all agree with final decisions and be able to give reasons for your decisions.

Steps:

1. Arrange yourselves so that every member of your team can see the examples.

2. Focus on the effect of each example on social interaction.

3. As a team, decide what qualities or characteristics all **Positive Examples** have in common. These characteristics define the social skill you are trying to identify.

4. Contrast the **Positive Examples** with the **Negative Examples**. The **Negative Examples** do not contain the characteristics of the social skill you are trying to identify.

5. Name the social skill that the **Positive Examples** illustrate.

6. Read each test example and determine whether it is a **Positive Example** of the social skill or a **Negative Example**. Be ready to give reasons for your decisions.

7. Sign your names to the activity sheet to indicate that you participated in the task, agree with decisions, and can justify your decision.

Discovering A Social Skill
Concept Attainment Activity Sheet

Focus: Focus on the effect of each statement on social interaction.
Do not focus on the length or punctuation.

Positive Examples	Negative Examples
1. We could take it one step further by . . .	O.K. Let's move on to the next question.
2. To add to your idea, I'd say . . .	Hey stupid! Give me a break!
3. Let's piggy-back on that idea.	No. I disagree. My idea is . . .
4. Along with that, we could say . . .	I don't understand.
5. On top of that . . .	I don't think that will work.
6. In addition to that . . .	That's a ridiculous idea!

Test Examples

7.   That's amazing!

8.   Is there anything we could add to that?

9.   Related to that is the idea of . . .

10. It's good enough the way it is.

11. Let's think of a way to take that idea one step further.

12. Make my day!

**Group Members'
Signatures:** _____

_____

B. Bennett, C. Rolheiser-Bennett, L. Stevahn (1991)
Cooperative Learning: Where Heart Meets Mind

Disagreeing in an Agreeable Way
A Sample Lesson on Teaching a Cooperative Skill

T-Chart

The teacher has cooperative teams generate T-Chart posters on ways members can disagree in agreeable ways **before** being involved in an activity requiring the discussion of a multi-faceted issue. Posters are added to after the activity as well as in subsequent lessons. A sample poster might be as follows:

"Disagreeing In An Agreeable Way"

See	Hear
Looks Like . . .	**Sounds Like . . .**
• Eye contact with subtle shake of the head	• "I understand what you are saying . . . we might also want to consider . . ."
• Smiling while you make your statement	• "I see your point, however . . ."
• Group members listening fully to one another's ideas before commenting	• "Your point is important, but I wonder if another idea might be . . ."
• Slight shoulder shrug and head shake	• "I don't agree because . . ."
etc.	• "That's an interesting idea, nonetheless . . ."
	• "You may want to consider . . ."

T-Chart

Social or Collaborative Skill: _____

See	Hear
Looks like...	Sounds like...

B. Bennett, C. Rolheiser-Bennett, L. Stevahn (1991)
Cooperative Learning: Where Heart Meets Mind

Social Skills:
Practical Applications

Given the information you've considered in this chapter, develop social skills lessons for application in your classroom. Discuss your plans with a colleague. Together, generate options for extending each lesson. (For example: How might you help students transfer the social skills to situations outside of the classroom?)

Notes:

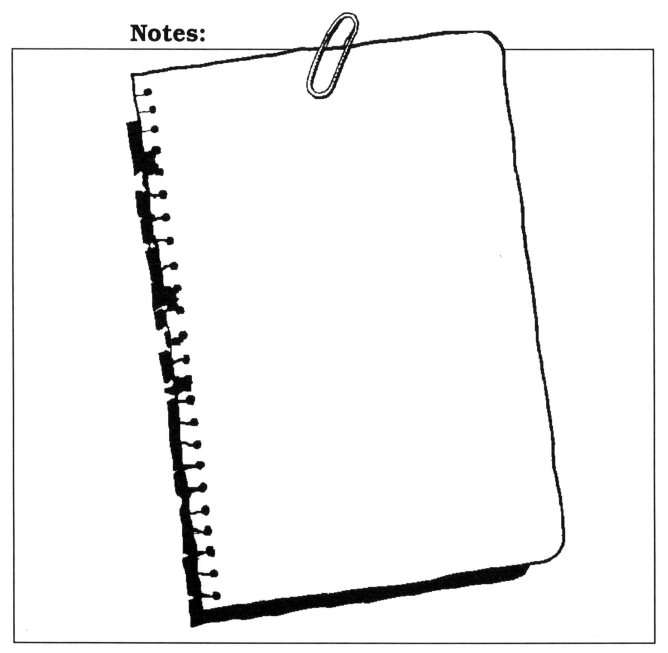

"The Human species seems to have a **relationship imperative**: We desire and seek out relationships with others, and we have personal needs that can be satisfied only through interacting with other humans. Career success, family success, friendships, and companionships all depend on building and maintaining relationships with other people. In fact, the most distinctive aspect of being alive is the potential for joy, fun, excitement, caring, warmth, and personal fulfillment in our relationships with other people."

- David Johnson (1986) -

B. Bennett, C. Rolheiser-Bennett, L. Stevahn (1991)
Cooperative Learning: Where Heart Meets Mind

Chapter 9

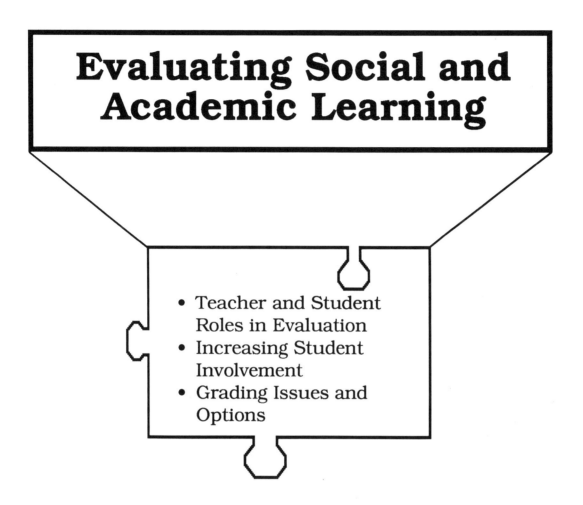

Evaluating Social and Academic Learning

- Teacher and Student Roles in Evaluation
- Increasing Student Involvement
- Grading Issues and Options

Overview

This chapter examines evaluation in cooperative learning. The chapter begins with questions that initiate personal reflection on evaluation in general, then refocuses attention on assumptions underlying effective application of cooperative strategies. Within this context, the chapter continues by exploring both teacher and student roles in the evaluation of cooperative learning. First, teacher considerations are outlined and sample forms for observation and feedback are provided. Next, ways to increase student involvement in the evaluation process are explored by analyzing a variety of evaluation instruments developed for student use. The chapter concludes by considering issues and options related to grading practices.

Evaluation in Your Teaching Situation

As teachers, we all approach student evaluation in similar, yet often diverse ways. Discuss your evaluation practices and beliefs with a colleague using the following questions as a guide.

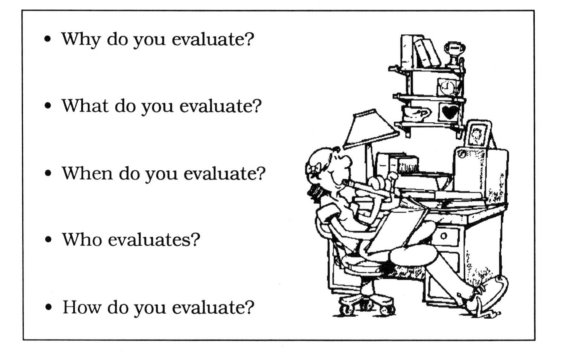

- Why do you evaluate?

- What do you evaluate?

- When do you evaluate?

- Who evaluates?

- How do you evaluate?

The practices and beliefs you discussed above establish a baseline from which to examine evaluation in cooperative learning. The following pages explore dimensions of evaluation in cooperative learning, starting with assumptions that underlie effective application of small group learning.

B. Bennett, C. Rolheiser-Bennett, L. Stevahn (1991)
Cooperative Learning: Where Heart Meets Mind

Assumptions for Effective Cooperative Learning

Remember, choosing to use Cooperative Learning means...

1 Small Heterogeneous Groups

2 Basic Elements
- Positive Interdependence
- Individual Accountability
- Face-to-face Interaction
- Social Skills
- Processing

3 A progression of student and teacher growth on a cooperative learning continuum

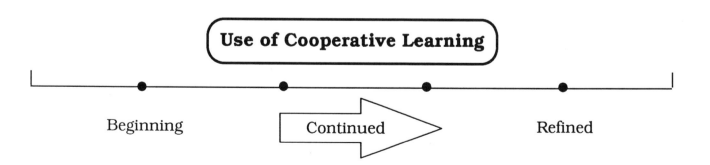

Use of Cooperative Learning

Beginning   Continued   Refined

Keep these three assumptions in mind as you explore issues and options related to evaluation in cooperative learning.

B. Bennett, C. Rolheiser-Bennett, L. Stevahn (1991)
Cooperative Learning: Where Heart Meets Mind

Evaluation and Cooperative Learning

In Cooperative Learning...

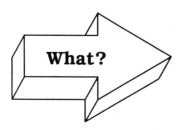
What?

Academic and social objectives demand evaluation of academic and social learning.

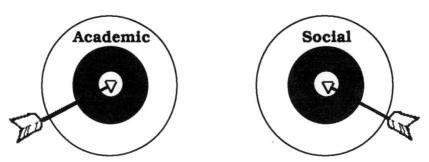

Why?

Purposes for evaluating include:

Formative
- diagnosis of needs and progress
- modification of objectives
- adjustment of teaching and learning

Summative
- measurement of learning outcomes
- assessment reports

Who?

Both teacher and students take active roles in formative and summative evaluation of academic and social learning.

Individual teachers need to decide:

- What the balance will be between teacher and student involvement in evaluation.

- How to facilitate student participation in evaluating self and peers in groupwork.

B. Bennett, C. Rolheiser-Bennett, L. Stevahn (1991)
Cooperative Learning: Where Heart Meets Mind

Exploring the Teacher's Role in Evaluation of Cooperative Learning

As a teacher, evaluating cooperative learning means. . .

1. Establishing evaluation criteria, involving students in establishing criteria when appropriate, and facilitating student understanding of evaluation criteria.

2. Gathering information on both the process and product of learning, through careful observation. Information gathering techniques include:

   - anecdotal records
   - tally sheets
   - checklists
   - rating scales
   - collections of student work

3. Providing feedback to students.

4. Facilitating student involvement in evaluation by helping students learn how to observe and gather information useful for evaluation.

The following pages outline several techniques for observation, including tally sheets, anecdotal records, and global observations. ➡

Tally Sheets

... are useful tools for gathering and sharing specific information about group interactions. The following procedures explain how a teacher might utilize a tally sheet during observation.

- Write the names of team members across the top of the tally grid.

- Write the names of social interaction skills to be observed in the first box of each row.

- When a student demonstrates one of the targeted skills during groupwork record a mark under that student's name in the corresponding skill box. For example, the tally below shows that Raoul contributed five ideas, asked for one idea, and complimented ideas two times.

- After teammates complete group work, have then examine their tally sheet and reflect on their involvement. The following page provides guidelines for facilitating this process.

Observations

Observer: _____

Date: _____

	Raoul	Sabrina	Joe
Gives ideas	ЖНТ	‖‖	‖‖
Asks for ideas	‖	‖	‖
Compliments ideas	‖	‖‖	ЖНТ

B. Bennett, C. Rolheiser-Bennett, L. Stevahn (1991)
Cooperative Learning: Where Heart Meets Mind

Guidelines for Tally Processing

1. Total columns and rows.

2. Show data to the group.

3. What does your group conclude about
   • participation?
   • group functioning?

4. Make sure each partner receives feedback on helpful behaviors!

5. Set a team goal for being even better in the future. (Together decide what you might do differently next time to improve.)

B. Bennett, C. Rolheiser-Bennett, L. Stevahn (1991)
Cooperative Learning: Where Heart Meets Mind

Anecdotal Observations

Observer's name:

Date:

Group observed:

In the squares below record examples of what group members do and say as they work on their cooperative task.

Behaviors to be Observed	Name	Name	Name
Compliments ideas			
Shares ideas and information			
Seeks ideas and information			
Other...			

B. Bennett, C. Rolheiser-Bennett, L. Stevahn (1991)
Cooperative Learning: Where Heart Meets Mind

Global Observations:
The Big Picture

Date: _____

Cooperative Task: _____

Stand back and observe the groups working.
Record what you see and hear, along with
some reflections. Jot down questions that
come to mind. For example, do you see body
language indicating frustration, tuning-out, or
excitement? Does the talk indicate students
are engaged in the task? Reflect on interesting observations.
What might be the reason(s) for their occurrence? How might you
use the observation for future planning?

Comments:

_____

_____

_____

_____

_____

_____

_____

Remember

... with guidance and practice, students can actively join teachers in the process of observing and gathering information for evaluation of cooperative interaction. As students learn to take an active role in observation, consider:

- limiting the number of skills to be observed

- giving all students opportunities to be observers

- limiting the time for student observation (e.g., 5 minutes of observation during a 20 minute cooperative activity)

- the importance of teaching students the behaviors they will be observing.

What other considerations would you include? With a colleague, discuss your particular teaching situation and develop a step-by-step plan for involving students in observation for evaluation.

B. Bennett, C. Rolheiser-Bennett, L. Stevahn (1991)
Cooperative Learning: Where Heart Meets Mind

Exploring Student
Involvement in Evaluation

Along with gathering information on group functioning, how can student involvement in evaluation of cooperative learning be extended?

WANTED!
**Student Involvement
in Evaluation**

The following forms engage students in evaluation. The forms have been clustered for examination. As you analyze the forms look for commonalities within each cluster. Think about...

- their purpose

- when they would be most useful

- how they relate to your present evaluation practices

- how they might be adapted for your students.

Cluster A

(Pages 139 to 145)

- What are the purposes of the forms in this cluster?

- When would these forms be most useful?

- How do these forms relate to your present evaluation practices?

- How might the forms in this cluster be adapted for your students?

B. Bennett, C. Rolheiser-Bennett, L. Stevahn (1991)
Cooperative Learning: Where Heart Meets Mind

Checking Out My Social Skills

A. Place a check in the boxes which you feel apply to you.

❏ I said things which made my partners feel good about themselves.

❏ I tried to smile even when I wasn't in agreement with another person's ideas.

❏ I was a good person to have in the group because I made other people feel good.

❏ It felt great to make other people happy.

❏ I made an effort to disagree in an agreeable way.

❏ I made sure that my voice didn't get TOO LOUD!

❏ I politely told other people to stay on task.

❏ I was nice when I told others that it was getting too noisy.

❏ I helped tidy up.

B. Please answer these questions in the spaces below:

1. What were some of the things you said when you disagreed in an agreeable way?

2. What could your group work on next time to work together better?

(Adapted from: Aldona Kasperazicius, 1990, Dufferin-Peel Roman Catholic School Board, Toronto, Ontario)

Self-evaluation

Using "**5**" as the highest degree and "**1**" as the lowest, decide to what degree you were successful in each of the following areas:

Circle one number

		Low				High
A	**Adhering to the rules**					
	• understanding and following the agreed upon procedure for the group discussion	1	2	3	4	5
B	**Contributing**					
	• helping the group plan its activities	1	2	3	4	5
	• helping others to achieve group goals	1	2	3	4	5
C	**Working cooperatively**					
	• understanding my responsibilities in the group	1	2	3	4	5
	• accomplishing my tasks (collecting information, organizing data, etc.)	1	2	3	4	5
	• helping to avoid or settle disagreements	1	2	3	4	5
	• helping the group stay on topic and accomplish its objectives	1	2	3	4	5
D	**Communication**					
	• making relevant statements	1	2	3	4	5
	• supporting opinions of group members with facts	1	2	3	4	5
	• using appropriate vocabulary when stating views	1	2	3	4	5
	• organizing my thoughts before and while speaking	1	2	3	4	5
E	**Organizing information and reaching conclusions**					
	• seeking information (asking for facts, expansion, or others' views)	1	2	3	4	5
	• clarifying statements (restating ideas, using examples)	1	2	3	4	5
	• summarizing (pulling ideas together, offering conclusions)	1	2	3	4	5

What is your overall evaluation of your contribution to the group effort?

_____

_____

_____

(1990, Durham Board of Education, Oshawa, Ontario)

B. Bennett, C. Rolheiser-Bennett, L. Stevahn (1991)
Cooperative Learning: Where Heart Meets Mind

Assessing My Skills as a Peer Tutor

Identify and explain one thing a member of your group learned as a result of you helping him or her.

_____

_____

_____

_____

_____

In the process of being a peer tutor you develop many skills. Discuss one skill that you have developed and explain how you learned it.

_____

_____

_____

_____

_____

Each member of your group made individual contributions to the group process. What did you learn from observing and asking questions about a group member's individual contributions? Explain your answer.

_____

_____

_____

_____

(1990, Durham Board of Education, Oshawa, Ontario)

Evaluating Myself

Review your completed group assignment.
How did you help your partner better understand
the material? Explain what you did.

_____

_____

_____

_____

_____

_____

_____

_____

_____

_____

_____

_____

_____

_____

_____

_____

_____

_____

_____

B. Bennett, C. Rolheiser-Bennett, L. Stevahn (1991)
Cooperative Learning: Where Heart Meets Mind

Processing Social Skills:
Personal Journal Entries

The following are sample entries from individual student journals (names have been changed for confidentiality). *

+ = things we did well
- = something we could do to improve next time

Checking for Understanding (Samuel)
+ "After I finished explaining something I would see if Doug could explain it back to me. After each time Doug explained to me about his book he would repeat it to make sure I understood."
- "One thing I need to improve on is to let Doug speak up more."

Taking Turns (Geoff's letter to Arn)
+ "Dear Arn, I would like you to know that your reminder about switching jobs helped me. I'm sure it helped Lucretta change the jobs more smoothly too."
- "One time when we needed to improve was when we got the hypothesis. Lucretta said, 'solve.' We just said, 'Yeah. Write it down.' We never bothered asking questions [like] why it went there or maybe that it didn't fit in. So next time we'll try to ask questions and have equal questioning time."

Staying on Task (Ellen)
+ "We said, 'keep on going' to encourage our group and to help them stay on task. We also said, 'that can't be' to try to figure out the question together."
- "One thing we did to distract people was we worked in a crowded area."

Commenting Positively (Ingrid)
+ " . . . I said to Samantha, 'Don't worry. Everyone makes mistakes', when she was writing down a word and she needed to erase it. And I said to Arn that he had a good idea when he extended off mine for our religion notes."
- " . . . What I'd like to improve on is: call my group members' names more often."

Taking Turns (Rajiv's letter to Kathy)
- "I noticed that you did not talk much. Maybe Darlene and I did too much talking because we had some good ideas, but when you talked you had some good ideas. One thing we have to improve on is equal time for jobs. I never did record."

Extending (Dominique)
+ "Today in science I extended ideas. For example, when Arn said, 'What if we tried something different?' and Sonya and I said, 'How about a shoe?'."
- "But we did not always agree and sometimes I didn't say what I felt."

Commenting Positively (Lydia)
+ "One time . . . Veronica and Catherine were arguing [about] what was the proper word to use, 'setting' or 'places', so I said, 'Catherine, Veronica, we could take a vote'."

Checking for Understanding (Serge) (Milios)
+ "One of the things we did was to make the person who was explaining repeat the phrase he said."
- "I would like to work on not always letting the group decide, and me just saying 'yes'."

(From John Mazurek's Grade 4/5 class, Dufferin-Peel Roman Catholic School Board, Toronto, Ontario)

Individual Evaluation

The social skill focus of this activity was:

_____

Think about your response to each question.
Write your response to each question in the space provided.

1. "Something I said or did that demonstrated the social skill was:

_____

_____

_____

_____."

2. "Something that I did to help the group work in a positive way was:

_____

_____

_____."

3. "I think I should work on:

_____

_____

_____."

B. Bennett, C. Rolheiser-Bennett, L. Stevahn (1991)
Cooperative Learning: Where Heart Meets Mind

Processing

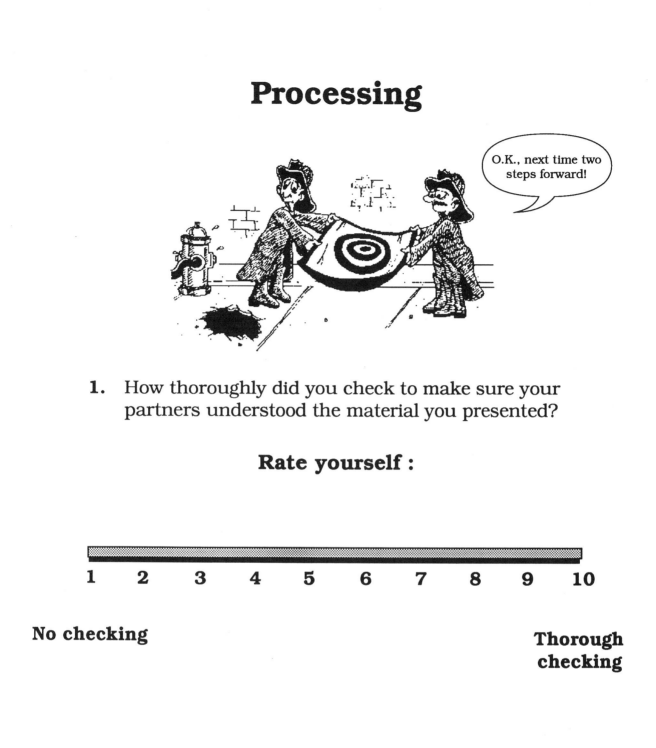

O.K., next time two steps forward!

1. How thoroughly did you check to make sure your partners understood the material you presented?

Rate yourself :

| 1 | 2 | 3 | 4 | 5 | 6 | 7 | 8 | 9 | 10 |

No checking   **Thorough checking**

2. Share your self-rating with your partners. Explain why you rated yourself as you did, and what you would do next time to improve your use of checking for understanding.

Cluster B

(Pages 147 to 156)

- What are the purposes of the forms in this cluster?

- When would these forms be most useful?

- How do these forms relate to your present evaluation practices?

- How might the forms in this cluster be adapted for your students?

B. Bennett, C. Rolheiser-Bennett, L. Stevahn (1991)
Cooperative Learning: Where Heart Meets Mind

Questions for Group Discussion

Select ONE box for group discussion.

1
- What did you do that helped your team work together?
- What can you do next time to help your team work together?

2
- How are you working as a group?
- What would you do differently next time?

3
- How did you feel?
- What did you notice?

4
- What was the best thing that happened in your group?
- What change would help you to be more successful?

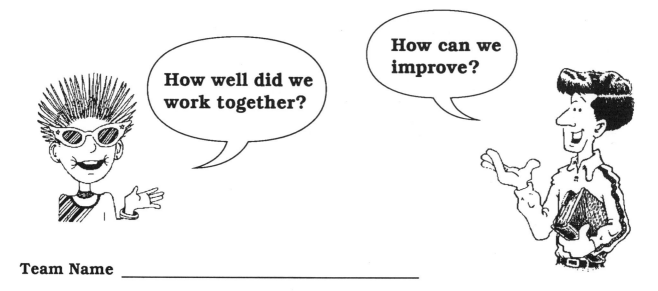

Team Name _____

Discuss, reach agreement, and color each bar on the graph up to the agreed level.

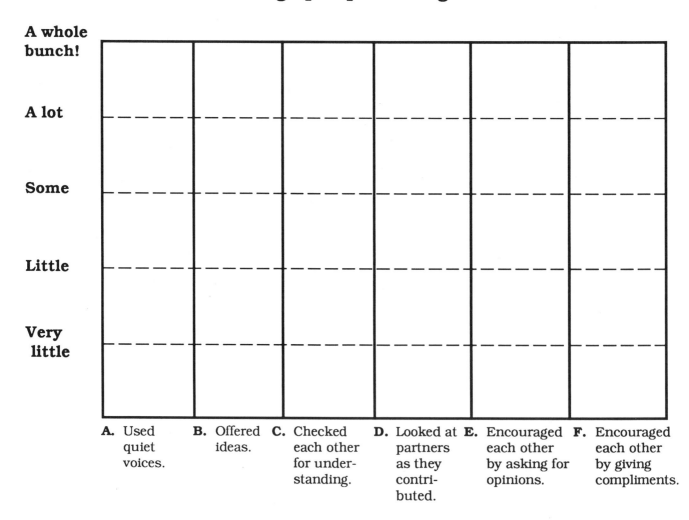

A whole bunch!

A lot

Some

Little

Very little

| A. Used quiet voices. | B. Offered ideas. | C. Checked each other for understanding. | D. Looked at partners as they contributed. | E. Encouraged each other by asking for opinions. | F. Encouraged each other by giving compliments. |

(Adapted from: Yolanda Edsinger, 1989)

B. Bennett, C. Rolheiser-Bennett, L. Stevahn (1991)
Cooperative Learning: Where Heart Meets Mind

How Did We Do?

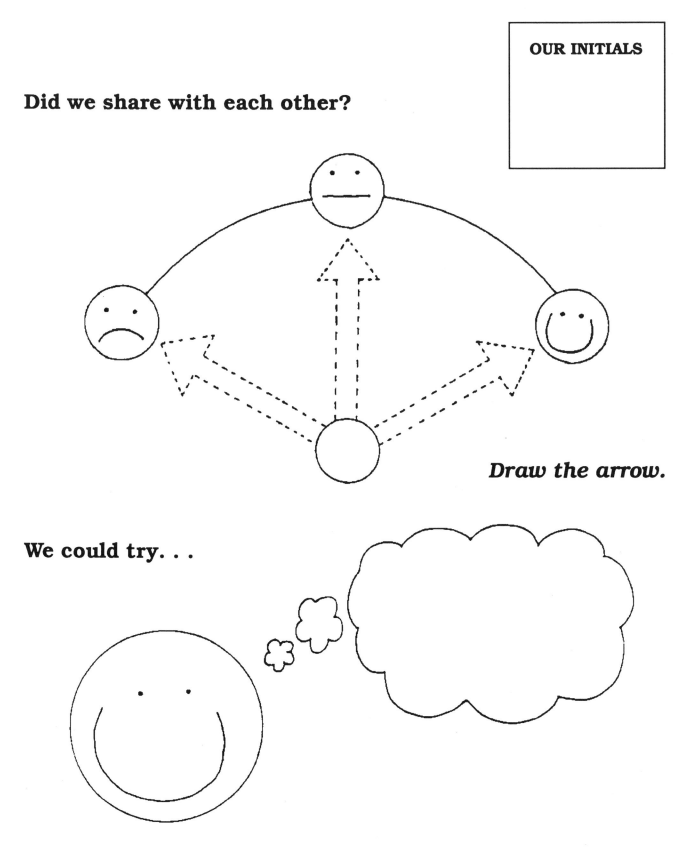

Did we share with each other?

OUR INITIALS

Draw the arrow.

We could try. . .

(Adapted from: Robin Meyers, 1988)

Group Evaluation

**Place a check on the blank that best represents
your group's evaluation of social skills.**

	seldom				always
We made certain that all members of our group understood the work.	——	——	——	——	——
We listened to the ideas and contributions of all group members.	——	——	——	——	——
We were patient when explaining difficult material to members within the group.	——	——	——	——	——
We shared the workload within the group.	——	——	——	——	——

What was your group particularly effective in doing? Explain the secret of your success?

_____

_____

_____

_____

_____

What would you do differently next time to enhance cooperation? Explain fully.

_____

_____

_____

_____

(Adapted from: 1990, Durham Board of Education, Oshawa, Ontario)

B. Bennett, C. Rolheiser-Bennett, L. Stevahn (1991)
Cooperative Learning: Where Heart Meets Mind

Group Mind Map:
Evaluating Our Success

Discuss how well your group functioned and draw a mind map that illustrates the "secrets of your success" (see pages 270-271 for information on mind mapping).

Secrets of our success!

Team Assessment

Complete the following questions as a team.

	Low				High

1. Did all of the members of our group contribute ideas?

    Low   **High**

1 2 3 4 5

2. Did all of the members of our group listen carefully to the ideas of other group members?

1 2 3 4 5

3. Did all of the members of our group encourage other members to contribute their thoughts and opinions?

1 2 3 4 5

4. Three ways that we helped each other learn the material were:

    ● _____

    ● _____

    ● _____

5. **a)** One difficulty our group had was (explain fully):

_____

_____

_____

    b) To resolve the situation we could:

_____

_____

_____

Group signatures: _____ _____

                       _____ _____

(1990, Durham Board of Education, Oshawa, Ontario)

B. Bennett, C. Rolheiser-Bennett, L. Stevahn (1991)
Cooperative Learning: Where Heart Meets Mind

Our Team Social Goal

Team Name: _____

Date: _____

Today we as teammates
all agree to work especially hard at _____

Your signatures: _____

_____

_____

- -

Did Your Team Meet Your Goal?

☐ **YES!** We met our goal by . . . (give examples):

☐ **No.** We will improve next time by . . . (give examples):

Your signatures: _____

_____

_____

Participation Pie

Divide the pie to illustrate how much each member of the group is participating in the task. Discuss the effectiveness of participation and any adjustments you might make for the remainder of the task.

B. Bennett, C. Rolheiser-Bennett, L. Stevahn (1991)
Cooperative Learning: Where Heart Meets Mind

Sharing Letters

Dear Partner,

Thank You For . . .

I think we can do better by...

Sincerely,

Processing A Social Skill:
"Disagreeing in agreeable ways"

Each person think of your response to the sentence and then tell the group. Please continue in roundrobin fashion until everyone has spoken.

1. "A statement or action that I did when disagreeing in an agreeable way was . . ."

2. "Something that you (tell the person to your right) did to help the group work in a positive way was . . ."

3. "Next time I think we could improve by... "

B. Bennett, C. Rolheiser-Bennett, L. Stevahn (1991)
Cooperative Learning: Where Heart Meets Mind

Cluster C

(Pages 158 to 159)

- What are the purposes of the forms in this cluster?

- When would these forms be most useful?

- How do these forms relate to your present evaluation practices?

- How might the forms in this cluster be adapted for your students?

Observing Another Group

A.   Your name: _____

B.   Name of the team you watched: _____

C.   They are working on the skill of: _____

D.   How well are they using this skill?

Needs a lot more improvement   **Outstanding!**

```
  ├────────────┼────────────┼────────────┼────────────┤
  1            2            3            4            5
```

E.   Give reasons for your rating: _____

_____

_____

_____

_____

B. Bennett, C. Rolheiser-Bennett, L. Stevahn (1991)
Cooperative Learning: Where Heart Meets Mind

Tally Sheet for Observing Cooperative Groups *

Observer: _____

Date: _____

Team Observed: _____

Behaviors To Be Observed	Name _____	Name _____	Name _____	Name _____
Other helpful behaviors . . .				

* **Note: Directions for using this tally sheet on page 132.**

B. Bennett, C. Rolheiser-Bennett, L. Stevahn (1991)
Cooperative Learning: Where Heart Meets Mind

Cluster D

(Pages 161 to 165)

- What are the purposes for the forms in this cluster?

- When would these forms be most useful?

- How do these forms relate to your present evaluation practices?

- How might the forms in this cluster be adapted for your students?

B. Bennett, C. Rolheiser-Bennett, L. Stevahn (1991)
Cooperative Learning: Where Heart Meets Mind

Self-evaluation
My Contribution to Our Group Project

YES   **NO**

_____ _____   **1.**   Does the introductory paragraph of my section specifically state the thesis and sub-topic areas?

_____ _____   **2.**   Have I developed the body of my section according to the introductory statement of thesis and sub-topics?

_____ _____   **3.**   Does each paragraph link up with the previous and following paragraphs?

_____ _____   **4.**   Does each paragraph have one central thought?

_____ _____   **5.**   Are the lengths of my sentences varied to avoid monotony?

_____ _____   **6.**   Have I refrained from drawing too much material from one source?

_____ _____   **7.**   Does the language sound like my own?

_____ _____   **8.**   Have I eliminated unnecessary repetition of content?

_____ _____   **9.**   Does my section accomplish the objective as stated in the introductory paragraph?

_____ _____   **10.**   Do my conclusions rest on the evidence presented in my section?

_____ _____   **11.**   Do all comments stem from my findings?

_____ _____   **12.**   As I read it over, is my section clear, does it make sense?

_____ _____   **13.**   Is it interesting to read?

_____ _____   **14.**   Does my section reflect my best effort?

_____ _____   **15.**   Is my section of the report neat and attractive?

_____ _____   **16.**   Have I incorporated creativity?

_____ _____   **17.**   Have I proofread my section to double-check spelling and punctuation?

_____ _____   **18.**   Are the pages in sequence with the remainder of the report?

_____ _____   **19.**   Have I provided a list of resources for the bibliography?

_____ _____   **20.**   Is the bibliography in correct form?

Adapted from: Ontario Secondary School Teachers' Federation. (1989). _Independent Learning: Process To Product._ **Toronto, Ontario.**

My Contribution to Our Group Presentation

Name: _____

Subject/Class: _____

Teacher: _____

Title or description of project: _____

_____

Date: _____

Evaluate your contribution to the group project using the following scale.

1	Unsatisfactory
2	Below average
3	Average
4	Above average
5	Outstanding

1. Originality and creativity of ideas ....

2. Clarity of presentation ....

3. Mastery of content ....

4. Quality of content ....

5. Care and attention to detail ....

6. Energy and enthusiasm ....

7. Organization ....

8. Originality and variety of presentation ....

9. Skill, expertise, and professionalism of presentation ...

10. Value and interest for the audience ....

Total

Adapted from: Ontario Secondary School Teachers' Federation. (1989). *Independent Learning: Process To Product.* Toronto, Ontario.

B. Bennett, C. Rolheiser-Bennett, L. Stevahn (1991) *Cooperative Learning: Where Heart Meets Mind*

How Did I Help My Group?

Name: _____

Group: _____

Date: _____

My task for the group assignment was:

_____

_____

_____

_____

What I did:

_____

_____

_____

_____

How I think my contribution contributed to the overall quality of the group product:

_____

_____

_____

_____

Assessing My Learning

- Review the assignment questions with your group.

- Discuss all questions, then complete the assignment individually.

- Which question were you better able to individually complete after discussion with your group? Explain.

_____

_____

_____

_____

_____

_____

_____

_____

_____

_____

_____

_____

B. Bennett, C. Rolheiser-Bennett, L. Stevahn (1991)
Cooperative Learning: Where Heart Meets Mind

Self-evaluation

Criteria:

Criteria:

List the academic criteria for evaluation that were developed cooperatively.

Rank your performance by circling the appropriate number.

	Low				High
1. _____	1	2	3	4	5
2. _____	1	2	3	4	5
3. _____	1	2	3	4	5
4. _____	1	2	3	4	5
5. _____	1	2	3	4	5

Steps I can take to improve:

_____

_____

_____

Teacher's Comments:

_____

_____

(Adapted from: 1990, Durham Board of Education, Oshawa, Ontario)

Cluster E

(Pages 167 to 173)

- What are the purposes for the forms in this cluster?

- When would these forms be most useful?

- How do these forms relate to your present evaluation practices?

- How might the forms in this cluster be adapted for your students?

B. Bennett, C. Rolheiser-Bennett, L. Stevahn (1991)
Cooperative Learning: Where Heart Meets Mind

Group Evaluation
of Our Written/Oral Report

		Strongly disagree				Strongly agree
1.	Our written/oral report has an introduction that states the thesis and sub-topics.	1	2	3	4	5
2.	Our written/oral report has a body that was developed according to the thesis and sub-topics.	1	2	3	4	5
3.	Our written/oral report has a conclusion that addresses the thesis.	1	2	3	4	5
4.	Our written/oral report contains material that supports our thesis.	1	2	3	4	5
5.	Our headings and visuals make our written/ oral report better understood.	1	2	3	4	5

6. Comments on our learning as a result of this assignment:

Here's the scoop!

_____

_____

_____

_____

_____

(Adapted from: 1990, Durham Board of Education, Oshawa, Ontario)

Group Evaluation of Our Oral Report

1. State the thesis and sub-topics of your group's oral report.

    _____

    _____

2. Explain how effectively your group's oral report developed the topics.

    _____

    _____

    _____

3. How did the audience respond to your oral report?

    _____

    _____

4. How effectively did you respond to questions asked by the audience? Justify your answer.

    _____

    _____

    _____

5. Describe what visual materials you used and how they enhanced your group's report.

    _____

    _____

    _____

6. Other comments:

    _____

    _____

B. Bennett, C. Rolheiser-Bennett, L. Stevahn (1991)
Cooperative Learning: Where Heart Meets Mind

Group Evaluation of
Our Research Project

Yes   **No**

_____ _____   **1.**   Have we clearly stated the purpose of our project?

_____ _____   **2.**   Have we refrained from drawing too much material from one source?

_____ _____   **3.**   Have we explained the project in our own words?

_____ _____   **4.**   Have we eliminated unnecessary repetition of content?

_____ _____   **5.**   Do our conclusions rest on the evidence collected?

_____ _____   **6.**   As we examine our project, does it make sense?

_____ _____   **7.**   Is it interesting?

_____ _____   **8.**   Does the project reflect our best effort?

_____ _____   **9.**   Is the presentation of our final project neat and attractive?

_____ _____ **10.**   Does the final project reflect creativity?

**Adapted from: Ontario Secondary School Teachers' Federation.
(1989).** _Independent Learning: Process To Product._ **Toronto, Ontario.**

B. Bennett, C. Rolheiser-Bennett, L. Stevahn (1991)
Cooperative Learning: Where Heart Meets Mind

Reflecting On Our Group Learning

1. List the steps that your group followed in preparing your group assignment.

    _____

    _____

    _____

    _____

2. What did your group learn from completing the assignment?

    _____

    _____

    _____

    _____

3. What did the people in your group learn that they might not have learned working alone?

    _____

    _____

    _____

4. Prepare one review question on your topic that could be used on an exam.

    _____

    _____

    _____

B. Bennett, C. Rolheiser-Bennett, L. Stevahn (1991)
Cooperative Learning: Where Heart Meets Mind

Group Evaluation of Our Project

Names: _____ _____

_____ _____

Subject/Class: _____

Teacher: _____

Title or Description of Project: _____

_____

_____

Date: _____

Evaluate your group project using the following scale.

| 1 Unsatisfactory |
| 2 Below average |
| 3 Average |
| 4 Above average |
| 5 Outstanding |

1. Originality and creativity of ideas _____

2. Clarity of presentation _____

3. Mastery of content _____

4. Quality of content _____

5. Care and attention to detail _____

6. Energy and enthusiasm _____

7. Organization _____

8. Originality and variety of presentation _____

9. Skill, expertise, and professionalism of presentation _____

10. Value and interest for the audience _____

TOTAL _____

Adapted from: Ontario Secondary School Teachers' Federation.
(1989). *Independent Learning: Process To Product.* Toronto, Ontario.

Team Assessment

1. Outline the steps followed by your group in preparing your report.

_____

_____

_____

_____

2. Sharing with others is an excellent strategy for learning. What did you learn from sharing your ideas with other groups?

_____

_____

_____

_____

3. How might you use what you learned from this assignment outside of the classroom?

_____

_____

_____

_____

B. Bennett, C. Rolheiser-Bennett, L. Stevahn (1991)
Cooperative Learning: Where Heart Meets Mind

Group Think!

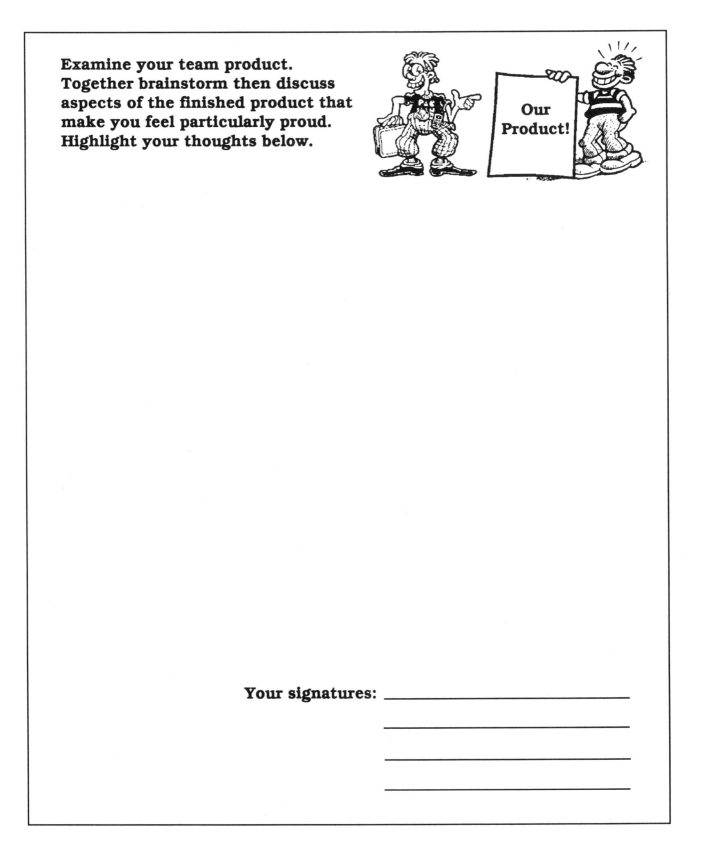

Examine your team product.
Together brainstorm then discuss
aspects of the finished product that
make you feel particularly proud.
Highlight your thoughts below.

Our
Product!

Your signatures: _____

_____

_____

_____

Cluster F

(Pages 175 to 179)

- What are the purposes of the forms in this cluster?

- When would these forms be most useful?

- How do these forms relate to your present evaluation practices?

- How might the forms in this cluster be adapted for your students?

B. Bennett, C. Rolheiser-Bennett, L. Stevahn (1991)
Cooperative Learning: Where Heart Meets Mind

Peer Evaluation of
Another Group's Presentation

		Low				High
1.	Outline/overview of the presentation	1	2	3	4	5
2.	Quality of information	1	2	3	4	5
3.	Delivery of material	1	2	3	4	5
4.	Quality of visuals	1	2	3	4	5
5.	Creativity	1	2	3	4	5

Strength(s) of the presentation observed:

_____

_____

_____

_____

_____

Suggestion(s) for improvement:

_____

_____

_____

_____

_____

(1990, Durham Board of Education, Oshawa, Ontario)

Evaluating the Work of Other Teams

1. What two things did you learn about the topic from the presentation?

    * _____

    * _____

2. Which part of the presentation was the most creative? Why?

    _____

    _____

    _____

3. What did the presenters do to capture the interest of their audience?

    _____

    _____

    _____

4. What suggestion might you offer to the group to strengthen their presentation?

    _____

    _____

    _____

5. Did the presentation make you want to learn more about the topic? Explain your answer.

    _____

    _____

(1990, Durham Board of Education, Oshawa, Ontario)

B. Bennett, C. Rolheiser-Bennett, L. Stevahn (1991)
Cooperative Learning: Where Heart Meets Mind

Anecdotal Peer Evaluation

After observing the presentation of another group, discuss and complete these questions with your own teammates.

What aspects of the group presentation were of greatest interest to you?

_____

_____

_____

_____

_____

_____

Explain what you learned from the other group after listening to how they developed their plans.

_____

_____

_____

_____

_____

Identify the positive features about the group's organization of information.

_____

_____

_____

_____

(1990, Durham Board of Education, Oshawa, Ontario)

Peer Evaluation of Group Presentations

Observer's Name: _____

Group Observed: _____

	Evident	Not Evident
• was organized and prepared for the presentation	_____	_____
• was knowledgeable about the topic presented	_____	_____
• demonstrated an ability to work together as a group	_____	_____
• presented information in a logical way	_____	_____
• was creative in their presentation	_____	_____
• stayed on topic and met their objectives	_____	_____
• encouraged participation from the audience	_____	_____

Strength(s) of the presentation:

_____

_____

_____

_____

Suggestion(s) for improvement:

_____

_____

_____

_____

(Adapted from: 1990, Durham Board of Education, Oshawa, Ontario)

B. Bennett, C. Rolheiser-Bennett, L. Stevahn (1991)
Cooperative Learning: Where Heart Meets Mind

Generating a Peer Evaluation Form
For Creative Presentations

- Well before the presentations, work with the class and develop a list of 10 things that you all decide are aspects of an excellent creative presentation. These become the EVALUATION CRITERIA. For example:

  - audience reaction
  - depth of research
  - audience interest generated in reading the same novel
  - organizing and planning
  - inventiveness
  - etc.

- Establish a MARKING SCALE. Together develop a description for each value on the scale. For example, agreed upon descriptions for a novel review might be:

  10 - so wonderful that it should tour all the schools in the area
  9 - wonderful; you plan to read the book as a result
  8 - very interesting
  7 - satisfactory; you understood it
  6 - good, but you would like to go through it again
  5 - well, at least they did something
  4 - needs more work
  3 - flawed
  2 - embarrassing
  1 - you ran screaming from the room
  0 - what presentation?

- The EVALUATION CRITERIA as well as the MARKING SCALE are printed and used by the students and the teacher.

(Adapted from: Diane Patterson, 1983, York Region Board of Education, Ontario)

Summarizing Student Involvement in Evaluation

The following diagram provides one framework for summarizing the students' role in evaluating Cooperative Learning.

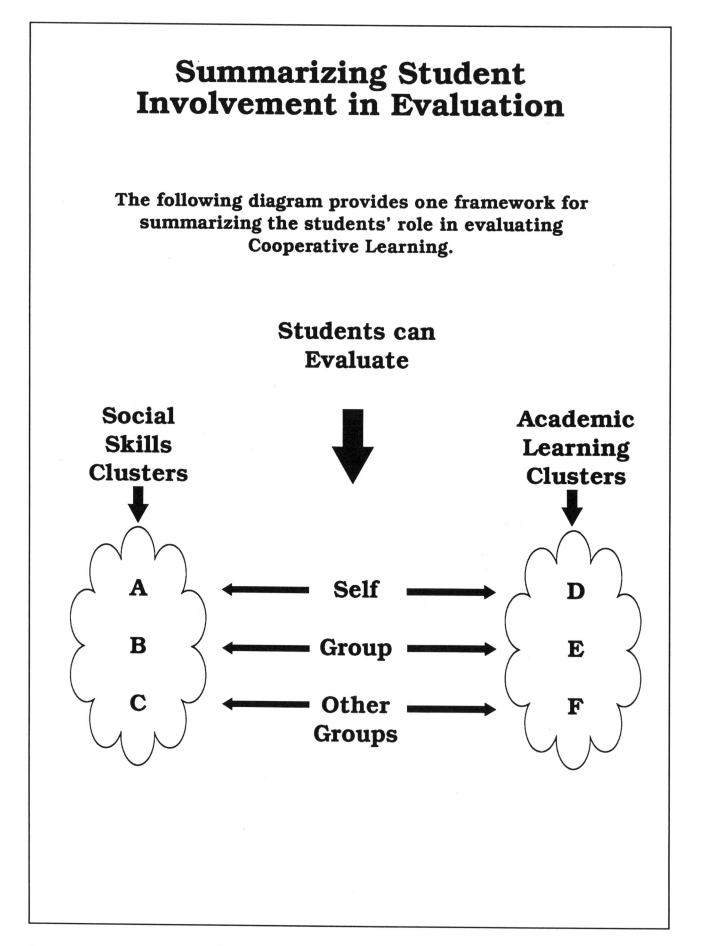

B. Bennett, C. Rolheiser-Bennett, L. Stevahn (1991)
Cooperative Learning: Where Heart Meets Mind

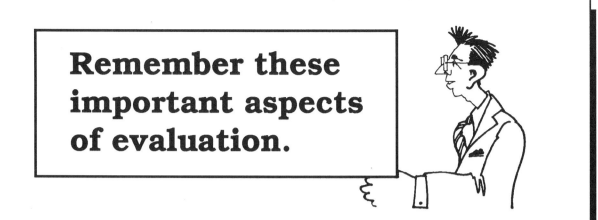

Remember these important aspects of evaluation.

- The teacher plays an active role in the ongoing decisions about evaluation of cooperative learning.

- Students can help decide what to evaluate, when to evaluate, who will evaluate, and how to evaluate. When students help to plan and carry out evaluation their motivation and sense of purpose in learning is strengthened.

- When students evaluate social skills they are engaging in processing — one of the Basic Elements of cooperative learning.

- Processing generally addresses two questions:
  1) How are we effectively using cooperative skills?
  2) How can we improve working together?

- Processing can involve individuals, small groups, or the entire class in reflection and discussion of social skills, as illustrated on the next page.

Processing

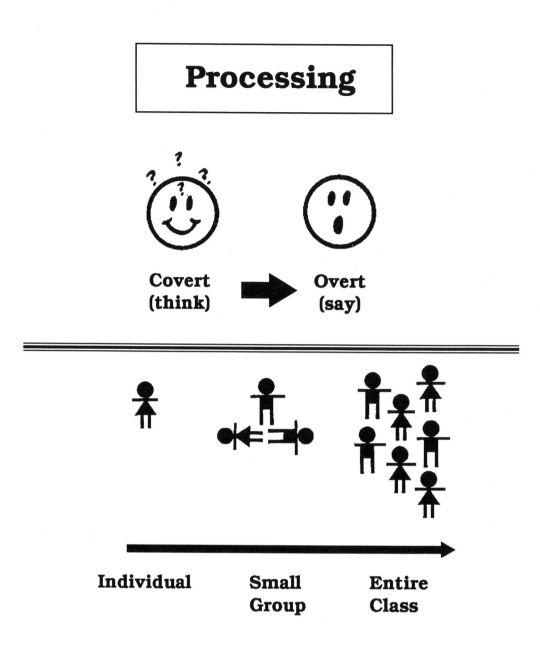

Covert (think) → **Overt (say)**

Individual **Small Group** **Entire Class**

"Members of a group engage in group processing when they discuss how well their group is functioning and how they may improve the group's effectiveness. More specifically, group processing may be defined as reflecting on a group session to describe what member actions were helpful and unhelpful and to make decisions about what actions to continue or change. The purpose of group processing is to clarify and improve the effectiveness of the members in contributing to the collaborative efforts to learn."

- Yager *et al* (1986) -

B. Bennett, C. Rolheiser-Bennett, L. Stevahn (1991)
Cooperative Learning: Where Heart Meets Mind

Your Plan...

Given your teaching situation, develop a plan for increasing student involvement in evaluation of cooperative learning. Remember, as your students become more skilled over time in working in cooperative groups their involvement in evaluation will also develop.

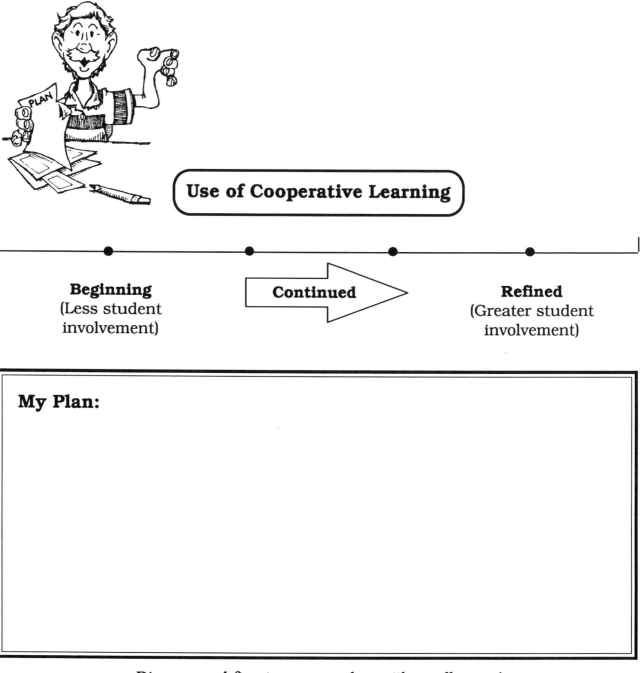

Use of Cooperative Learning

Beginning
(Less student
involvement)

Continued

Refined
(Greater student
involvement)

My Plan:

Discuss and fine-tune your plan with a colleague!

Anticipate Obstacles

Obstacles may arise as you carry out your plan for involving students in evaluation of cooperative groupwork. Some of the more common obstacles include:

- Limited Time

- Vague Assessments

- Lack of Involvement or Investment in Processing

- Blaming Teammates for Lack of Success

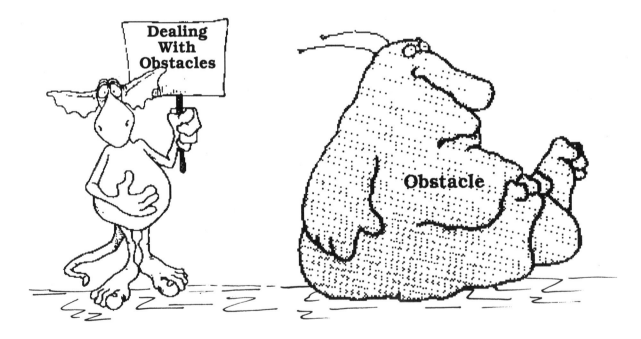

Options for dealing with these obstacles are outlined on the pages that follow.

B. Bennett, C. Rolheiser-Bennett, L. Stevahn (1991)
Cooperative Learning: Where Heart Meets Mind

Obstacle: Limited Time

As you begin using cooperative learning it may be difficult to process social and academic performance given limited time for lessons, as well as unexpected adjustments that must be made throughout instruction. Suggestions for dealing with this obstacle include:

- Quick processing at the end of the lesson (e.g., students respond to processing statements with hand signals to indicate agreement, disagreement, or uncertainty; students privately reflect on processing questions, or quickly share reactions)

- Processing midway through cooperative groupwork (e.g., the teacher stops teams, facilitates processing, then challenges students to implement changes for improvement during the remainder of the activity; the teacher interacts with each team during groupwork and guides group processing)

- Place priority on social processing (e.g., by processing before debriefing academic performance; by discussing academic performance the next day; by giving written feedback on the academic product; by having students finish part of the team assignment at home, if appropriate)

- Incorporate processing questions into the academic assignment (e.g., two questions on the assignment sheet are processing questions)

- Individual processing for homework (e.g., journals or folder writing).

What additional ideas do you have for dealing with this obstacle?

B. Bennett, C. Rolheiser-Bennett, L. Stevahn (1991)
Cooperative Learning: Where Heart Meets Mind

Obstacle: Vague Assessments

Initially, students may evaluate group functioning in vague terms (e.g., "We did great!"; "We worked O.K."; "We need to work together better."). To move students toward more specific analysis and discussion we might:

- Probe for clarification when students give vague responses (e.g., "What did you do that showed cooperation?"

- Model the procedure for processing, using phrases that specifically describe behaviors

- Provide specific feedback on behaviors to each group (e.g., show your written observations to teammates or play back audio or videotapes of their group interaction)

- Provide sentence starters that demand specific examples of behavior for completion (e.g., "You really helped our team when you...") or provide a statement that invites students to provide specific alternatives for completion (e.g., As a team, we need to concentrate on: 1. Asking each other for justification: "Please explain your reason to us." 2. Including everyone: "We need to hear what Erika thinks." 3. Supporting continued effort: "Give it a try and we will coach you.")

- Set a group goal to become more detailed in analyzing performance

- Train students to observe and give teammates specific feedback for use in evaluation.

Specifically, this is what I saw...

What additional ideas do you have for dealing with this obstacle?

B. Bennett, C. Rolheiser-Bennett, L. Stevahn (1991)
Cooperative Learning: Where Heart Meets Mind

Obstacle: Lack of Involvement or Investment in Processing

Sometimes students stay uninvolved or exhibit a lack of seriousness in processing (which results in quick, superficial discussion or messy, incomplete written processing reports). To deal with these problems, structure processing as you would any cooperative task:

- Explain the purpose and importance of processing (older students may benefit by inviting a respected person from the community to speak to the class about the importance of social skills in the workplace, act as an observer with the teacher during groupwork, or provide specific feedback to teams and the class on behaviors observed)

- Assign different, yet interconnected roles for processing (e.g., the roles of Interviewer, Responder, and Recorder can be rotated in a team of three to ensure that each partner responds to processing questions)

- Ask for one written report that all teammates agree upon and sign

- Emphasize improvement as a purpose for processing (e.g., establish baseline data, then apply incentive interdependence to the improvement of academic scores or processing behaviors)

- Incorporate processing into the academic assignment (e.g., provide teams with one math sheet that contains 10 word problems and 2 processing questions)

- Teach the skills needed for involved and invested processing (e.g., active listening, disagreeing in agreeable ways)

- Process the processing. Particularly, discuss with students how it feels to process (recognizing mutual feelings of awkwardness, embarrassment, or self-consciousness can help students overcome initial apprehensiveness toward processing).

What additional ideas do you have for dealing with this obstacle?

Obstacle: Blaming Teammates for Lack of Success

Sometimes teammates blame one another when the team does not fully achieve the criteria for success. When this happens, negative actions become the focus, rather than positive behaviors for improvement. The result can be the promotion of helplessness rather than interdependence. To facilitate positive, helpful discussions for improvement of academic and social performance:

- Model and role play procedures for positive team discussions

- Provide sentence starters that focus attention on improvement in positive ways

- Establish rules for processing that will promote positive discussions on improvement (e.g., Use the word "we" when discussing improvements: "I think we need to concentrate on...")

- Ensure that teammates celebrate successes and express appreciation to one another for cooperative efforts. They may benefit from teacher modeling of validating comments.

What additional ideas do you have for dealing with this obstacle?

B. Bennett, C. Rolheiser-Bennett, L. Stevahn (1991)
Cooperative Learning: Where Heart Meets Mind

Exploring Grading Practices in Cooperative Learning

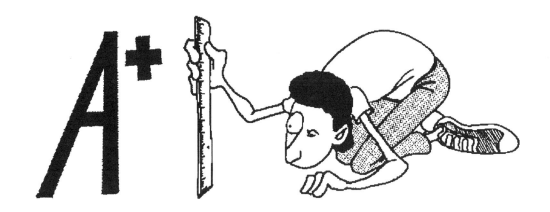

How does the assignment of grades relate to evaluation of social and academic objectives in cooperative learning?

In most cases, the results of cooperative learning will be:

- one group product (e.g., one set of answers, one collage, one lab report, one presentation)

- individual products from teamwork (e.g., personal compositions developed and edited cooperatively, personal exams that follow cooperative study)

- use of social interaction skills that promote cooperative relationships (e.g., complimenting, giving help, asking for help, taking turns, involving everyone).

Given these types of outcomes, individual teachers must decide when it is appropriate to assign grades as well as how to assign grades. **Questions to Guide Grading Decisions** follow, along with explorations of the following options:

- No grade is assigned

- Teammates share a single group grade

- Individual grades are assigned

- Several grading options are combined

Questions to Guide Grading Decisions

Use these questions to guide your thinking as you explore grading options on the pages that follow.

1. What is the purpose of the assignment/activity?

2. What is the duration of the assignment/activity?

3. How much guidance/practice/reflection have students had with...
   - the academic task?
   - social skills for cooperative interaction?

4. Where is your class on the Cooperative Learning Continuum?

5. What other considerations might be important in guiding your decisions about grading practices in cooperative learning?

B. Bennett, C. Rolheiser-Bennett, L. Stevahn (1991)
Cooperative Learning: Where Heart Meets Mind

No Grade is Assigned

At times, you may decide that grading cooperative learning outcomes is not appropriate. This option should be considered especially when:

- the purpose of the cooperative activity or assignment is skill development through practice and feedback or to gather data for formative evaluation of learning progress

- the cooperative activity or assignment will take a relatively short period of time (in proportion to other activities or assignments designed to help students accomplish learning objectives)

- the teacher is introducing and teaching basic social interaction skills for successful groupwork

- the students are initially learning the cooperative skills necessary for academic and social success in groups

- teams are newly formed or ad hoc in nature

- the teacher and students are in "beginning use" stages on the cooperative learning continuum (see page 129)

If these circumstances exist, approach grading with caution. Instead of grading, it may be more appropriate to let the cooperative experience be one of learning for future performances that will be graded.

Evaluation processes are important and need to take place regardless of whether grades are assigned. To maximize learning, involve students in evaluation of both academic and social outcomes (perhaps using evaluation forms like the samples on pages 145 - 186). With students, carefully analyze actions that contributed to success, as well as behaviors that will enhance future performance,

Even when students become skilled with cooperative strategies, you may still choose to involve students in cooperative activities primarily for the purpose of study and mastery of knowledge and skills. Accordingly, individual grades would be determined by performance on individual assignments (e.g., homework or exams) designed to assess mastery.

Teammates Share a Single Group Grade

Determining a single grade that teammates share may be appropriate when:

- cooperative groups produce one shared product

- teammates have had previous successful cooperative experiences with one another (i.e., teammates have developed a sense of shared identity, commitment, and care through previous cooperative activities)

- the purpose of the cooperative activity or assignment is to provide data for a summative measure of learning progress

- the duration of the activity or preparation of the assignment takes a relatively long period of time (in proportion to other experiences designed to help students accomplish learning objectives)

- teammates clearly perceive their interdependent situation and actively employ social interaction skills necessary for productive cooperative work (i.e., teammates skillfully demonstrate the basic elements of cooperative learning during groupwork... which means groups truly are cooperative!)

- teams have opportunities to fine-tune the cooperative outcomes being graded prior to final grading

If you choose to utilize a group grade that all teammates will share, make certain students can actively employ the social interaction skills necessary for a positive experience (e.g., asking for help, assisting in supportive ways, involving everyone, listening carefully, raising questions, disagreeing in agreeable ways, reaching consensus). If students are initially learning these skills, it may be more appropriate for the cooperative experience to be one of practice and improvement for future experiences that will be graded.

When students are ready for the single group grade, be sure all students clearly understand the grading criteria (established by teacher, students or both), as well as the method for determining the mark. Ensuring that each team has a checklist of the criteria prior to the cooperative activity should help students better evaluate their performance while they work. Be sure teammates have ample opportunities to check, question, discuss, and contribute to each other's work prior to final grading. Carefully monitoring teamwork and intervening when necessary will ensure these cooperative behaviors occur. You also might require all teammates to sign completed products indicating agreement and satisfaction with the final outcome before it is graded.

continued...

B. Bennett, C. Rolheiser-Bennett, L. Stevahn (1991)
Cooperative Learning: Where Heart Meets Mind

When groups produce one product, determining a single group grade becomes a matter of applying the pre-established criteria. When group members produce individual products through teamwork, a single group grade can be determined by first marking individual products according to the pre-set criteria, then averaging or accumulatively combining the individual marks for a single team score (see the sample below). Although both the averaging and accumulative score methods for determining a group grade produce equivalent results, the motivational impact on students may be quite different. For example, when the averaging method is employed, the sum of individual scores is divided by the number of teammates in the group. The resulting averaged score may make teammates with the highest individual marks feel that their efforts are not fully credited. Alternatively, when the accumulative score method is employed, the sum of individual scores becomes the total group score. In this case, teammates are more likely to feel fully credited for their efforts. Both methods produce equivalent grades.

Grading Scale	Individual Scores on Products From Teamwork	Group Grade: Averaging Method	Group Grade: Accumulative Score Method
90 - 100% A 80 - 89% B 70 - 79% C 60 - 69% D 0 - 59% F	Armondo +5/10 Katie +9/10 Sonja +10/10	10 points possible Team Average: 24/3 = 8 Team Score: +8/10 Team Grade: B	30 points possible (10 pts. per teammate) Accumulative Team Score: +24/30 Team Grade: B

Finally, if you decide to assign a single group grade for social interaction, be sure to document specific cooperative behaviors you observe. Tally grids are particularly useful for this purpose (e.g., see page 132).

Individual Grades are Assigned

Individual grades may be appropriate when:

- individual products are developed through cooperative groupwork (e.g., compositions, reports, blueprints)

- individual assignments or exams are administered to measure and report individual accomplishment of cooperative study

- teammates have devoted a great deal of time cooperatively preparing individual products or studying for individual exams (in proportion to time spent on other learning activities)

- individual mastery of knowledge or skills needs to be assessed and reported at the end of a unit of study

- students initially are learning the cooperative skills necessary to assist one another throughout groupwork

If these circumstances exist, you may decide to determine individual grades in the same way that you already grade individualistic assignments. If you choose to grade individuals on social interaction, be sure to document your observations.

Even when groups submit one product, you still may decide to individually grade students on their roles, ability to explain or defend the group product, or their use of social interaction skills during groupwork.

B. Bennett, C. Rolheiser-Bennett, L. Stevahn (1991)
Cooperative Learning: Where Heart Meets Mind

Several Grading Options are Combined

Given your situation, it may be appropriate to combine several grading options. The following examples illustrate several possibilities.

- Teammates produce individual products through groupwork. Two academic grades are determined: an individual grade for the individual product as well as a shared team grade by averaging. The two grades can be recorded separately or be combined into one overall academic mark. A third grade for cooperative interaction may also be added.

- Teammates produce one group product. Two grades are determined. First, teammates share a single group grade on the finished product. Second, teammates are graded individually on how well they executed their assigned roles during the cooperative activity. The two grades can be recorded separately or be combined into one overall mark. A third grade for cooperative interaction may also be added.

- Teammates earn individual scores on exams that follow cooperative study. The scores are averaged to determine whether teammates will also earn bonus points to be added to their individual exam scores (e.g., if every partner in the group scores at least 80 percent on the exam, then every partner will earn 5 bonus points to be added to their individual exam scores).

- Academic grades are combined with grades for cooperative behavior (e.g., 30% of an individual's overall grade is based on participation, 35% on group academic scores, and 35% on individual academic scores).

- Students develop personal portfolios containing a variety of measures to document learning progress.

What other combinations make sense in your teaching situation?

Developing Your Plan for Grading Cooperative Learning *

On the page that follows...

- List the types of group and individual products from teamwork that you assign when employing cooperative learning (columns 1 and 2).

- List the social interaction skills you have taught and expect students to utilize during groupwork (column 3).

- Use the **Questions to Guide Grading Decisions** on page 190 and determine which grading options are most appropriate for your students.

> Discuss your options with a colleague...
> and together explore the implications of each choice.

---

* See also: Clarke, J., Wideman, R., & Eadie, S. (1990). *Together We Learn*. Scarborough, Ontario: Prentice-Hall Canada.

B. Bennett, C. Rolheiser-Bennett, L. Stevahn (1991)
Cooperative Learning: Where Heart Meets Mind

Grading Practices

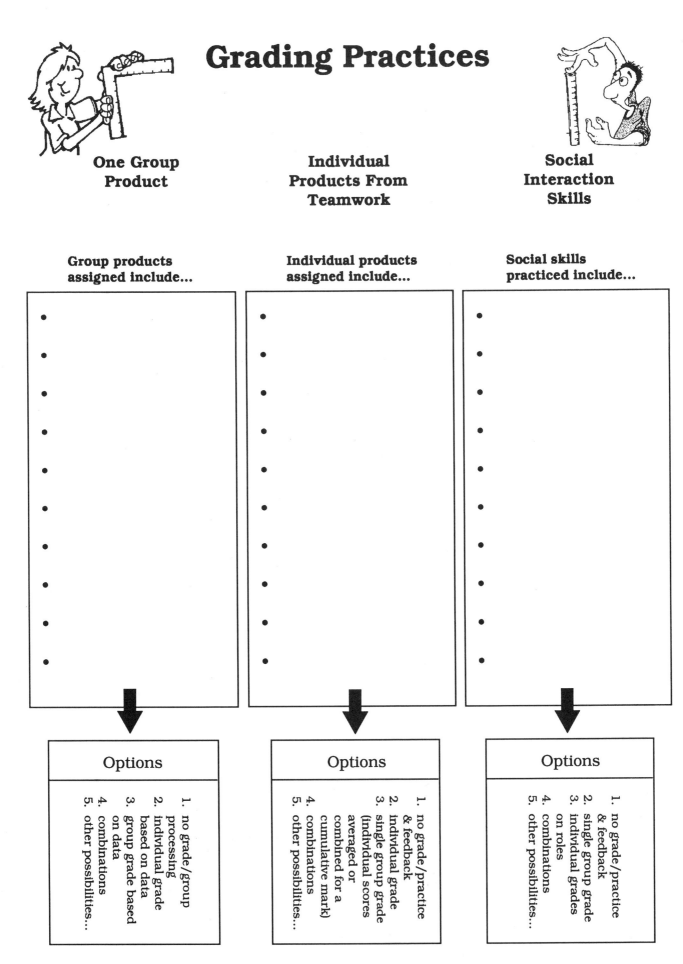

One Group Product

Individual Products From Teamwork

Social Interaction Skills

Group products assigned include...

-
-
-
-
-
-
-
-
-

Individual products assigned include...

-
-
-
-
-
-
-
-
-

Social skills practiced include...

-
-
-
-
-
-
-
-
-

Options

1. no grade/group processing
2. individual grade based on data
3. group grade based on data
4. combinations
5. other possibilities...

Options

1. no grade/practice & feedback
2. individual grade
3. single group grade (individual scores averaged or combined for a cumulative mark)
4. combinations
5. other possibilities...

Options

1. no grade/practice & feedback
2. single group grade
3. individual grades on roles
4. combinations
5. other possibilities...

B. Bennett, C. Rolheiser-Bennett, L. Stevahn (1991)
Cooperative Learning: Where Heart Meets Mind

Remember . . .

- Approach "shared group grades" with caution. Students need practice and a certain degree of competence with cooperative learning to be able to effectively deal with shared marks. When students have learned how to cooperatively work with one another, have confidence in their abilities, and have developed a sense of trust and commitment, shared marks are not threatening, but rather, perceived as fair.

- Consider the pros and cons, as well as the motivational implications of the grading methods you employ.

- Document social skill observations by recording specific behaviors. The information is useful for grading as well as providing feedback for processing.

- Students are motivated to be involved in learning when the learning experience is perceived as personally meaningful. Group rewards that are fun, that capture imagination, and that focus on shared celebrations of success (like the examples on page 61) may be most effective in motivating students to work together and learn. When learning outcomes need to be measured and reported, grades will reflect student accomplishments.

B. Bennett, C. Rolheiser-Bennett, L. Stevahn (1991)
Cooperative Learning: Where Heart Meets Mind

Chapter 10

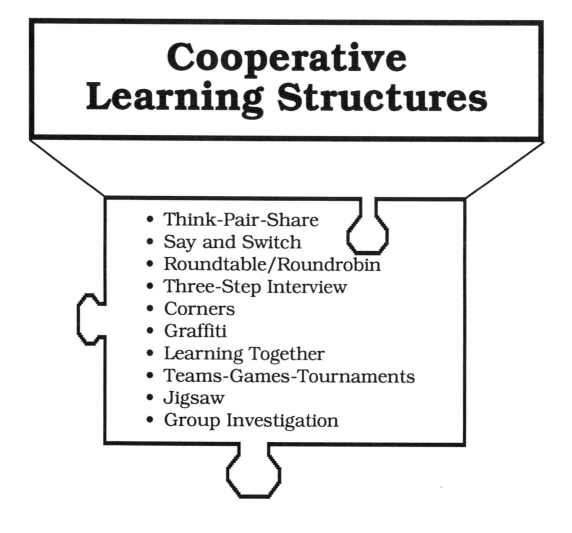

Cooperative Learning Structures

- Think-Pair-Share
- Say and Switch
- Roundtable/Roundrobin
- Three-Step Interview
- Corners
- Graffiti
- Learning Together
- Teams-Games-Tournaments
- Jigsaw
- Group Investigation

Overview

This chapter briefly examines a number of cooperative learning structures including: Think-Pair-Share, Say and Switch, Roundtable/ Roundrobin, Three-Step Interview, Corners, Graffiti, Learning Together, Teams-Games-Tournaments, Jigsaw, and Group Investigation. The questions that start the chapter initiate personal reflection on classroom experimentations with cooperative structures. Then, both simpler and more complex structures are described and applications explored. The chapter concludes by examining interrelationships between cooperative structures and basic elements of cooperative learning.

Structures for Cooperative Learning

Every cooperative activity has a specific structure (i.e., a particular procedure that can be described step-by-step).

- How have you structured cooperative activities?
- Which were simpler to set up?
- Which were simplest for students to follow?
- Which were more complex?
- What skills did students need to be successful with that structure?

Step 1 _____

Step 2 _____

Step 3 _____

A variety of simple and more complex cooperative structures are described in the pages that follow. When using any of these structures, the content may change but the procedures for engaging in the activity (i.e., the structure) remain the same. Consider each structure described and how it might be useful in your teaching.

B. Bennett, C. Rolheiser-Bennett, L. Stevahn (1991)
Cooperative Learning: Where Heart Meets Mind

Think-Pair-Share

Think-Pair-Share (Kagan, 1990) is a cooperative structure in which partners privately think about a question (or issue, situation, idea, etc.), then discuss their responses with one another. As a relatively simple structure that can be implemented quickly, Think-Pair-Share can be incorporated into almost any form of instruction. It is particularly useful for actively involving all students during lectures.

Formulate-Share-Listen-Create (Johnson, Johnson, & Bartlett, 1990) is a similar structure in which teammates first privately formulate responses, each share and listen in turn, then together create a new answer or perspective through discussion and elaboration. It too has widespread application and encourages students to stretch their thinking.

By promoting focused, short-term, purposeful talk among students, informal cooperative learning structures like Think-Pair-Share and Formulate-Share-Listen-Create can initially ease students into cooperative peer relationships. As students learn to work cooperatively on more complex team tasks, these informal structures can be used to facilitate group interaction.

How might you utilize **Think-Pair-Share** or **Formulate-Share-Listen-Create** in your teaching? The following pages outline procedures and may be useful when introducing the structures to students.

1. Think

2. Pair

3. Share

B. Bennett, C. Rolheiser-Bennett, L. Stevahn (1991)
Cooperative Learning: Where Heart Meets Mind

• *Formulate*

... an answer individually

• *Share*

... your answer with a partner

• *Listen*

... carefully to your partner's answer

• *Create*

... a new answer through discussion

Say and Switch

Say and Switch is a cooperative structure in which partners sequentially take turns responding to a question or discussion topic at signalled (and sometimes unpredictable) intervals. After the discussion topic is identified, the first partner begins to respond while the second carefully listens. At the signal, roles switch and the second partner responds while the first carefully listens. When the switch occurs, the challenge for the second partner is to continue (*or* complete) the first partner's line of thought before introducing new ideas. Several switches may take place throughout the period of time allotted for discussion. **Say and Switch** is particularly useful as a structure for reviewing, rehearsing, or checking for understanding. In addition, it holds both students accountable to participate.

Sample Topic: Environmental Responsibility in Manufacturing

- *Say*

> Legislation should require manufacturers to use recycled material in production. The technology exists and ...

> ... if we don't apply it we run the risk of totally depleting our nonrenewable resources. However, that will increase manufacturing costs. Consumers may not be willing to pay higher prices in the marketplace. Another solution might be ...

- *Switch*

How might you utilize **Say and Switch** in your teaching?

B. Bennett, C. Rolheiser-Bennett, L. Stevahn (1991)
Cooperative Learning: Where Heart Meets Mind

Roundtable/Roundrobin

Roundtable (Kagan, 1990) is a cooperative structure in which one paper and pencil are systematically passed around the group. For example, one partner writes an idea, then passes the paper and pencil to the partner on the left. A variation of the procedure is to have each partner hold and use a different colored writing tool while the paper gets passed. This visually reinforces that all partners are contributing equally while also allowing the teacher to document individual contributions.

Roundrobin (Kagan, 1990) is the oral form of Roundtable. Each teammate verbally contributes an idea to the group in a systematic, "around-the-group" fashion.

Roundtable

(written contribution,
then paper passes to the left)

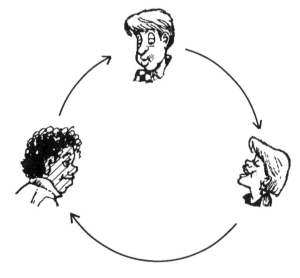

Roundrobin

(verbal contribution,
then turn passes to the left)

How might you utilize **Roundtable or Roundrobin** in your teaching?

Three-Step Interview

Three-Step Interview (Kagan, 1990) is a cooperative structure in which teammates interview one another on a particular topic. For example, in a team of three, partner A interviews Partner B, while Partner C records key aspects of the response. Roles rotate after each interview, allowing all members the opportunity to be interviewed.

In a group of 4, the three steps can progress as follows:
1. A interviews B while C simultaneously interviews D.
2. Roles reverse, with B now interviewing A, and D interviewing C.
3. The group of 4 reconvene with each person sharing their partners response.

Three-Step Interview can be incorporated into any type of lesson, while the content of the interview can be virtually anything. For example, this structure can be used:

- as an anticipatory set – "What are the questions you would like to explore related to this topic?" or "What do you already know about this topic?"
- to share personal experiences or express opinions – "What 3 qualities do you most value in a friend and why?"; "If you could go 'back to the future,' where would you go? What time period would you choose? What social changes would you make?" (See pages 249 and 250 for more examples.)
- to summarize the learning in a lesson – "What would you like to know more about as a result of our lesson today?"; "What was the most meaningful idea for you today and why? What will you do to apply today's learning?"
- to review homework – "What were the key points from last night's reading?"; "What was the most interesting part of your homework – the most difficult?"
- to explore concepts in content areas – "How does your family attend to environmental issues?"; "How did you solve the math problem?"; "What is your hypothesis or prediction at this point?"

The Three-step Interview is a natural structure for practicing a range of social skills, in particular listening and communication skills (e.g., active listening, use of open-ended questions, probing, clarifying, etc.).

How might you utilize the **Three-Step Interview** in your teaching? The following page outlines the procedure and may be useful when introducing the structure to students.

B. Bennett, C. Rolheiser-Bennett, L. Stevahn (1991)
Cooperative Learning: Where Heart Meets Mind

Three-Step Interview

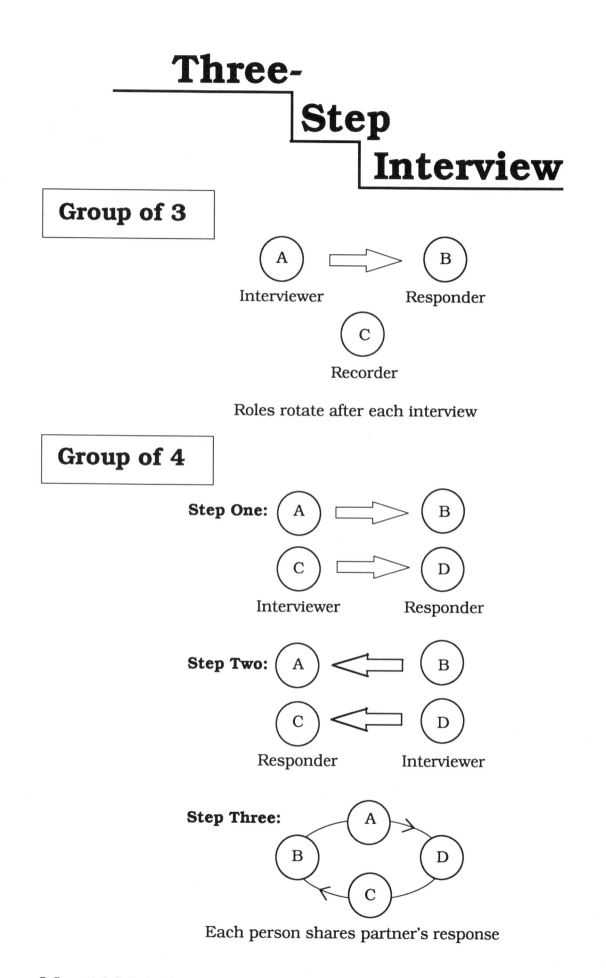

Group of 3

A — Interviewer ⇒ B — Responder

C — Recorder

Roles rotate after each interview

Group of 4

Step One: A ⇒ B

C ⇒ D

Interviewer — Responder

Step Two: A ⇐ B

C ⇐ D

Responder — Interviewer

Step Three:

B — A — D — C

Each person shares partner's response

B. Bennett, C. Rolheiser-Bennett, L. Stevahn (1991)
Cooperative Learning: Where Heart Meets Mind

Corners

Corners (Kagan, 1990) is a cooperative structure that enables students to choose and discuss a particular dimension of a topic. To facilitate the activity, different dimensions of a topic are posted in designated corners of the room. Then, each student selects a particular dimension in response to a question asked by the teacher, and moves to the appropriate corner. For example, suppose the names of different characters from a storybook or novel are posted in each corner. The teacher might ask: "Who was your favorite character?" or "Which character would you most like to meet?" or "Which character do you think was most responsible for the dilemma?" Once in their selected corner, students pair up to discuss the reasons for their choice. Students might also address additional questions designated to foster critical thinking around the topic.

After discussion, the teacher randomly selects pairs from each corner to report their thinking to the class. By having representatives from each corner present their viewpoints, varying perspectives and rationale for selection emerge. Teachers or students can determine the topics and dimensions for discussion. For example, the following topics and corresponding dimensions might be posted.

Volleyball Skills: Serve, Bump, Set, Spike
("What skill would you most like to develop?")

Current Issues: Poverty, Drug abuse, Crime, Pollution
("If you were the leader of your country, which issue would be your top priority?")

**Geographical
Regions:** South America, Europe, Africa, Australia
("What region would you most like to study?")

**Controversial
Issues:** Strongly agree, Disagree, Agree, Strongly disagree
("All forms of violence should be censored on television" or
"All students are treated fairly at our school.")

**Community
Interview:** 75% and above, 50 - 75%, 25 - 50%, less then 25%
("Predict the percentage of people who will respond affirmatively to the survey.")

B. Bennett, C. Rolheiser-Bennett, L. Stevahn (1991)
Cooperative Learning: Where Heart Meets Mind

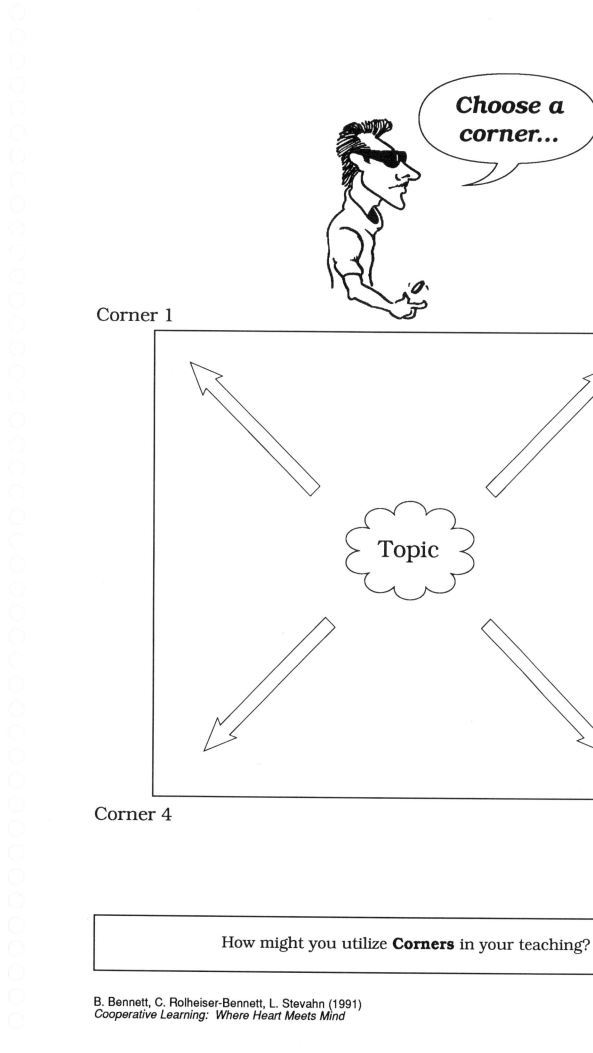

How might you utilize **Corners** in your teaching?

B. Bennett, C. Rolheiser-Bennett, L. Stevahn (1991)
Cooperative Learning: Where Heart Meets Mind

Graffiti

Graffiti (Gibbs, 1987) is a cooperative structure that facilitates brainstorming and also doubles as a group energizer. Each cooperative group of 3 or 4 is given a piece of butcher paper and different colored felt pens (one for each group member allowing each individual's contribution to be tracked). Then each group is given a different question, topic, issue, or statement to which they respond. For example, "I feel happiest when..." or "What words come to mind when you think of the ideal school classroom?" or "Ways to conserve energy," etc. For a short period of time every group in the room writes their "graffiti" (words, phrases, graphics) on their particular topic. The teacher then stops them, asks each group to pass their graffiti sheet to the next group and the process repeats itself, with each group now responding to the new topic. The process continues until a group's original sheet returns to them. Then, as a group they read all of the "new" comments, discuss and summarize. They may also wish to categorize the comments in order to draw conclusions or present a brief summary presentation to the class. Note that if the class is large, each topic could be repeated once, so instead of 8 topics, there might only be 4, and rotation would only occur to half the class (while the other half rotated through the same topics at the same time).

Another variation of graffiti is to have each group follow the same initial step as outlined above. The only difference is when the teacher stops them the first time, all members depart from their group, leaving their graffiti sheet behind. Over the next number of minutes all class members can go to any other graffiti sheet in the class and add their comments/visuals to it. They cannot return to any one graffiti sheet unless they've contributed to all the others. At the end of the designated time allotment, team members return to their original graffiti sheet to read, discuss, summarize, and possibly present it (as outlined in the previous variation).

Graffiti works very effectively as an anticipatory set or closure activity, or as an energizer during any lesson where generation of ideas is desired.

How might you utilize **Graffiti** in your teaching? What variations might you try? The following page outlines the procedures and may be useful when introducing the structure to students.

B. Bennett, C. Rolheiser-Bennett, L. Stevahn (1991)
Cooperative Learning: Where Heart Meets Mind

Graffiti Steps

Step 1

Each group writes graffiti on assigned topic for _____ minutes.

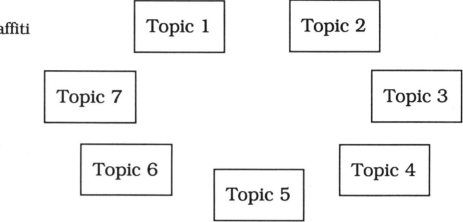

Step 2

Groups stop, then pass their sheet to the next group. (Variation: Group members leave home base and individually walk from table to table, adding graffiti to other sheets.)

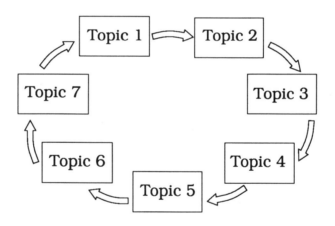

Step 3

Sheets are passed until original graffiti sheet returns to the home group. (Variation: After _____ minutes return to your original graffiti.)

Step 4

Each group...
- Reads
- Discusses
- Summarizes
- Presents

} ... their graffiti ideas.

B. Bennett, C. Rolheiser-Bennett, L. Stevahn (1991)
Cooperative Learning: Where Heart Meets Mind

Learning Together

Learning Together (Johnson & Johnson, 1991) is characterized by teammates in small heterogeneous groups working cooperatively to accomplish mutual learning goals. Together, teammates work on an academic task which often involves preparing a single cohesive team product (such as one set of answers, one illustration, one report, etc.). Social skills needed for successful teamwork are directly taught, practiced, reinforced, and processed. Groups that achieve the pre-established criteria for success mutually share rewards (intrinsic pride from accomplishment and, if appropriate, extrinsic awards).

Typically referred to as a conceptual approach, Learning Together is based on the presence of five basic elements of cooperative learning (i.e., positive interdependence, individual accountability, face-to-face interaction, social skills, and group processing). Although specific directions may vary between different Learning Together tasks, the basic elements of cooperative learning are carefully incorporated into each Learning Together experience. The sample cooperative lessons in Chapter 12 illustrate a variety of Learning Together lessons.

How might you utilize **Learning Together** in your teaching? The Cooperative Learning Lesson Planning Guides in Chapter 13 may be useful for developing your own Learning Together lessons.

B. Bennett, C. Rolheiser-Bennett, L. Stevahn (1991)
Cooperative Learning: Where Heart Meets Mind

Teams-Games-Tournaments

Teams-Games-Tournaments (Slavin, 1986) is a cooperative structure in which teammates cooperatively study to master learning, then individually apply their learning in a competitive game. Specifically, heterogeneous Cooperative Teams (i.e., mixed ability groups) are formed to study or review learning from previous teaching. Then, individuals move to homogeneous Tournament Teams (i.e., equal ability groups) to compete in a game based on the learning. Typically, the game is one in which students take turns answering questions. Individuals win points for each question correctly answered. After the tournament, students return to their Cooperative Teams with their individual scores. Each Cooperative Team calculates a Total Team Score and winning teams are recognized.

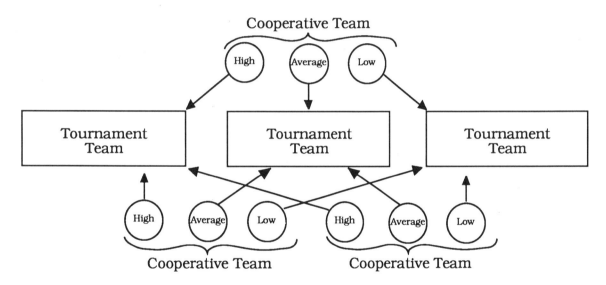

In addition to providing students with opportunities to practice cooperative skills necessary for productive study and review, Teams-Games-Tournaments also provide opportunities to practice and process social skills that comprise good sportsmanship. Prior to the tournaments, discuss with students what it means to be a good sport, challenging them to describe specific examples. Also, discuss the benefits of good sportsmanship to increase the likelihood that students will compete with one another in fun, appropriate ways.

> How might you utilize **Teams-Games-Tournaments** in your teaching? The following pages provide sample directions and materials. Consider ways you would adapt the example to meet the learning needs of your students.

Teams-Games-Tournaments:
Sample Directions

(1) Select a name for your Cooperative Team (three teammates).

(2) With your Cooperative Team, study or review _____.

   Time: _____

(3) Move to your Tournament Team (three people).

(4) Each Tournament Team gets:

   One envelope of Question Cards (see page 218)
   One Tally Sheet (see page 216 or 217)

   ROLES: Quizzer   ☞ Reads Question Card

           Responder   ☞ Answers the question

           Recorder   ☞ Marks points for correct
                            answers on the Tally Sheet

   NOTE: Roles and materials rotate after each turn.
           Every individual gets the same number of turns to answer
           questions (e.g., 10 turns each).

(5) Return to your Cooperative Team with your individual score.

(6) Calculate a total Cooperative Team score by adding individual scores.
     Record the total on your Cooperative Team Total Score Sheet (see page 215),
     then submit the sheet to the teacher.

(7) Winning <u>teams</u> will be recognized!

(Note: Teachers have the option of recognizing the highest scoring team or any teams achieving over a preset
    criterion.)

                                    B. Bennett, C. Rolheiser-Bennett, L. Stevahn (1991)
Cooperative Learning: Where Heart Meets Mind

Teams-Games-Tournaments:
Cooperative Team Total
Score Sheet*

Team Name: ───────────────────────

Your Name _____ **Score** _____

Your Name _____ **Score** _____

Your Name _____ **Score** _____

**Total
Team
Score**

---

* Cooperative teams use this page to calculate their total team score after participating in the tournament.

Teams-Games-Tournaments:
Tally Sheet*

Cooperative Team Name	Question										Total
	1	2	3	4	5	6	7	8	9	10	

* Tournament Teams may use this page to record individual points for correct answers. The name of the Cooperative Team that each individual represents is written on the sheet before the tournament begins. Individuals take their scores back to their Cooperative Teams, respectively.

B. Bennett, C. Rolheiser-Bennett, L. Stevahn (1991)
Cooperative Learning: Where Heart Meets Mind

Teams-Games-Tournaments
Individual Tally Sheet*

Your Name _____

Directions: Mark ✓ or ✗.

1. _____

2. _____

3. _____

4. _____

5. _____

6. _____

7. _____

8. _____

9. _____

10. _____

= Total Correct

---

* It may be easier for students to use Individual Tally Sheets during the tournament (as opposed to the group tally sheet on the preceding page). When this option is chosen, each student brings an Individual Tally Sheet to the Tournament Team where the sheets are exchanged for scoring during the competition. After the tournament, individuals bring their completed tally sheets back to their Cooperative Teams, respectively.

Preparing Question Cards

- Draw identical boxes on both sides of an 8 ¹/₂ x 11 paper.

Front		Back	
Question #1	Question #6	Answer #6	Answer #1
Question #2	Question #7	Answer #7	Answer #2
Question #3	Question #8	Answer #8	Answer #3
Question #4	Question #9	Answer #9	Answer #4
Question #5	Question #10	Answer #10	Answer #5

- Write questions on the front (one question per box).

- Write answers on the back. Carefully match each answer to the corresponding question on the front.

- Make a double-sided copy, cut boxes, and place cards in an envelope.

- Prepare one set of Question Cards for each Tournament Team.

Note: Each set of Question Cards should contain enough questions for each individual to respond to a new question every turn during the tournament. For example, when Tournament Teams consist of three individuals and each individual will respond 10 times, each set of Question Cards needs to contain at least 30 different questions.

B. Bennett, C. Rolheiser-Bennett, L. Stevahn (1991)
Cooperative Learning: Where Heart Meets Mind

Jigsaw

Cooperative **Jigsaw** structures (e.g., Aronson, 1980; Johnson, Johnson, & Holubec, 1990; Kagan, 1990) are basically characterized by teammates within a Cooperative Group each becoming expert on different aspects of one topic of study. For example, if a Cooperative Group is studying the topic of "Japanese Culture," one teammate could become an expert on "traditional values," another an expert on "government structures," and the third an expert on "current issues." After developing individual expertise on the assigned subtopic, teammates take turns teaching one another. The Cooperative Group goal is that all teammates master all aspects of the major topic.

Before presenting and teaching to the Cooperative Group, students form Expert Groups comprised of individuals from different Cooperative Groups who have the same assigned subtopic (e.g., two students from different groups studying "current issues" would meet as expert partners on that subtopic). Together, expert partners study their subtopic and plan effective ways to teach important information when they return to their Cooperative Groups. After teaching and checking takes place back in Cooperative Groups, individual mastery of the topic is evaluated (e.g., students respond when called upon during whole class questioning, write individual exams, or draw individual concept maps). The following diagram illustrates the basic jigsaw process.

Cooperative Groups
(material assigned)

Expert Groups
(study and prepare)

Cooperative Groups
(teach and check)

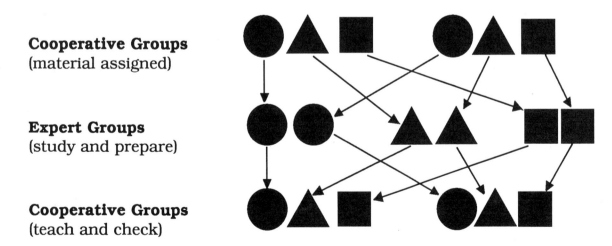

How might you utilize **Jigsaw** in your teaching? The following pages outline two variations of Jigsaw. Consider ways you would adapt the examples to meet the learning needs of your students. What other variations of Jigaw might you try?

Basic Jigsaw

Step 1: Arrange Cooperative Groups & Assign Material

Within each Cooperative Group, teammates are assigned different material to learn and present to one another (e.g., the first teammate is assigned page 1, the second teammate is assigned page 2, and the third teammate is assigned page 3).

Step 2: Expert Groups Study and Prepare Presentations

Expert Groups are formed by pairing students with the same assigned material (e.g., the person in Cooperative Group A who was assigned page 1 will meet with the person in Cooperative Group B who was assigned page 1). Expert partners read and study their material together, plan effective ways to teach their material, and plan ways to check for comprehension of Cooperative Group teammates.

Step 3: Return to Cooperative Groups for Teaching and Checking

Individuals return to their Cooperative Groups. Cooperative Group members take turns presenting their material to one another. The team goal is for all group members to master all of the material presented.

Step 4: Individual and Group Accountability

Groups are accountable for ensuring that all members master all of the material. Individuals may be asked to demonstrate mastery in a variety of ways (e.g., by writing an exam, responding orally to random questions, or making a presentation on material taught by teammates).

B. Bennett, C. Rolheiser-Bennett, L. Stevahn (1991)
Cooperative Learning: Where Heart Meets Mind

Jigsaw Variation*

Cooperative Groups
meet and each teammate
is assigned different
material to learn.

Preparation Pairs
meet and students with
the same assigned material
together read and prepare
to teach their material.

Practice Pairs
meet to rehearse and
fine-tune presentations
as well as gain additional
ideas from one another.

Cooperative Groups
reconvene and teammates
take turns presenting and
teaching their material
to one another.

Mastery
is assessed through whole
class debriefing, oral
quizzing, individual exams,
class presentations, etc.

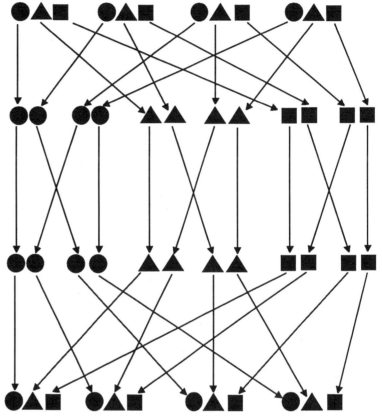

* Adapted from: Johnson, D.W., Johnson, R.T., & Holubec, E.J. (1990). *Cooperation in the Classroom* (rev. ed.). Edina, MN: Interaction Book Company.

Group Investigation

Group Investigation (Sharan & Hertz-Lazarowitz, 1980; Sharan & Sharan, 1990) is a cooperative structure that enables students to plan and carry out a course of study. This includes identifying a topic for investigation, planning and carrying out the investigation, and preparing a final presentation. This structure is a more complex one in that students are involved in multifaceted learning tasks that demand greater student autonomy and group self-direction.

The following pages describe the six stages in the Group Investigation process:

1. **Grouping**
2. **Planning**
3. **Investigating**
4. **Organizing**
5. **Presenting**
6. **Evaluating**

How might you utilize **Group Investigation** in your teaching? What adaptations would you make?

B. Bennett, C. Rolheiser-Bennett, L. Stevahn (1991)
Cooperative Learning: Where Heart Meets Mind

Group Investigation

Stage 1: Grouping

Identifying the topic for investigaiton and organizing the students into research groups

Step 1: Present the Topic
- Present a multi-faceted topic to the class which will trigger a variety of reactions. Present the topic as a question to define scope and set the tone of the inquiry (e.g., "What can we learn from a study of pioneer life in Upper Canada?" or "What can we learn about our culture through media?"
- Have students scan a variety of resources (films, texts, picture books, magazines, articles, etc.) to stimulate inquiry.

Step 2: Clarify the Topic
- The class compiles a list of questions for group inquiry. A variety of methods can be used, including:
  - a) Whole class – Students raise questions they would like to investigate and compile a list.
  - b) Small group – In groups of four students record ideas for investigation and report to the whole class. A class discussion of all lists results in one shared list.
  - c) Individual – Students write down their own questions and progress with their planning to larger groups (e.g., pairs, quartets). Questions are compared at each step and repetition eliminated until a single list is compiled.

Step 3: Identify Sub-topics
- The list of questions compiled by the class are classified into categories. The categories become the sub-topics for the group investigation.

Step 4: Form Investigation Groups
- Students select the sub-topic of their choice and form groups accordingly. If a large group forms around a popular sub-topic, that group may be divided to limit numbers. Although student choice of inquiry topics is paramount, teachers may also need to consider heterogeneity of groups.

B. Bennett, C. Rolheiser-Bennett, L. Stevahn (1991)
Cooperative Learning: Where Heart Meets Mind

Group Investigation

Stage 2: Planning

Group planning for investigation

Step 1: Clarify the Task
- Each group explores its sub-topic and formulates a researchable problem. Focus questions are developed to outline the scope of the inquiry.

Step 2: Develop an Action Plan
- Each group plans a course of action by:
  - a) deciding what aspects of the sub-topic are to be investigated by each group member (e.g., Will each member investigate a different aspect or will members investigate in pairs?);
  - b) establishing individual deadlines for reporting back to the group;
  - c) determining the resources needed to carry out the task;
  - d) re-examining the original plan to consider alternatives if group members are not happy;
  - e) completing a worksheet (see next page) that structures the planning stage and records all group members' progress;
  - f) determining job responsibilities, including materials manager, coordinator of group discussions, recorder for whole class reporting, worksheet and steering committee representative. This last role involves hearing other group's reporting plans and helping to schedule final presentations.

B. Bennett, C. Rolheiser-Bennett, L. Stevahn (1991)
Cooperative Learning: Where Heart Meets Mind

Planning Sheet for Group Investigation

Research Topic:
State the group investigation sub-topic in question form.

_____

Group Members and Roles:
Coordinator, Recorder, Resource Person, Steering Committee, etc.

	Name	Role
1.	_____	_____
2.	_____	_____
3.	_____	_____
4.	_____	_____

Specific Group Research Assignments:

	Name	Specific Task
1.	_____	_____
2.	_____	_____
3.	_____	_____
4.	_____	_____

Resources:
A. Books and Documents:

_____

_____

B. People:

_____

_____

C. Sites, Artifacts, and Audio-Visual:

_____

_____

(Bob Walker, 1990, Durham Board of Education, Oshawa, Ontario)

Group Investigation

Stage 3: Investigating

Carrying out the investigation

Step 1: Prepare a Daily Plan
- Group members complete an action plan sheet for each investigation day (see next page).

Step 2: Research the Sub-topic
- Group members gather information from a variety of sources.

Step 3: Analyze and Evaluate the Data
- Group members assess the relevance of the collected data relative to their specific research topic.

Step 4: Apply the Data
- Group members apply their share of new knowledge to "solving" the group research problem.

B. Bennett, C. Rolheiser-Bennett, L. Stevahn (1991)
Cooperative Learning: Where Heart Meets Mind

Our Group's Daily Investigation Action Plan

Date: _____

Group Plan:

	Name	**Action**
1.		

2. _____

3. _____

4. _____

Possible Action Plan Ideas

- Researching in the Resource Center
- Summarizing notes on a visit to a site
- Interviewing a resource person
- Reading a relevant article
- Viewing a specific audiovisual resource
- Sharing information
- Analyzing and evaluating data collected
- Comparing the findings of group members
- Discussing conclusions
- Assisting a team member
- Writing an inter-group summary
- Other...

(Bob Walker, 1990, Durham Board of Education, Oshawa, Ontario)

Group Investigation

Stage 4: Organizing

Preparing for a Final Report

Step 1: Select the Report Vehicle
- The group, in conjunction with the teacher, decides the presentation format to be used to share findings with the rest of the class. Possible presentation formats include:
  - exhibits
  - learning centers
  - guided tours
  - slide presentations
  - models
  - written reports
  - dramatic presentations
  - other...

Step 2: Plan the Report
- Group members discuss individual roles in the final report.
- Group members complete a report to the steering committee upon completion of their presentation plan (see next page).

Step 3: Construct the Report
- Group members complete individual assignments or responsibilities for the final presentation.

B. Bennett, C. Rolheiser-Bennett, L. Stevahn (1991)
Cooperative Learning: Where Heart Meets Mind

Report to Steering Committee

Group Research Topic:

_____

Group Members:

1. _____

2. _____

3. _____

4. _____

Presentation Format:

_____

Role of Each Group Member in the Presentation:

1. _____

_____

2. _____

_____

3. _____

_____

4. _____

_____

Request for Special Materials:

_____

_____

Reporting Schedule (to be completed by Steering Committee):

_____

_____

_____

(Bob Walker, 1990, Durham Board of Education, Oshawa, Ontario)

Group Investigation

Stage 5: Presenting

Presenting the Final Report

Step 1: Present the Report
- Groups present their final reports to the class in accordance with a posted schedule.

Step 2: React to the Report
- Members of the other groups (audience) voice their reactions to what they saw and heard.

B. Bennett, C. Rolheiser-Bennett, L. Stevahn (1991)
Cooperative Learning: Where Heart Meets Mind

Group Investigation

Stage 6: Evaluating

Assessing the research process and product

Step 1: Establish the Criteria
- The teacher and students establish the criteria for evaluation of the group investigation by addressing the following questions:
  - What are we looking for in an effective group investigation? (criteria for process)
  - What are we looking for in the presentation of the product? (criteria for product).

Step 2: Clarify the Components
- Clarification might include:
  a) teacher and student roles in the evaluation process
  b) plans for formative and summative evaluation
  c) the weighting between evaluation of process and product
  d) the ratio of individual to group marks
  e) how and why anecdotal and numerical evaluation instruments will be used.

Step 3: Check for Understanding
- Be certain that the students understand at the outset how they are to be evaluated in the group investigation activity.
- Have the students complete an Evaluation Sheet (see page 233) to check for understanding of the components to be used.

Group Investigation

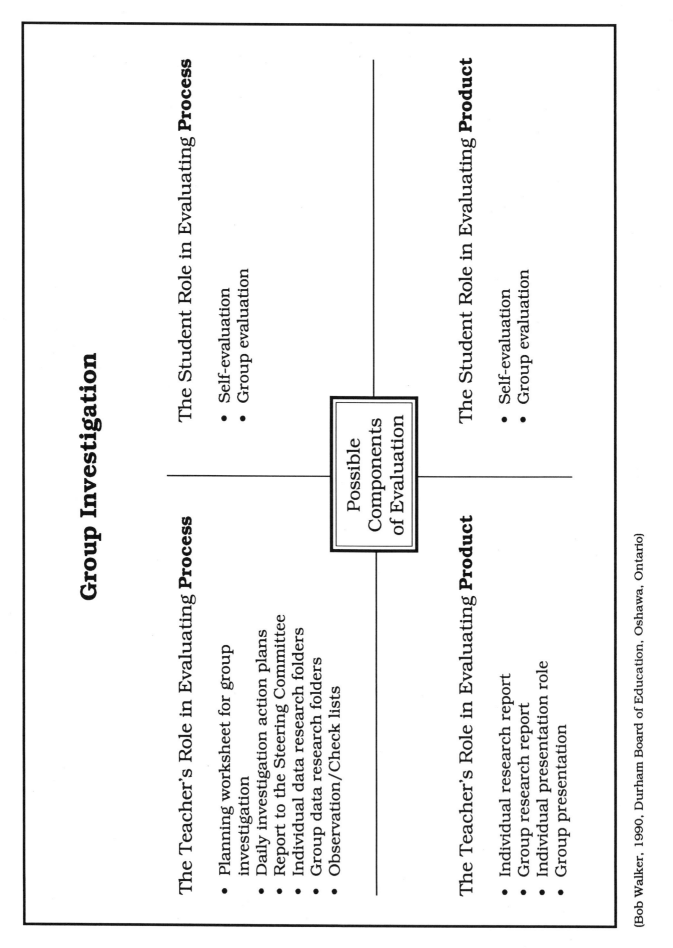

The Teacher's Role in Evaluating **Process**

- Planning worksheet for group investigation
- Daily investigation action plans
- Report to the Steering Committee
- Individual data research folders
- Group data research folders
- Observation/Check lists

The Student Role in Evaluating **Process**

- Self-evaluation
- Group evaluation

Possible Components of Evaluation

The Teacher's Role in Evaluating **Product**

- Individual research report
- Group research report
- Individual presentation role
- Group presentation

The Student Role in Evaluating **Product**

- Self-evaluation
- Group evaluation

(Bob Walker, 1990, Durham Board of Education, Oshawa, Ontario)

B. Bennett, C. Rolheiser-Bennett, L. Stevahn (1991)
Cooperative Learning: Where Heart Meets Mind

Evaluation

How will I be evaluated in the Group Investigation?

... of the Process   (Weighting =   %)

Possible Components:	Check if Included	How the Evaluation Component will be Used
• The Planning Worksheet for Group Investigation		
• The Daily Investigation Action Plan		
• Report to the Steering Committee		
• Individual Research Folders		
• A Group Research Folder		
• Teacher Observation of the Group		
• Teacher Observation of Individuals in the Group		
• Group Evaluation		
• Self-Evaluation		
• Other...		

... of the Product   (Weighting =   %)

Possible Components:	Check if Included	How the Evaluation Component will be Used
• Individual Research Report		
• Group Research Report		
• Individual Presentation Role		
• Group Presentation		
• Group Self-Evaluation		
• Peer Evaluation of Other Group Presentations		
• Other...		

(Bob Walker, 1990, Durham Board of Education, Oshawa, Ontario)

Group Investigation Evaluation
Process

Name: _____

Sub-topic: _____

Group Members: 1. _____   3. _____

2. _____   4. _____

My Component: _____

Process Criteria:

What we are hoping to see taking place in our group as we work toward production of our final product:

1. _____

2. _____

3. _____

4. _____

A. How effective were **we** as a group in meeting the criteria?   **OR**

B. As a group member, how effective was **I** in meeting the criteria?

_____

_____

_____

A. How can **the group** improve?   **OR**   B. How can **I** improve?

_____

_____

_____

(Bob Walker, 1990, Durham Board of Education, Oshawa, Ontario)

B. Bennett, C. Rolheiser-Bennett, L. Stevahn (1991)
Cooperative Learning: Where Heart Meets Mind

Group Investigation Evaluation
Product

Name: _____

Sub-topic: _____

Group Members: 1. _____   3. _____

 2. _____   4. _____

My Component: _____

Product Criteria:

What are we looking for in the presentation of the product?

1. _____

2. _____

3. _____

4. _____

A. How effective were **we** as a group in meeting the criteria?   **OR**
B. As a group member, how effective was **I** in meeting the criteria?

_____

_____

_____

A. How can **the group** improve?   **OR**   B. How can **I** improve?

_____

_____

_____

(Bob Walker, 1990, Durham Board of Education, Oshawa, Ontario)

B. Bennett, C. Rolheiser-Bennett, L. Stevahn (1991)
Cooperative Learning: Where Heart Meets Mind

Exploring Connections

Exploring Connections Between Cooperative Structures and the Basic Elements of Cooperative Learning

The diagram that follows illustrates a perspective on interrelationships between cooperative structures (Chapter 10) and the basic elements of cooperative learning (Chapter 4).

Cooperative structures provide step-by-step direction for facilitating cooperative experiences. Whether simpler or more complex, each structure is characterized by a set of procedures. Knowing and becoming skilled with a variety of structures enables teachers to select and employ the structures best suited to particular learning situations, needs, and purposes. Teaching students a repertoire of structures also more readily enables groups to engage in a variety of cooperative activities and develop a range of cooperative skills.

However, regardless of the structure employed, the five basic elements of cooperative learning fundamentally underlie effective group functioning. Successful cooperative experiences are supported by the presence, strength, and meaningfulness of each basic element. Consequently, when considering a cooperative structure, designing a cooperative experience, or trying to prevent anticipated difficulties, it is helpful to ask: How is positive interdependence embedded in the structure of the activity? How might it be strengthened? What social skills need to be taught, practiced, and processed for students to be successful with the structure? How does the structure hold students accountable for social and academic learning?

By conceptually understanding and skillfully applying the basic elements of cooperative learning, along with a variety of specific structures, teachers can facilitate powerful cooperative experiences in the classroom.

B. Bennett, C. Rolheiser-Bennett, L. Stevahn (1991)
Cooperative Learning: Where Heart Meets Mind

A Perspective: Connections Between Basic Elements of Cooperative Learning and Cooperative Structures

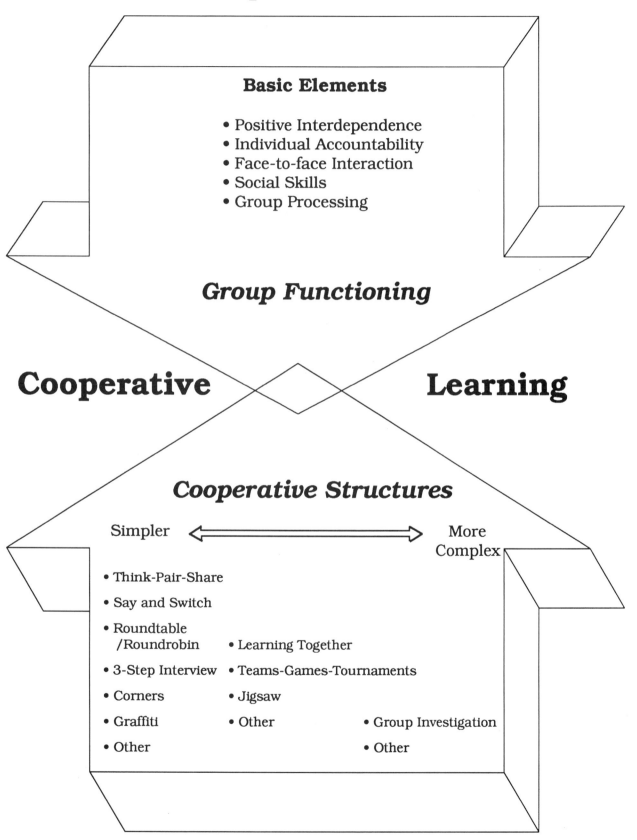

Basic Elements

- Positive Interdependence
- Individual Accountability
- Face-to-face Interaction
- Social Skills
- Group Processing

Group Functioning

Cooperative   **Learning**

Cooperative Structures

Simpler ⟷ More Complex

- Think-Pair-Share
- Say and Switch
- Roundtable /Roundrobin   • Learning Together
- 3-Step Interview   • Teams-Games-Tournaments
- Corners   • Jigsaw
- Graffiti   • Other   • Group Investigation
- Other   • Other

B. Bennett, C. Rolheiser-Bennett, L. Stevahn (1991)
Cooperative Learning: Where Heart Meets Mind

Summary

As you experiment with various cooperative structures, remember ...

- Numerous cooperative structures exist in addition to those outlined in this chapter.

- Appropriately selecting structures involves considering where your students are on a continuum of use (e.g., beginning stages versus practiced and refined use), prerequisite skills of students (social and academic), and learning outcomes targeted.

- The basic elements of cooperative learning support effective groupwork and can be used as measures of success. Considering the basic elements when utilizing any structure increases the likelihood of achieving cooperative interaction and productive learning.

B. Bennett, C. Rolheiser-Bennett, L. Stevahn (1991)
Cooperative Learning: Where Heart Meets Mind

Part III

Applying Cooperative Learning in Your Classroom

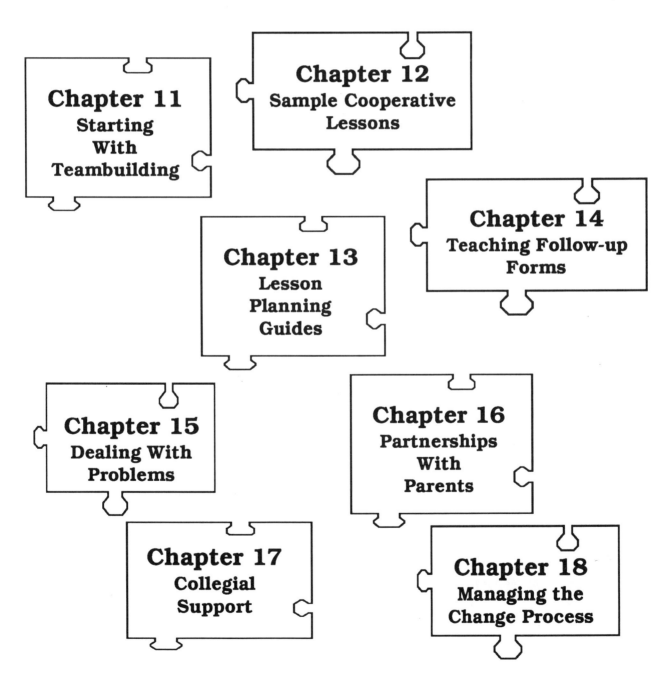

Chapter 11
Starting
With
Teambuilding

Chapter 12
Sample Cooperative
Lessons

Chapter 13
Lesson
Planning
Guides

Chapter 14
Teaching Follow-up
Forms

Chapter 15
Dealing With
Problems

Chapter 16
Partnerships
With
Parents

Chapter 17
Collegial
Support

Chapter 18
Managing the
Change Process

B. Bennett, C. Rolheiser-Bennett, L. Stevahn (1991)
Cooperative Learning: Where Heart Meets Mind

Part III

Applying Cooperative Learning in Your Classroom

Overview

This section deals with practical aspects of implementing cooperative learning in the classroom. Specifically:

- **Chapter 11 – Starting With Teambuilding** considers the importance of teambuilding when getting started and provides sample activities.

- **Chapter 12 – Sample Cooperative Lessons** presents a variety of sample cooperative lessons applicable across subjects and grade levels.

- **Chapter 13 – Lesson Planning Guides** contains Cooperative Learning Lesson Planning Guides for personal planning.

- **Chapter 14 – Teaching Flollow-up Forms** contains Teaching Follow-up forms for personal reflecting and dialoguing on classroom practice.

- **Chapter 15 – Dealing With Problems** identifies typical problems that arise during the implementation of cooperative learning and overviews some problem-solving processes for dealing with these.

- **Chapter 16 – Partnerships with Parents** explores ways to develop partnerships with parents when applying cooperative learning and includes sample letters that describe cooperative groupwork and address common parental concerns.

- **Chapter 17 – Collegial Support** explores the importance of collegial support in the process of implementing cooperative strategies and suggests activities for ongoing professional development among colleagues.

- **Chapter 18 – Managing the Change Process** considers important aspects of managing change for long-term implementation of cooperative learning.

B. Bennett, C. Rolheiser-Bennett, L. Stevahn (1991)
Cooperative Learning: Where Heart Meets Mind

Chapter 11

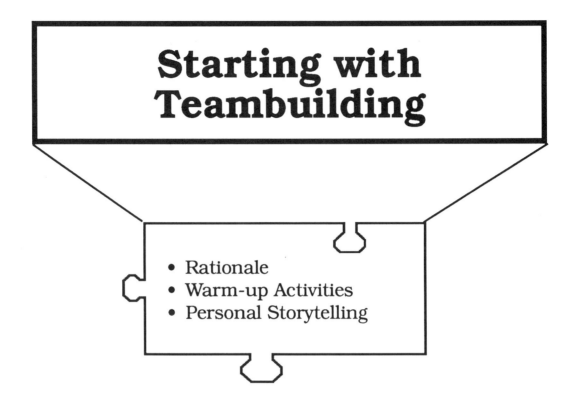

Starting with Teambuilding

- Rationale
- Warm-up Activities
- Personal Storytelling

Overview

Teambuilding activities that enable students to share personal stories and respectfully listen to one another, play an important role in developing the trust, care, and commitment needed for productive cooperative groupwork. This chapter begins with a rationale for teambuilding, followed by a variety of sample warm-up and teambuilding activities. Each activity is designed to foster meaningful connections among students and develop group cohesiveness.

A Place to Begin...

"By letting you know me, I allow you to like me. By disclosing myself to you, I create the potential for trust, caring, commitment, growth, and self-understanding. How can you care for me if you do not know me? How can you trust me if I do not demonstrate my trust in you by disclosing myself to you? How can you be committed to me if you know little or nothing about me? How can I know and understand myself if I do not disclose myself to friends? To like me, to trust me, to be committed to our relationship, to facilitate my personal growth and self-understanding, and to be my friend you must know me."

- David W. Johnson (1986) -

Getting started with cooperative learning means helping students to interact in ways that will foster appreciation and acceptance, respect and trust, care and commitment. Team-building activities can accomplish this purpose by enabling meaningful self-disclosure and active, interested listening among partners. In short, that means giving students opportunities to talk with one another about "things that really matter": personal interests, unique talents, memorable experiences, present concerns, and future aspirations.

The following pages describe sample teambuilding activities designed to enable safe, yet meaningful, personal sharing among students. Some of the activities are brief and can be integrated into cooperative lessons, while other activities constitute entire lessons. Regardless, when teambuilding activities are implemented consistently, team cohesiveness will more likely evolve.

As you consider the following teambuilding activities, discuss these questions with a colleague:

• Which activities are suitable for your teaching situation?

• Which activities could you adapt for use in your classroom?
  What adaptations would you make?

• What additional activities would be effective for teambuilding in your situation?

B. Bennett, C. Rolheiser-Bennett, L. Stevahn (1991)
Cooperative Learning: Where Heart Meets Mind

Warming-Up

Complete this chart for yourself, then interview your partners. How are you all alike?

	Self	Partner	Partner
1. Your birthplace			
2. Country you would like to visit			
3. Favorite holiday spot			
4. Favorite ice cream flavor			
5. Best school memory			
6. Favorite time of day			
7. Favorite season of the year			
8. Favorite recreational activity			
9. Your hero/heroine			
10. Favorite subject			
11. A special friend			
12. Favorite book			
13. Most respected world leader			
14. Favorite food			
15. Most important world issue			
16. Favorite local place to visit			
17.			
18.			

What Do We Have in Common?

Make a list of things you as teammates have in common. List as many items as you can discover. Here are some questions to get you started:

- Do you all like pizza? Other foods?

- Do you share the same hobby? Other interests?

- Do you like the same type of music?

- Are you all involved with athletics?

- Is there a particular television show that you all like?

- Do you like to read the same type of books?

- Do you have the same type of pets at home?

- Are your favorite colors the same?

- Others...

Next Step...

Based on what you have in common, agree on a team name and logo!

B. Bennett, C. Rolheiser-Bennett, L. Stevahn (1991)
Cooperative Learning: Where Heart Meets Mind

People Bingo!

Sharing one **People Bingo** board with teammates, read the statements in each box. Write your initials in the boxes that contain statements that are true for you. Your partners should also initial any statements that are true for them. Can you score a team **Bingo** (i.e., 3 boxes in the same row, column, or diagonal initialed by all teammates)?! Which statements are true for every teammate?

Born in another country	Has red hair	Dislikes liver
Has an unusual hobby	Had a job where you wore a uniform	Favorite color is yellow
Is wearing something wild and crazy	Has more than four brothers and sisters	Can tell a funny story about school

Create a **People Bingo** for your students using the page that follows.

People Bingo!

Sharing one **People Bingo** board with teammates, read the statements in each box. Write your initials in the boxes that contain statements that are true for you. Your partners should also initial any statements that are true for them. Can you score a team **Bingo** (i.e., 3 boxes in the same row, column, or diagonal initialed by all teammates)?! Which statements are true for every teammate?

_____	_____	_____
_____	_____	_____
_____	_____	_____

B. Bennett, C. Rolheiser-Bennett, L. Stevahn (1991)
Cooperative Learning: Where Heart Meets Mind

True or False?!

Write three statements about yourself, two false and one true. Mix the order of your statements, then ask your teammates to guess which statement is true.

Paper Caper

Take a piece of paper and change it in a way that will reveal something about yourself to your partners that they probably do not know. You may wish to fold, crunch, rip, or draw on your paper. Ask your partners to guess what you are trying to reveal. For example, the fellow below has made a paper airplane, revealing his interest in international travel.

(Adapted from: Teresa Cantlon, 1988, C & M Education Consultants, Portland, Oregon)

B. Bennett, C. Rolheiser-Bennett, L. Stevahn (1991)
Cooperative Learning: Where Heart Meets Mind

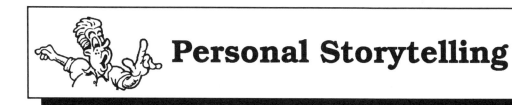 **Personal Storytelling**

Questions that promote storytelling about personally significant events, experiences, or concerns can be powerful for teambuilding. Teammates often listen more carefully and respectfully to one another when interesting personal stories are shared. Questions to initiate personal storytelling include the following:

1. What is your favorite place in the whole world? Why?

2. Where do you go to "re-energize" yourself? What makes it revitalizing?

3. Think back to kindergarten. In what ways are you still the same? How have you changed?

4. What is the story behind your name? How did you get your name? Have you ever had a nickname? What was it? Did you like it? What name would you have chosen?

5. Have you ever been in danger? Did you know it at the time? How did you survive the situation?

6. Think back to special celebrations in your early childhood. Which celebration is particularly memorable? What made it so special?

7. Who is your all-time favorite teacher? Why?

8. What was your favorite toy or activity as a kid?

9. What is the most difficult thing you've ever done?

10. What has been the proudest moment in your life? What lead up to that moment?

11. Who is someone you trust? What did that person do to win your trust?

12. What is your favorite holiday? Why?

13. What are three of your all-time favorite songs? What makes those songs personally significant?

14. What is the most frustrating experience that you have had with a computer? What is the best discovery you've made with a computer?

15. Who is your favorite hero or heroine? What qualities do you admire in that person (or character)?

16. What leader do you most admire? Why?

17. What would you look for in a "best friend?"

18. Who in history would you most like to meet? Why? What would you like to ask that person?

19. If you could visit or live anywhere (besides here), where would it be? Why?

20. If you could witness (or take part in) any event in history, what would it be? Why?

21. If you could change one event in history, what would it be?

22. Do you believe in "love at first sight?" What makes you believe or disbelieve?

23. Can money buy success (or happiness)? Explain your rationale.

24. What would you do with one hundred dollars?

25. If you could go "back to the future," where would you go? What time period would you choose? What social changes would you make?

26. _____

27. _____

28. _____

29. _____

30. _____

What questions can you add? Use the blank spaces above to write additional questions for use in your teaching situation. Try to develop questions that are interesting, relate to lesson objectives, and will be "taken to heart" by students.

B. Bennett, C. Rolheiser-Bennett, L. Stevahn (1991)
Cooperative Learning: Where Heart Meets Mind

Teambuilding Through Interviews

Questions for teambuilding like those on the previous two pages can be systematically discussed by groups at the start of cooperative experiences. The following interview format is an effective structure to use.

In a team of three, each student takes responsibility for one of the following roles: **Interviewer**, **Responder**, or **Recorder**. Using an interview grid like the one below, the first teambuilding question is written at the top of the first column. The first interviewer then asks one partner to respond to the question while the other partner briefly writes a summary of the response in the box next to the responder's name.

Using the interview grid below to illustrate the process, Sarah would begin by interviewing Omar while Josh briefly recorded Omar's response in the box next to Omar's name. Then roles would rotate so that Omar could interview Josh while Sarah recorded Josh's response in the box next to Josh's name. A third rotation of roles would complete the process, enabling Josh to interview Sarah while Omar recorded Sarah's response in the box next to her name.

The interview grid can be stored in a team folder, always ready for "warm-up" interviews when the team meets!

Name	Question #1 What makes you happy?	Question #2	Question #3
Sarah	Having reliable friends		
Omar	Taking walks with grandfather		
Josh	Playing hockey - especially league games!		

Friendship Interview

Considering how friendships evolve gives insight into the process of developing cooperative relationships among teammates.

Individually...

List the names of several true friends. Try to focus on individuals outside of your immediate family. Select one friend from your list who you would like to talk about during an interview.

Cooperatively...

Conduct "friendship interviews" with one another using the following roles: **Interviewer**, **Responder**, **Recorder**. Rotate roles after each interview.

Interview Questions
(While interviewing, add questions of your own!)

1. How did you and your friend meet each other? Where were you? Was it an unexpected meeting?

2. What was your reaction when you first met?

3. What activities did you initially do together? Did you participate in any events together? What were they?

4. At what point did you feel that the friendship was special?

5. Has your friendship survived conflicts or disagreements? How did you feel during the disagreement? What did you do to resolve the conflict?

6. Have you ever struggled together? How did you feel during the struggle? After the struggle?

7. How does your friend enrich your life?

Group Processing...

- What do your "friendship stories" have in common?
- How did you feel about sharing your story? About listening to your partners' stories?
- Did you see any "friendship qualities" occurring among yourselves during the interviews? What were they?
- What can we learn from your stories about developing friendships in cooperative teams?

B. Bennett, C. Rolheiser-Bennett, L. Stevahn (1991)
Cooperative Learning: Where Heart Meets Mind

Helping Hands Interview

Individually...

Recall a situation you were in where you really needed a "helping hand"... and someone came through for you.

Cooperatively...

Interview one another to learn about each partner's story. Use the following roles and rotate after each interview:

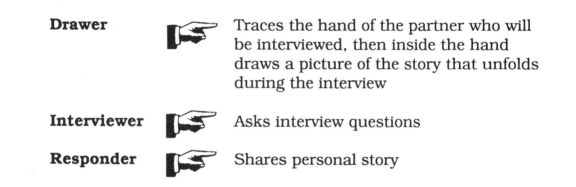

Drawer — Traces the hand of the partner who will be interviewed, then inside the hand draws a picture of the story that unfolds during the interview

Interviewer — Asks interview questions

Responder — Shares personal story

Sample Interview Questions

1. Have you ever needed a "helping hand?"

2. Did you ask for help or did someone notice you needed help and volunteered without your asking?

3. Who came through for you?

4. What did that person do to lend a hand?

5. How did you feel when that person gave you a helping hand?

Group Processing...

- How were you "helping hands" for one another during this activity?
- What did your partners do to show they really cared about you and your experiences?

(Adapted from: Child Development Project, San Ramon, California)

"We Believe..." *

This activity is designed to enable members of a community (e.g., classroom, school, department) to share values, beliefs, hopes, and achievements with one another. Such personal sharing fosters greater understanding and appreciation for the particular contributions each member brings to the group. Directions and materials for the activity follow. Storycards included are for adults, however, these can be readily adapted for any student group.

Sharing Personal Stories

1. In your group of 5 each person randomly select one of the story cards that follow.
2. Take 10 minutes to read and reflect on your story, jotting down any notes that may help you in sharing your thoughts with your group.
3. Take turns sharing and discussing your stories.

Developing A Statement... "We Believe"

1. What common values do you see being shared in the various messages each group member presented?
2. Is there a common thread weaving its way through the sharing that has taken place?
3. Based on your discussion, develop a "We Believe" statement that expresses your common beliefs.
4. Record your statement on the "We Believe" crest (see page 257).

Symbolizing Your Statement

1. What symbols visually express the beliefs in your "We Believe" statement?
2. Agree on a visual representation and portray it on your "We Believe" crest.
3. Sign your crest to show support!

Lived Action

1. As an individual, reflect for a few moments about your group's "We Believe" statement. Think about how the statement will translate into action for you. Record your thoughts on the "Lived Action" sheet (see page 258).
2. Share one "Lived Action" with your teammates that you would like to implement based on the "We Believe" statement. Be as concrete and specific as possible.

Sharing

1. Each group prepare to read your "We Believe" statement to the class and explain the significance of the symbol(s) on your crest.
2. Prepare a class crest, combining the symbols from each group in the class.

* (Adapted from: Marie Whelan, 1988, Edmonton Catholic Schools, Edmonton, Alberta)

B. Bennett, C. Rolheiser-Bennett, L. Stevahn (1991)
Cooperative Learning: Where Heart Meets Mind

Story Cards

Storycard #1

Symbols are important in our lives. We often place symbols in our workplace as a reminder of values that are important to us. A candle as a symbol of light or a butterfly as a symbol of growth are a few examples that come to mind.

Think about a symbol that has some value to you in your role as an educator. Share your thoughts about this symbol, why it is of value, and what makes it significant to you. Your sharing time will be approximately five minutes.

Storycard #2

Take the time to think about a teacher who played a significant role in your development during your years as a student. Why was this teacher someone you valued? How did this teacher give special direction to your life? What special qualities did this teacher possess?

Reflecting back on this teacher, is there a value that can be taken from this experience and brought to life in your present role?

You will be asked to share your thoughts about this teacher with your group. Sharing time will be approximately five minutes.

Storycard #3

Take the time to think about a student who has played a significant role in your development as an educator. This would be a student, who for one reason or another, has helped you to focus on your growth or direction as a teacher.

You will be asked to share your thoughts on this student, why this student has made a difference, and how this student has impacted your growth as a teacher. Sharing time will be approximately five minutes.

Storycard #4

As teachers we share many unique experiences which cause us to focus or develop in a particular direction. Think back to a specific experience that has played a significant role in your development as a teacher; an experience that has impacted your growth.

You will be asked to share this experience with your group. In what way did this experience cause you to move forward in your growth as a teacher? Sharing time will be approximately five minutes.

Storycard #5

Teachers possess certain qualities that are special – qualities that enable others to grow and develop. From your personal point of view, what do you believe are the three most important qualities a teacher should possess? Think about these qualities and the value they bring into the lives of others.

You will be asked to share these qualities, their value to you personally, and their significance in the development of others. Sharing time will be approximately five minutes.

B. Bennett, C. Rolheiser-Bennett, L. Stevahn (1991)
Cooperative Learning: Where Heart Meets Mind

"We Believe..." Crest

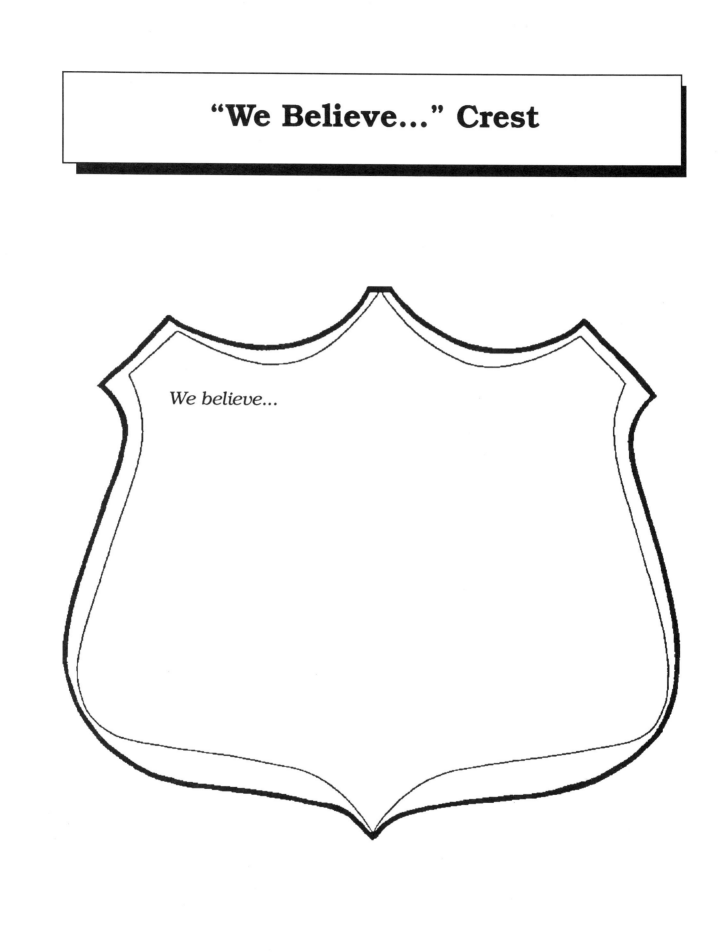

We believe...

Lived Action

You are invited to close your eyes for a few minutes and reflect about your group's "We Believe" statement. Think about how this belief statement will translate into lived action for you... here... at school. Record your idea below in a concrete *action* format. You will be asked to share your idea with your group.

Remember...

Facilitating effective groupwork begins with students learning to appreciate one another on a personal level.

Time spent on warm-ups and teambuilding reaps rewards as students begin to value one another as unique individuals.

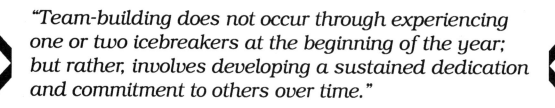

"Team-building does not occur through experiencing one or two icebreakers at the beginning of the year; but rather, involves developing a sustained dedication and commitment to others over time."

- Carol Rolheiser-Bennett, Laurie Stevahn,
& Barrie Bennett (1991) -

B. Bennett, C. Rolheiser-Bennett, L. Stevahn (1991)
Cooperative Learning: Where Heart Meets Mind

Chapter 12

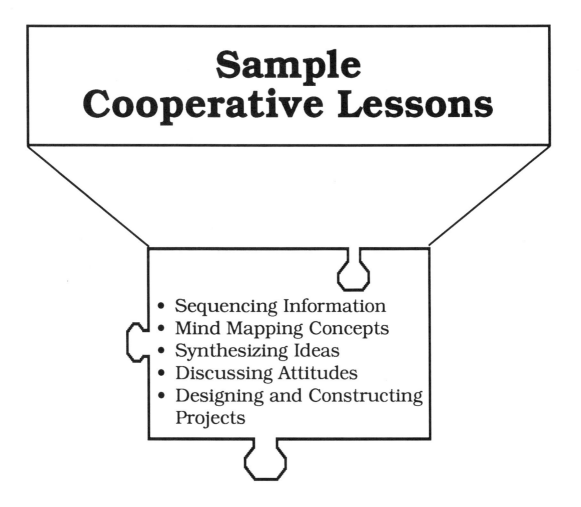

Sample Cooperative Lessons

- Sequencing Information
- Mind Mapping Concepts
- Synthesizing Ideas
- Discussing Attitudes
- Designing and Constructing Projects

Overview

This chapter contains a sampling of cooperative lessons adaptable across curricula and ages. Each lesson illustrates how the basic elements of cooperative learning work in combination. Sample lessons include:

- Sequencing Information
- Mind Mapping Concepts
- Synthesizing Ideas
- Discussing Attitudes
- Designing and Constructing Projects

The questions that start the chapter can be used to guide analysis of each lesson as well as facilitate possible applications and adaptations in your classroom.

Questions to Guide Analysis of Cooperative Learning Lessons

The following questions can be used to guide your analysis of the sample lessons.

1. Where could you apply the following sample cooperative lessons? How would you adapt each lesson to meet the learning needs of your students?

2. How might positive interdependence be strengthened in each lesson? What alternatives for structuring positive interdependence might you employ?

3. What social interaction skills will your students most need to successfully accomplish the cooperative tasks in the sample lessons?

4. Would you teach the needed social interaction skills prior to facilitating the cooperative lesson? In conjunction with the cooperative lesson? After the cooperative lesson (i.e., once the need for particular social skills is recognized by students from their experience)?

5. Where do you see evidence of the basic elements of cooperative learning in each lesson? How are the basic elements interconnected? How do the basic elements support one another?

6. What cooperative lessons could you create that would also have wide applicability (e.g., cooperative problem-solving, writing, editing, oral reading, reading comprehension, spelling)?

Cooperative Learning Lessons

B. Bennett, C. Rolheiser-Bennett, L. Stevahn (1991)
Cooperative Learning: Where Heart Meets Mind

COOPERATIVE LEARNING -- LESSON PLANNING GUIDE

DATE: _____

NAME: _____

ACADEMIC OBJECTIVE: _Sequence a set of items:_

GRADE LEVEL: _Adaptable_

a) _Apply understanding by determining correct order._

b) _Evaluate by prioritizing/defending rank order._

SOCIAL OBJECTIVE: _Encouraging Participation_

SUBJECT: _Adaptable_

I ORGANIZATIONAL DECISIONS PRIOR TO TEACHING

GROUPS: **SIZE:** _3_

ASSIGNMENT:
- ☒ Heterogeneous
- ☐ Homogeneous

Method: _____

ARRANGING THE ROOM:
- ☐ Desk Clusters
- ☐ Chair Clusters
- ☐ Floor clusters
- ☒ Tables
- ☐ Other...

MATERIALS:
- ☒ Shared
- ☐ Individual

LIST:
One set of items to sequence per group (e.g., paperstrips, cards, illustrations)

II SETTING THE LESSON — Sequencing Information

POSITIVE INTERDEPENDENCE:	ACADEMIC TASK DIRECTIONS:	CRITERIA FOR SUCCESS:	INDIVIDUAL ACCOUNTABILITY:	INTRODUCING SOCIAL BEHAVIORS:
☒ GOAL—one group product	Together...	• Correct order.	• Individuals will sign the completed group product to indicate participation, agreement, and ability to explain.	• Encouraging Participation
☒ INCENTIVE—choose where to display	1. Examine each item.	OR		
☒ RESOURCE—one set of items	2. Arrange items in the correct order.	Justifiable order.		
☒ ROLE—Cardmover, Checker, Pacer	OR	• Ability to explain rationale.	• Teacher will "spot-check" while groups are working.	
☒ ENVIRONMENT—team table	Rank order items and justify.			
☐ SEQUENCE	3. Agree and be able to explain.			
☐ IDENTITY				
☐ OUTSIDE FORCE				
☐ SIMULATION				

VERBAL	NONVERBAL
• What do you think?	• Eye contact
• Good idea!	• Head nod
• We need to hear from...	• Lean toward partners

III MONITORING AND INTERVENING

WHO WILL MONITOR GROUP WORK?

TEACHER ☒

TEACHER/STUDENTS ☐

HOW WILL MONITORING BE DONE?

INFORMAL NOTES ☒

FORMAL OBSERVATION SHEET ☐

WHAT BEHAVIORS WILL BE MONITORED?
- Encouraging Participation
- Reaching Agreement
- ...also: * Listening to Ideas
        * Clean-up of Materials

IV EVALUATING THE PRODUCT AND PROCESS OF GROUPWORK

ACADEMIC FEEDBACK:
(How will academic learning be evaluated?)

The teacher will:
(a) check the finished product of each group.
(b) provide feedback to group members.

SOCIAL SKILL PROCESSING:
(How will students' reflect on social interactions?)

Self-evaluation, by: _____

In Small Group, by: _rating themselves on participation_

Whole Class, by: _discussing what worked well and possible improvements_

Directions: Cut. Put in order.

Cartoons by John Migliore.

© Al Migliore

B. Bennett, C. Rolheiser-Bennett, L. Stevahn (1991)
Cooperative Learning: Where Heart Meets Mind

– *Sample Sequencing Lesson* –
Cartoon Frames

Directions: With your partner --
- sequence the cartoon frames and be prepared to tell the story *or*
- sequence the cartoon frames and write the captions *or*
- add your own cartoon frame(s) to the beginning and/or end, and write the captions for the entire story

The Exam

Cartoons by John Migliore.

– *Sample Sequencing Lesson* –
Cartoon Frames

Directions: With your partner --
- sequence the cartoon frames and be prepared to tell the story *or*
- sequence the cartoon frames and write the captions *or*
- add your own cartoon frame(s) to the beginning and/or end, and write the captions for the entire story

The Principal's Office

© John Migliore

Cartoons by John Migliore.

B. Bennett, C. Rolheiser-Bennett, L. Stevahn (1991)
Cooperative Learning: Where Heart Meets Mind

– *Sample Sequencing Lesson* –
Steps in Solving an Equation for Math

Directions: Cut and scramble the steps. Sequence in correct order to solve.

Solve	93 X + 42 = 53 X + 7
	93 X + 42 - 42 = 53 X + 7 - 42
	93 X = 53 X - 35
	93 X - 53 X = 53 X - 53 X - 35
	40 X = - 35
	(1 /40) (40X) = (1/40) (-35)
	X = - 35 / 40
	X = -7/8

COOPERATIVE LEARNING -- LESSON PLANNING GUIDE

DATE: _____

NAME: _____

ACADEMIC OBJECTIVE: Demonstrate understanding of a concept/topic.

GRADE LEVEL: Adaptable

SOCIAL OBJECTIVE: Supportively Suggesting Alternatives & Involving Everyone

SUBJECT: Adaptable

I ORGANIZATIONAL DECISIONS PRIOR TO TEACHING

GROUPS: **SIZE:** 4

ASSIGNMENT:
- ☒ Heterogeneous
- ☐ Homogeneous

ARRANGING THE ROOM:
- ☐ Desk Clusters
- ☐ Chair Clusters
- ☐ Floor clusters
- ☒ Tables
- ☐ Other...

Method: _____

MATERIALS:
- ☒ Shared
- ☐ Individual

LIST:
Each team receives...
- one sheet of butcher paper
- one set of felt markers
- one Mind Map Guide

II SETTING THE LESSON Mind Mapping Concepts

POSITIVE INTERDEPENDENCE:	ACADEMIC TASK DIRECTIONS:	CRITERIA FOR SUCCESS:	INDIVIDUAL ACCOUNTABILITY:	INTRODUCING SOCIAL BEHAVIORS:
☒ GOAL – one team product ☒ INCENTIVE – the map itself ☒ RESOURCE – one set of materials ☒ ROLE – see next page ☒ ENVIRONMENT – team table ☐ SEQUENCE ☐ IDENTITY ☐ OUTSIDE FORCE ☐ SIMULATION	1. Prepare a mind map on (any concept/topic). 2. Use all components of mind mapping. *See the "Team Directions" on the next page.*	• Complete the team task. • Everyone involved. • Everyone agree. • Everyone can explain the team mind map.	• Sign team mind map to indicate you participated, agree, and can explain ideas/decisions. • Be ready to represent your team if randomly called.	• Involve everyone! • Suggest alternatives in helpful and supportive ways!

III MONITORING AND INTERVENING

WHO WILL MONITOR GROUP WORK?
- TEACHER ☒
- TEACHER/STUDENTS ☐

HOW WILL MONITORING BE DONE?
- INFORMAL NOTES ☒
- FORMAL OBSERVATION SHEET ☐

WHAT BEHAVIORS WILL BE MONITORED?
- Involvement (Contributing Ideas)
- Suggesting Alternatives Supportively
- ...also: * Listening   * Reaching Agreement

IV EVALUATING THE PRODUCT AND PROCESS OF GROUPWORK

ACADEMIC FEEDBACK:
(How will academic learning be evaluated?)

Each team presents its mind map to the class. Other teams ask questions and tell what they liked about the mind map.

SOCIAL SKILL PROCESSING:
(How will students' reflect on social interactions?)

Self-evaluation, by: discussing effectiveness and possible changes

In Small Group, by: _____

Whole Class, by: teams presenting assessments and ideas

B. Bennett, C. Rolheiser-Bennett, L. Stevahn (1991)
Cooperative Learning: Where Heart Meets Mind

– *Sample Mind Mapping Lesson* – Mind Mapping Team Directions

Academic Task:

1. Prepare a mind map on the following topic:

   _____

2. Use all of the component parts of an effective mind map (see pages 270 and 271).

Roles:

A. Drawer: Maps team ideas

B. Materials Manager: Collects necessary materials

C. Map Checker: Ensures map has all component parts

D. Scout: Scouts out ideas from other groups

E. Timekeeper: Monitors time (this role can be combined with any of the above roles)

Social Skill Focus:

Make suggestions in helpful and supportive ways !!

Accountability:

Team success depends on each of you being able to explain every aspect of your team mind map. Sign your name to the map when you can do this — and are certain that your partners can, too!

– *Sample Mind Mapping Lesson* –
Strategy: Mind Mapping *

Definition: Mind mapping is a strategy that encourages the learner to visually record learning. The process establishes connections and helps the learner understand relationships between different concepts and ideas.

Component Parts:

Defined Center contains the central concept or topic.

Emphasis highlights the important information by use of bubbles, arrows, or wavy lines.

Colors facilitate retention and aid the organization of different concepts.

Key Words function as triggers to release additional and connected ideas.

Chains provide the connections or links to further establish and create relationships between ideas.

Visualizations such as illustrations, novel shapes, and pictorial details, facilitate retention.

* See: Buzan, T. (1983). *Use Both Sides of Your Brain* (rev. ed.). New York: E.P. Dutton.

B. Bennett, C. Rolheiser-Bennett, L. Stevahn (1991)
Cooperative Learning: Where Heart Meets Mind

– Sample Mind Mapping Lesson –
Mind Mapping: Component Parts

Remember:

- Images precede words.
- Mapping involves a minimum of words and images to communicate meaning.
- The map is a mental picture that promotes fluency and organization of thoughts.

B. Bennett, C. Rolheiser-Bennett, L. Stevahn (1991)
Cooperative Learning: Where Heart Meets Mind

– *Sample Mind Mapping Lesson* –
Processing Mind Mapping

Individual Processing:

How helpful were you in accomplishing the team goal?

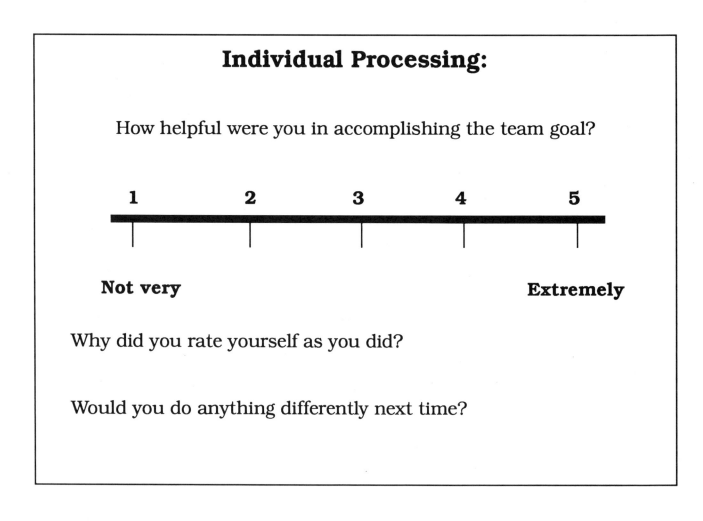

| 1 | 2 | 3 | 4 | 5 |

Not very   **Extremely**

Why did you rate yourself as you did?

Would you do anything differently next time?

Small Group Processing:

What was the best thing about working with your teammates?

What adjustments might you make to fine-tune your collaborative efforts?

B. Bennett, C. Rolheiser-Bennett, L. Stevahn (1991)
Cooperative Learning: Where Heart Meets Mind

COOPERATIVE LEARNING -- LESSON PLANNING GUIDE

DATE: _____
NAME: _____

ACADEMIC OBJECTIVE: To develop ⟶ creative thinking (synthesize ideas).
⟶ reasoning ability (evaluate ideas).
GRADE LEVEL: _Adaptable_

SOCIAL OBJECTIVE: Validating the Ideas of Others
SUBJECT: _Adaptable_

I ORGANIZATIONAL DECISIONS PRIOR TO TEACHING

GROUPS: **SIZE:** 3

ASSIGNMENT:
☒ Heterogeneous
☐ Homogeneous

ARRANGING THE ROOM:
☐ Desk Clusters
☐ Chair Clusters
☐ Floor clusters
☒ Tables
☐ Other...

Method: _____

MATERIALS:
☒ Shared
☐ Individual

LIST:
Each team receives...
• one sheet of writing paper
• one pencil
• one sheet of butcher paper
• one set of felt markers

II SETTING THE LESSON

POSITIVE INTERDEPENDENCE:	ACADEMIC TASK DIRECTIONS:	CRITERIA FOR SUCCESS:	INDIVIDUAL ACCOUNTABILITY:	INTRODUCING SOCIAL BEHAVIORS:
☒ GOAL — one team product	*Synthesizing Ideas*	• Finished team product.	• Signature on finished team product to indicate participation.	• Validating the ideas of others during all phases of the activity.
☒ INCENTIVE — present & post	1. Brainstorm items— randomly select one	• Teammates carry out all roles.		
☒ RESOURCE — shared paper/pens	2. Change/Improve/Develop	• Validation of ideas evident.	• Team presenter randomly selected.	
☒ ROLE — see next page	3. Draw			
☒ ENVIRONMENT — team table	4. Name			
☒ SEQUENCE — rotate roles	5. Present			
☒ IDENTITY— name invention				
☒ OUTSIDE FORCE— "sell your product"	(See the directions on the pages that follow.)			
☒ SIMULATION — you are inventors				

III MONITORING AND INTERVENING

WHO WILL MONITOR GROUP WORK?
TEACHER ☒
TEACHER/STUDENTS ☐

HOW WILL MONITORING BE DONE?
INFORMAL NOTES ☐
FORMAL OBSERVATION SHEET ☒
(use tally sheet during drawing phase of activity)

WHAT BEHAVIORS WILL BE MONITORED?
• Validating Ideas of Others

IV EVALUATING THE PRODUCT AND PROCESS OF GROUPWORK

ACADEMIC FEEDBACK:
(How will academic learning be evaluated?)

Individuals are randomly selected to present their team product to the class. Class may respond by telling what they like best about the product and why.

SOCIAL SKILL PROCESSING:
(How will students' reflect on social interactions?)

Self-evaluation, by: discussing "Secret of Our Team Success"

In Small Group, by: discussing "secrets of success"

Whole Class, by: sharing "secrets of success" (...& discussing other applications for the skills)

– *Sample Lesson: Synthesizing Ideas* –
"That's a Great Idea!"

Task: Develop a new product!

Social Skill: Validate the ideas of others.

Part One:

In your group brainstorm a list of types of transportation. Be creative. You have 3 minutes!

Circle the 5th item from the bottom of your list.

Part Two:

Your challenge is to change the circled item to make it the best way to get to school. You can add any improvements that you like. Be original!

Sequential Roles:

1) **Idea Person** — Makes a suggestion for how to improve the circled item.

2) **Validator** — Responds by saying, "That's a great idea because . . . !"

3) **Recorder** — Writes the suggested improvement on a team list.

Note: **Roles rotate for each new idea.**

B. Bennett, C. Rolheiser-Bennett, L. Stevahn (1991)
Cooperative Learning: Where Heart Meets Mind

continued...

Part Three:

Make a drawing of your selected means of transportation, including all improvements generated in Part Two.

Roles:

1) **Reader** — Reads an item from the list

2) **Drawer** — Draws that item

3) **Coach** — Encourages and makes helpful suggestions to the drawer

Note: **Roles may rotate for each item drawn. Also, remember idea validation!**

Part Four:

Give your new product a name and be prepared to "unveil" it to the public, highlighting its finest features. Any individual in your group may be called upon to do the sharing. Be sure to sign all names to the product, indicating your participation in its creation.

Part Five:

Present your product and post it for others to see. Discuss the secrets of your team's success. What enabled you to work well together?

COOPERATIVE LEARNING -- LESSON PLANNING GUIDE

DATE: _____

NAME: _____

ACADEMIC OBJECTIVE: Analyze songs to understand public attitudes toward war.

GRADE LEVEL: Adaptable

SOCIAL OBJECTIVE: Encourage Participation & Reach Consensus
(while both are important focus on one)

SUBJECT: Adaptable

I ORGANIZATIONAL DECISIONS PRIOR TO TEACHING

GROUPS: SIZE: 3

ASSIGNMENT: _____

ARRANGING THE ROOM:
- ☒ Heterogeneous
- ☐ Homogeneous

- ☒ Desk Clusters
- ☐ Chair Clusters
- ☐ Floor clusters
- ☐ Tables
- ☐ Other...

Method: _____

MATERIALS:
- ☒ Shared
- ☐ Individual

LIST: One per team...
- Question Sheet
- Song Sheet
- Textbook
- Pen/Pencil

II SETTING THE LESSON   Discussing Attitudes

POSITIVE INTERDEPENDENCE:	ACADEMIC TASK DIRECTIONS:	CRITERIA FOR SUCCESS:	INDIVIDUAL ACCOUNTABILITY:	INTRODUCING SOCIAL BEHAVIORS:
☒ GOAL—one finished product	Together...	• Completed Question Sheet.	• Students sign the Question Sheet to indicate agreement and understanding.	• Encourage all teammates to participate!
☒ INCENTIVE—"bonus" if appropriate	1. Listen to the songs and follow the words on the Song Sheet.	• All agree.		
☒ RESOURCE—one set of materials		• All explain and defend answers.		
☒ ROLE—Reader, Recorder, Checker	2. Complete the Question Sheet.		• Teacher will randomly call on students to respond for their team.	or
☒ ENVIRONMENT— desks clustered	3. Reach consensus on all answers.			• Reach consensus
☐ SEQUENCE				
☐ IDENTITY				
☐ OUTSIDE FORCE				
☐ SIMULATION				

III MONITORING AND INTERVENING

WHO WILL MONITOR GROUP WORK?

TEACHER ☒

TEACHER/STUDENTS ☐

HOW WILL MONITORING BE DONE?

INFORMAL NOTES ☒

FORMAL OBSERVATION SHEET ☐

WHAT BEHAVIORS WILL BE MONITORED?
- Encouragement & Participation
- Listening & Checking for Understanding while reaching consensus

IV EVALUATING THE PRODUCT AND PROCESS OF GROUPWORK

ACADEMIC FEEDBACK:
(How will academic learning be evaluated?)

Students will provide feedback on questions by teacher randomly calling.

SOCIAL SKILL PROCESSING:
(How will students' reflect on social interactions?)

Self-evaluation, by: jotting down ways to improve

In Small Group, by: _____

Whole Class, by: Teacher sharing observations & students identifying helpful behaviors

B. Bennett, C. Rolheiser-Bennett, L. Stevahn (1991)
Cooperative Learning: Where Heart Meets Mind

– *Sample Lesson: Discussing Attitudes* –
Attitudes Toward War

Task:

1)   Follow the words on the songsheet as you listen to the songs.

2)   Discuss and answer each question on the QUESTION SHEET. Everyone in your group must agree on final answers and be able to explain each answer.

3)   During discussion, the **READER** will read aloud any passages in the songs or textbook helpful to answering the questions.

4)   The **RECORDER** will write your group's final answers on the QUESTION SHEET.

5)   The **CHECKER** will make sure everyone in your group agrees on each answer and can explain each answer.

Social Expectation:

Everyone participates and contributes ideas.
Teammates encourage each other!

Accountability:

You must be able to provide and explain an answer for each question if randomly asked.

– Sample Lesson: Discussing Attitudes –
Question Sheet

1. _____ was a popular song about war during _____.
   (title)   (years/era)
   What do you believe is the major message of that song?

2. What attitudes or emotions are conveyed by the song?

3. How do the posters illustrated in your textbook on page _____ reflect similar attitudes to those you identified in the song?

4. Why might the public have had those attitudes during that year/era?
   List several reasons.

5. Have public attitudes changed toward involvement in war since that year/era?
   Give reasons to support your answer.

6. What factors might influence changes in attitudes toward war?
   Make a list.

7. Do you think that a major world power like the United States could ever remain neutral in an outbreak of war? State your position and defend your answer with several reasons.

Note: When you sign your name to this sheet, it means that you agree with each answer and can explain/defend each answer.

Signatures: _____
_____
_____
_____

B. Bennett, C. Rolheiser-Bennett, L. Stevahn (1991)
Cooperative Learning: Where Heart Meets Mind

– Sample Lesson: Discussing Attitudes –
Songs

In this lesson dealing with war and super-powers, the focus is on the United States. The following songs about war may be used in this lesson. If possible, have students listen to the recording of the selected songs. Additional songs to consider are listed in the October issue of Social Education (journal of the National Council for the Social Studies), featuring a special section on "Studying U.S. History Through Songs." Also, consider having students analyze other popular media such as films, novels, news publications, posters, slogans, etc.

Patriotic songs about war include...

"Over There"
(1917)

"There's a
Star Spangled
Banner Waving
Somewhere"
(1942)

"Soldier's
Last Letter"
(1944)

"Sink the Bismark"
(1960)

"The Ballad of the
Green Berets"
(1966)

"The Fightin' Side
of Me"
(1970)

"In America"
(1980)

Others...

War?

Anti-war songs include...

"Eve of Destruction"
(1965)

"Fortunate Son"
(1969)

"War"
(1970)

"Military
Madness"
(1971)

"Stop the War Now"
(1971)

"Undercover
(of the Night)"
(1983)

"I Ain't Marching
Anymore"
(1983)
(n.d.)

Others...

COOPERATIVE LEARNING -- LESSON PLANNING GUIDE

DATE: _____

NAME: _____

ACADEMIC OBJECTIVE: To identify the factors that determine the ability

GRADE LEVEL: Adaptable

of a ship to hold cargo by constructing a series of boats.

SOCIAL OBJECTIVE: *Encouraging Alternative Ideas/Supportively Pacing the Team/Being Honest
*(Choose one)

SUBJECT: Science

I ORGANIZATIONAL DECISIONS PRIOR TO TEACHING

GROUPS: SIZE: 4

ASSIGNMENT:
☒ Heterogeneous
☐ Homogeneous

ARRANGING THE ROOM:
☐ Desk Clusters
☐ Chair Clusters
☐ Floor clusters
☒ Tables
☐ Other...

MATERIALS:
☒ Shared
☐ Individual

LIST:
Each team receives...
• tub with water
• plasticene
• marbles
• paper and pencil for designs

Method: by science ability

II SETTING THE LESSON Designing and Constructing Projects

POSITIVE INTERDEPENDENCE:	ACADEMIC TASK DIRECTIONS:	CRITERIA FOR SUCCESS:	INDIVIDUAL ACCOUNTABILITY:	INTRODUCING SOCIAL BEHAVIORS:
☒ GOAL — effective boat design	See "Team Directions" on the page that follows.	• A boat design that will hold at least 13 marbles for 5 seconds.	• A design sketch for each person.	• Encouraging alternative ideas
☒ INCENTIVE — satisfaction!				
☒ RESOURCE — shared materials		• Identify factors that affected the ability of your boat to hold cargo.	• Roles carried out.	• Supportively pacing the team
☒ ROLE — see next page				
☒ ENVIRONMENT — stay in team area			• A completed self-evaluation sheet for each person.	• Being honest
☒ SEQUENCE — roles rotate		• Use of targeted social skills within your group.		* (Choose one)
☒ IDENTITY — name boat or design team				
☒ OUTSIDE FORCE — must float 5 seconds				
☒ SIMULATION — you are a "design team"				

III MONITORING AND INTERVENING

WHO WILL MONITOR GROUP WORK?

TEACHER ☒

TEACHER/STUDENTS ☐

HOW WILL MONITORING BE DONE?

INFORMAL NOTES ☒

FORMAL OBSERVATION SHEET ☐

WHAT BEHAVIORS WILL BE MONITORED?
• Encouraging alternative ideas
• Supportively pacing the team
• Being honest

IV EVALUATING THE PRODUCT AND PROCESS OF GROUPWORK

ACADEMIC FEEDBACK:
(How will academic learning be evaluated?)

Each team will share factors affecting the ability of a ship to hold cargo.

SOCIAL SKILL PROCESSING:
(How will students' reflect on social interactions?)

Self-evaluation, by: written self-evaluation question sheet

In Small Group, by: completing written group evaluation sheet

Whole Class, by: discussing how social skills were evidenced

B. Bennett, C. Rolheiser-Bennett, L. Stevahn (1991)
Cooperative Learning: Where Heart Meets Mind

– *Sample Lesson: Designing & Constructing* – Boat Construction

Academic Task:

Construct a plasticene boat that will bouy up as many marbles as possible for at least 5 seconds before sinking. From the experience, identify the factors that determine the ability of a ship to hold cargo.

Social Task: _____

Note: Teacher and/or students select one social interaction skill (e.g., encouraging alternative ideas, supportively pacing the group, extending ideas, or critiquing in positive ways).

Roles:

1. **Designer** — designs a vessel
2. **Tester** — places the marbles in the vessel (timer from another group verifies the test)
3. **Timer** — times another group's test
4. **Critical Inquirer** — makes suggestions for improvement for the next design
   Note: Roles rotate for each new design.

Directions:

1. Get bucket, water, marbles, design paper, pencil, and plasticene.

2. **Designer** draws a sketch with dimensions and suggestions from the team and then constructs the boat.

3. When ready, get a **Timer** from another team and the **Tester** places in the marbles.

4. **Critical Inquirer** states what is wrong and re-sketches the boat. Roles then rotate so that the Critical Inquirer becomes the Designer, the Designer the Tester, etc.. Repeat the process until each person has designed a boat or until 25 minutes has elapsed.

Note: There should be four sketches that show attempts at improvement. All members must sign their name to their sheet indicating they carried out their assigned task with integrity. In addition, you must name and be prepared to market your "ship" based on the factors enabling your ship to carry cargo.

continued...

– *Sample Lesson: Designing & Constructing* –
Boat Construction
Self-Evaluation Questions

Complete and file in team folder for future reference.

1. What did you learn about yourself while working in this group?

2. What were your strengths in working cooperatively in the group?

3. What cooperative skills would you like to improve next time you work in a group?

4. Give an example of how you used the identified collaborative skill in the group activity just completed.

B. Bennett, C. Rolheiser-Bennett, L. Stevahn (1991)
Cooperative Learning: Where Heart Meets Mind

continued...

– *Sample Lesson: Designing & Constructing* –
Boat Construction
Group Evaluation

Complete and file in team folder for future reference.

1. How well we used the collaborative skill:

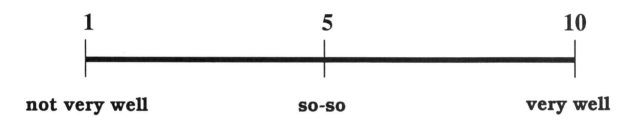

1	5	10
not very well	**so-so**	**very well**

Discuss and record why you gave your group this rating.

2. Our goal for next time we practice this skill:

"The art of teaching is the art of assisting discovery."

- Mark Van Doran -

B. Bennett, C. Rolheiser-Bennett, L. Stevahn (1991)
Cooperative Learning: Where Heart Meets Mind

Chapter 13

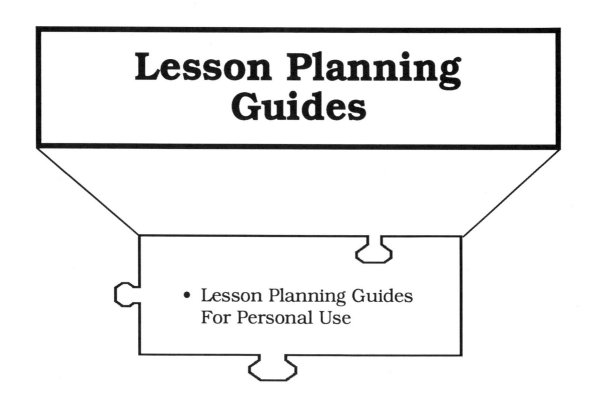

Lesson Planning Guides

- Lesson Planning Guides
  For Personal Use

Overview

This chapter contains Cooperative Learning Lesson Planning Guides for personal planning. Two formats are provided, each incorporating the basic elements of cooperative groupwork as outlined in Chapter 4. When using the forms to design cooperative lessons, you may wish to refer to the annotated guide that starts the chapter.

COOPERATIVE LEARNING -- LESSON PLANNING GUIDE
* Explanation of How to Use This Form *

DATE: _____

NAME: _____

ACADEMIC OBJECTIVE: What academic learning will be targeted?

GRADE LEVEL: _____

SOCIAL OBJECTIVE: What social interaction skills will be practiced?

SUBJECT: _____

I ORGANIZATIONAL DECISIONS PRIOR TO TEACHING

GROUPS:

SIZE:
- Start small
- Consider nature of task, skills of students, and time

ASSIGNMENT:
- ☐ Heterogeneous (mixed grouping)
- ☐ Homogeneous (similar grouping)

Method: How will you establish the groups (i.e., procedures)?

ARRANGING THE ROOM:
- ☐ Desk Clusters
- ☐ Chair Clusters
- ☐ Floor clusters
- ☐ Tables
- ☐ Other...

MATERIALS:
- ☐ Shared
- ☐ Individual

LIST: What materials are needed?

II SETTING THE LESSON

POSITIVE INTERDEPENDENCE:	ACADEMIC TASK DIRECTIONS:	CRITERIA FOR SUCCESS:	INDIVIDUAL ACCOUNTABILITY:	INTRODUCING SOCIAL BEHAVIORS:
☐ GOAL ☐ INCENTIVE ☐ RESOURCE ☐ ROLE ☐ ENVIRONMENT ☐ SEQUENCE ☐ IDENTITY ☐ OUTSIDE FORCE ☐ SIMULATION *what goal will be utilized?*	• What procedures will the students follow to complete the task? • How will the directions be explained? • Do the students need a demonstration?	• How will accomplishment be measured (social and academic)? • How will the students become aware of the criteria?	• How will individuals be held responsible for learning? • What will motivate students to be involved?	• How will social behaviors be taught and reinforced? • Plan to focus on one social behavior.

III MONITORING AND INTERVENING

WHO WILL MONITOR GROUP WORK?
- ☐ TEACHER
- ☐ TEACHER/STUDENTS

HOW WILL MONITORING BE DONE?
(e.g., global observation or anecdotal notes) ☐ INFORMAL NOTES
(e.g., tally sheets or checklists) ☐ FORMAL OBSERVATION SHEET

WHAT BEHAVIORS WILL BE MONITORED?
In addition to the expected social skills that will be monitored, are there other behaviors you will observe?

IV EVALUATING THE PRODUCT AND PROCESS OF GROUPWORK

ACADEMIC FEEDBACK:
(How will academic learning be evaluated?)

SOCIAL SKILL PROCESSING:
(How will students' reflect on social interactions?)

Self-evaluation, by: _____

In Small Group, by: _____

Whole Class, by: _____

See Chapter 9 on "Evaluation" for examples.

B. Bennett, C. Rolheiser-Bennett, L. Stevahn (1991)
Cooperative Learning: Where Heart Meets Mind

COOPERATIVE LEARNING -- LESSON PLANNING GUIDE

NAME: _____
GRADE LEVEL: _____
SUBJECT: _____

DATE: _____
ACADEMIC OBJECTIVE: _____
SOCIAL OBJECTIVE: _____

I ORGANIZATIONAL DECISIONS PRIOR TO TEACHING

| GROUPS: | SIZE: | ASSIGNMENT: ☐ Heterogeneous ☐ Homogeneous Method: _____ | ARRANGING THE ROOM: ☐ Desk Clusters ☐ Chair Clusters ☐ Floor clusters ☐ Tables ☐ Other... | MATERIALS: ☐ Shared ☐ Individual LIST: |

II SETTING THE LESSON

POSITIVE INTERDEPENDENCE:	ACADEMIC TASK DIRECTIONS:	CRITERIA FOR SUCCESS:	INDIVIDUAL ACCOUNTABILITY:	INTRODUCING SOCIAL BEHAVIORS:
☐ GOAL				
☐ INCENTIVE				
☐ RESOURCE				
☐ ROLE				
☐ ENVIRONMENT				
☐ SEQUENCE				
☐ IDENTITY				
☐ OUTSIDE FORCE				
☐ SIMULATION				

III MONITORING AND INTERVENING

WHO WILL MONITOR GROUP WORK?

TEACHER ☐
TEACHER/STUDENTS ☐

HOW WILL MONITORING BE DONE?

INFORMAL NOTES ☐
FORMAL OBSERVATION SHEET ☐

WHAT BEHAVIORS WILL BE MONITORED?

_____
_____

IV EVALUATING THE PRODUCT AND PROCESS OF GROUPWORK

ACADEMIC FEEDBACK:
(How will academic learning be evaluated?)

SOCIAL SKILL PROCESSING:
(How will students' reflect on social interactions?)

Self-evaluation, by: _____
In Small Group, by: _____
Whole Class, by: _____

COOPERATIVE LEARNING -- LESSON PLANNING GUIDE

DATE: _____
ACADEMIC OBJECTIVE: _____
SOCIAL OBJECTIVE: _____

NAME: _____
GRADE LEVEL: _____
SUBJECT: _____

I ORGANIZATIONAL DECISIONS PRIOR TO TEACHING

GROUPS: **SIZE:** ____ **ASSIGNMENT:** ☐ Heterogeneous ☐ Homogeneous

ARRANGING THE ROOM:
☐ Desk Clusters
☐ Chair Clusters
☐ Floor clusters
☐ Tables
☐ Other...

MATERIALS: ☐ Shared ☐ Individual

LIST:

Method: ____

II SETTING THE LESSON

POSITIVE INTERDEPENDENCE:	ACADEMIC TASK DIRECTIONS:	CRITERIA FOR SUCCESS:	INDIVIDUAL ACCOUNTABILITY:	INTRODUCING SOCIAL BEHAVIORS:
☐ GOAL				
☐ INCENTIVE				
☐ RESOURCE				
☐ ROLE				
☐ ENVIRONMENT				
☐ SEQUENCE				
☐ IDENTITY				
☐ OUTSIDE FORCE				
☐ SIMULATION				

III MONITORING AND INTERVENING

WHO WILL MONITOR GROUP WORK?
TEACHER ☐
TEACHER/STUDENTS ☐

HOW WILL MONITORING BE DONE?
INFORMAL NOTES ☐
FORMAL OBSERVATION SHEET ☐

WHAT BEHAVIORS WILL BE MONITORED?
_____
_____

IV EVALUATING THE PRODUCT AND PROCESS OF GROUPWORK

ACADEMIC FEEDBACK:
(How will academic learning be evaluated?)

SOCIAL SKILL PROCESSING:
(How will students' reflect on social interactions?)

Self-evaluation, by: _____
In Small Group, by: _____
Whole Class, by: _____

B. Bennett, C. Rolheiser-Bennett, L. Stevahn (1991)
Cooperative Learning: Where Heart Meets Mind

Cooperative Learning
Lesson Planning Guide

Subject Area: _____

Grade Level: _____

Lesson Description: _____
_____
_____
_____
_____
_____
_____

Objectives: Academic: _____
_____
_____

Social: _____
_____
_____
_____

Materials: _____
_____
_____
_____
_____
_____

**Organizational
Decisions:**
Group Size: _____
Assignment to groups: _____
_____
_____
Room Arrangement: _____
_____
_____

continued...

Task Directions: _____
_____
_____
_____
_____
_____
_____

**Positive
Interdependence:** _____
_____
_____
_____
_____
_____

**Individual
Accountability:** _____
_____
_____
_____
_____
_____

Criteria for Success: _____
_____
_____
_____

**Evaluation of...
Academic Learning:** _____
_____
_____
_____

Social Learning (Processing):

❑ Self-evaluation, by: _____
_____

❑ In Small Groups, by: _____
_____

❑ Whole Class, by: _____
_____

B. Bennett, C. Rolheiser-Bennett, L. Stevahn (1991)
Cooperative Learning: Where Heart Meets Mind

Chapter 14

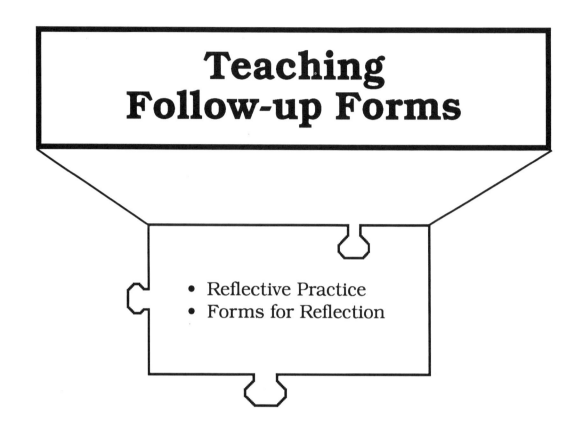

Teaching Follow-up Forms

- Reflective Practice
- Forms for Reflection

Overview

This chapter contains Teaching Follow-up forms for personal reflection on cooperative lessons. The chapter begins by considering the importance of reflective practice for professional growth, as well as how the forms can contribute to effective peer coaching and collegial sharing. An annotated form for reference precedes the forms for personal use.

Reflective Practice

Reflection plays an important role in enhancing professional growth. It can lead to:

- creating your own meaning (personalization)
- understanding situation-specific complexities
- problem-setting and solving
- critical inquiry
- synthesis of ideas
- connection-making
- examination and revision
- guiding future action

Reflection is essential to continued growth for both teachers and students as they experiment with cooperative learning. Examining how cooperative learning works in your own teaching situation leads to personal discovery as theory takes on practical meaning and practical knowledge contributes to theory. Reflection also provides opportunities to explore questions and issues that arise within your specific context. From this, refinements, new techniques, and additional questions evolve.

Reflection on any aspect of teaching is powerful in and of itself. Moreover, when it occurs in the context of ongoing critical inquiry (e.g., action research), the building of instructional repertoire, and collaboration with other colleagues, then life long professional learning is nurtured (Fullan, Bennett, & Rolheiser-Bennett, 1990). The effect of reflection, therefore, goes far beyond just implementing cooperative learning. It lies at the heart of classroom and school improvement efforts.

The Teaching Follow-up form that follows can guide personal reflection about cooperative learning. After teaching a cooperative lesson, record your thoughts about successes, frustrations and possible revisions. Keep the basic elements of cooperative learning in mind as you analyze various dimensions of the lesson.

When collaborating with others reflection is enhanced. You may wish to use the form as a tool to guide discussion or peer coaching interactions. Consider asking your "coach" to record your reflection on the form while you share aloud.

B. Bennett, C. Rolheiser-Bennett, L. Stevahn (1991)
Cooperative Learning: Where Heart Meets Mind

Teaching Follow-up

Explanation of How to Use This Form

Name: _____ School: _____

Lesson/Subject: _____ Date: _____

1. Successes Experienced

- What worked well?

- What pleased you?

- How did students evidence success?

2. Problems Encountered

- What frustrated you?

- What was problematic?

- Describe any disappointments.

3. Possible Revisions

- What changes would you make if you were teaching this lesson again?

- What revisions would deal specifically with the problems you encountered?

4. Critical or Interesting Incidents

- What was unexpected?

- What intrigued you?

- What questions were raised in your mind?

5. I shared this lesson with...
Collaborating with others promotes growth in implementing cooperative learning.
- Who can you share your successes with?
- Who can you problem-solve with?

B. Bennett, C. Rolheiser-Bennett, L. Stevahn (1991)
Cooperative Learning: Where Heart Meets Mind

Teaching Follow-up

Name: _____ *School:* _____

Lesson/Subject: _____ *Date:* _____

1. Successes Experienced

2. Problems Encountered

3. Possible Revisions

4. Critical or Interesting Incidents

5. I shared this lesson with...

B. Bennett, C. Rolheiser-Bennett, L. Stevahn (1991)
Cooperative Learning: Where Heart Meets Mind

Teaching Follow-up

Name: _____ *School:* _____

Lesson/Subject: _____ *Date:* _____

1. Successes Experienced

2. Problems Encountered

3. Possible Revisions

4. Critical or Interesting Incidents

5. I shared this lesson with...

B. Bennett, C. Rolheiser-Bennett, L. Stevahn (1991)
Cooperative Learning: Where Heart Meets Mind

"What you do about what you don't know is, in the final analysis, what determines what you will ultimately know."

- Eleanor Duckworth (1987) -

"We must move to ways of thinking, and to plans and programs by which teachers reflect on themselves as knowing, teaching beings."

- Teacher Education in Ontario (1987) -

"Cooperative learning communities that develop the capacity of young people to reflect upon the quality of their interactions, to candidly critique the here-and-now situation, to determine needed changes, and to take meaningful action together would be a magnificent resource for our field to give the world. What if hundreds of thousands of people so internalized the reflection process for systems change that they carried it into their future families, neighborhood organizations and work groups? ... I truly believe the cooperative learning movement has more to offer the children of tomorrow than we have yet realized."

- Jeanne Gibbs (1990) -

B. Bennett, C. Rolheiser-Bennett, L. Stevahn (1991)
Cooperative Learning: Where Heart Meets Mind

Chapter 15

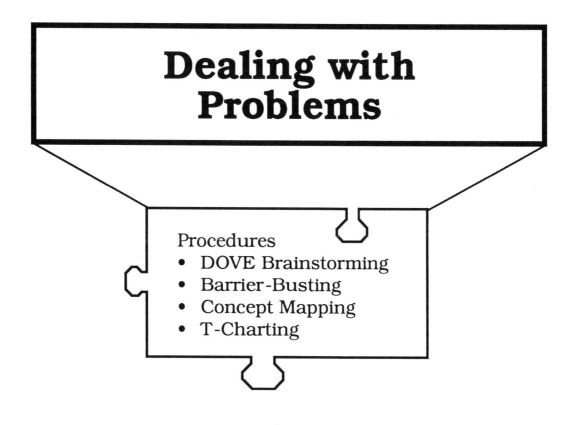

Dealing with Problems

Procedures
- DOVE Brainstorming
- Barrier-Busting
- Concept Mapping
- T-Charting

Overview

This chapter presents a variety of procedures that can be used to develop possible solutions to difficulties that may arise when facilitating cooperative groupwork. The chapter begins by noting typical problems associated with groupwork and invites teachers to list additional concerns. Four procedures for collaborative problem-solving follow, including: DOVE Brainstorming, Barrier-Busting, Concept Mapping, and T-Charting. Each is explained and illustrated with an example.

The Problem-Solving Process

Students learn to work cooperatively through experience. Despite carefully structured lessons, problems commonly occur when students are initially learning to work together. Typical problems include:

- Noise Level
- The Easy Rider
- The Anti-group Student
- The Unmotivated Student
- Keeping On-task
- Time
- Groups Finishing at Different Rates
- One Group Product: Who Takes It Home?
- Absences

What difficulties or frustrations have you encountered when facilitating cooperative lessons?

-
-
-
-
-
-
-
-
-

Through practice and with your persistence, many of these problems can be solved as students develop cooperative skills, experience increased success, and learn to value one another.

Along the way, it is helpful to collaboratively generate options for action. The pages that follow describe and illustrate four problem-solving procedures that you and your colleagues can use to deal with the concerns listed above. The procedures include: DOVE Brainstorming, Barrier-Busting, Concept Mapping, and T-Charting. Experiment with each as you continue to support one another in the problem-solving process!

B. Bennett, C. Rolheiser-Bennett, L. Stevahn (1991)
Cooperative Learning: Where Heart Meets Mind

DOVE Brainstorming

Collaborative brainstorming is fundamental to productive problem-solving because: "None of us is as smart as all of us!"

By pooling knowledge of effective teaching, understanding of the basic elements of cooperative learning, and practical classroom experience, teachers can develop a range of options for possible action to solve problems that arise during groupwork.

DOVE Brainstorming (Bellanca, 1990) is one procedure teams of teachers can use to generate solutions to problems. After identifying and clarifying a particular problem, teachers brainstorm ideas to deal with the problem using the DOVE rules:

Defer judgement—accept all ideas, list
     everything, evaluate later

Opt for original and off-beat—anything
     goes, especially different and crazy ideas

Vast numbers of ideas are best—get many
     ideas, the more the better

Expand by association—piggyback off of
     each other's ideas

DOVE Brainstorming may be applied in a variety of ways. The pages that follow describe extensions of the DOVE process.

Barrier-Busting

The aim of **Barrier-Busting** is to prevent or eliminate barriers that inhibit cooperative learning. The procedure is described below.

With a team of supportive colleagues...

One Teacher	• describes a barrier, problem, or concern related to cooperative learning

Time!

Time to plan or facilitate the lesson?

Colleagues	• check their understanding of the problem and ask questions for clarification if necessary • use DOVE Brainstorming (see page 299) to generate a list of possible solutions

To facilitate...
- start with pairs
- start with simple or familiar tasks like sequencing
- repeat a structure to develop routines so directions can briefly be reviewed
- process social skills mid-activity

The Teacher	• listens and records all suggestions • when brainstorming is completed, tells colleagues which idea looks most promising and briefly describes next steps to put the selected idea into action • reports results to colleagues at the next meeting

I'm going to try stopping teams mid-activity to process ...maybe even intervene in each group to make it personal.

The team recycles the process so that every teacher in the group has an opportunity to target a barrier and gain insights from colleagues.

B. Bennett, C. Rolheiser-Bennett, L. Stevahn (1991)
Cooperative Learning: Where Heart Meets Mind

Concept Mapping

Concept Mapping (Bellanca, 1990) facilitates critical thinking about problems as teachers systematically contribute and make connections between possible solutions. The following description outlines the process.

Step 1: Meet with a team of supportive colleagues.

Step 2: Target a problem and record it in the center of a piece of paper.

Step 3: Clarify dimensions of the problem by briefly discussing underlying causes.

Step 4: Systematically develop a map of possible solutions to the problem by passing the paper around the team in a "roundtable" fashion (see page 205). When it is your turn, you may contribute an idea or pass. If you contribute an idea, designate whether your idea constitutes a **main** or **supportive** solution to the problem and decide where to connect your idea to the map. Circle main ideas and write supportive ideas on extending branches (see the example below). DOVE Brainstorming rules apply throughout the process (see page 299).

Step 5: After passing the paper around the team several times, discuss insights and make plans to implement selected ideas.

Step 6: Set a future meeting date to share results of actions taken.

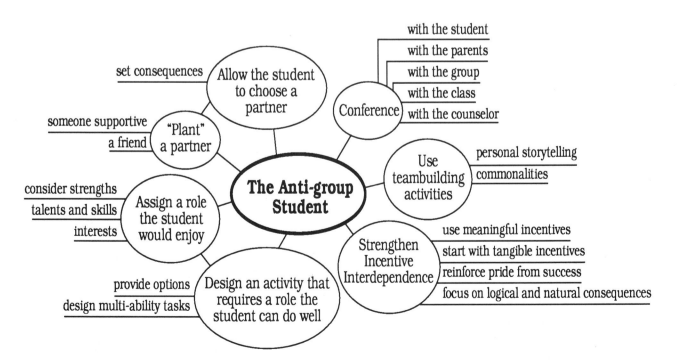

T-Charting

T-charting is a particularly useful technique for preplanning teacher interventions that may be necessary when inappropriate student behavior is observed during groupwork. Steps in the procedure are as follows:

- With a group of supportive colleagues, identify a situation that may call for teacher intervention during student groupwork.

- Together, clarify dimensions of the situation by discussing possible reasons for the inappropriate student behavior.

- Use DOVE Brainstorming (see page 299) to generate possible approaches to intervening. What might you say and/or do to carry out the intervention? Record all ideas on a T-Chart (see the example below).

- Discuss the ideas you would like to try. Ask your colleagues which ideas they would be inclined to try.

- Role play the situation several times to give each teacher in the group an opportunity to rehearse selected ideas.

Intervention T-Chart	
Incident: *A student displays extreme anger during groupwork*	
What the teacher might **say**:	What the teacher might **do**:
• "Close your books. We need to talk." • "Stop. Something's not right here." • "What's happening in this group?" • "How are each of you feeling right now? Why? Let's hear from everyone." • "You sound angry. What's happening?" • "What steps can you take as a group to solve the problem?" • "I'll be back to check on your progress."	• Sit eye-to-eye with students as a member of their team. • Be in their space. • Turn the group assignment sheet over. • Touch a student on the shoulder or arm if appropriate. • Convey a sense of seriousness about solving the problem (e.g., through facial expressions, gestures, tone of voice).

B. Bennett, C. Rolheiser-Bennett, L. Stevahn (1991)
Cooperative Learning: Where Heart Meets Mind

Chapter 16

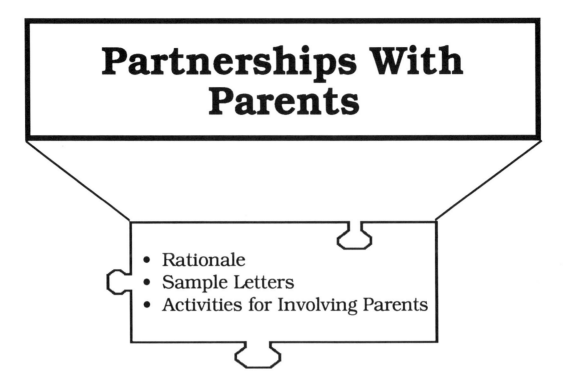

Partnerships With Parents

- Rationale
- Sample Letters
- Activities for Involving Parents

Overview

This chapter explores the importance of developing supportive partnerships with parents when employing cooperative strategies in the classroom. The questions that start the chapter initiate thinking about parental concerns regarding groupwork, as well as what parents should know about cooperative learning. This is followed by an argument for actively involving parents in student learning. Sample letters to parents follow, each designed to briefly explain cooperative learning, address concerns, and invite interaction and support. The chapter concludes with guidelines for developing initial letters to parents and suggestions for actively involving parents and the community in supporting cooperative learning.

Involving Parents – A Personal Reflection

Why is it important to involve parents as active participants in student learning?

What concerns do parents have about cooperative learning?

What do parents want to know?

What would you like parents to know?

Brainstorm ways you might involve parents as partners in the cooperative learning process.

B. Bennett, C. Rolheiser-Bennett, L. Stevahn (1991)
Cooperative Learning: Where Heart Meets Mind

A Rationale for Parent Involvement

Educators who use cooperative learning are doing so to nurture student development of lifelong skills... skills that transcend the walls of the classroom. To accomplish this goal partnerships with parents are essential. Those partnerships can be fostered by communicating with parents about why cooperative learning is being used in the classroom and school, as well as how it is being used.

By seeking their input about what is important regarding their child's learning, by listening to their concerns, by inviting feedback about classroom activities, and by eliciting their active support both in school and at home, we enable parents to become active partners in classroom and school improvement efforts.

As Michael Fullan (1991) notes:

> *"The closer the parent is to the education of the child, the greater the impact on child development and educational achievement."*

Communicating With Parents

Communication with parents is essential in developing effective partnerships. A letter home might be one way of helping parents understand cooperative learning and how it is going to be used in their child's classroom. The following letters serve as examples. How might you adapt the letters to reflect your context?

School District
Letterhead and School Address

August (year)

Dear Parent(s),

This is an exciting time to be an educator! Many effective programs and strategies have emerged. At the forefront is Cooperative Learning, where students work together to accomplish shared goals. This is done in small groups where students learn assigned material as well as social skills to facilitate group cooperation. Each student is accountable for his or her individual effort, as well as for the success of all group members.

I see Cooperative Learning as a strategy that adds a new dimension to the learning in our room. Research informs us that this grouping strategy provides an opportunity for students to learn interpersonal skills, group and individual responsibility, and to experience success in a group situation. The importance of Cooperative Learning is emphasized as we realize that each skill learned extends to areas outside of the classroom --- to the world of work and everyday living.

Cooperative Learning may sound like the latest educational concept, but in fact it has been implemented successfully as early as the late 19th century. Since that time, extensive research around the world has dispelled the myth that all students must learn at the same rate. Cooperative Learning shows us that group members can discuss, edit, check and correct the work of their fellow classmates without working on the same material or at the same rate. In the long run, the mutual collaborative skills promote a comfortable environment that ensures the success of any participating member.

I plan to meet with you during Parent Conference Week in early November. At that time I hope to discuss with you the benefits of Cooperative Learning and other effective strategies we are using in our classroom. You are also welcome to come and observe or participate in our class at any time.

Sincerely,

Teacher's Name

(Adapted from: Donna Zukowski, 1988, Adna School District, Adna, Washington)

B. Bennett, C. Rolheiser-Bennett, L. Stevahn (1991)
Cooperative Learning: Where Heart Meets Mind

(School Letterhead)

September,

Dear Parent(s),

Another school year has started! Many wonderful learning opportunities are planned, and we look forward to having you and your child share these experiences with us.

We are eager to help all students develop to their potential-- mastery of facts, development of critical thinking skills, and the fostering of a positive attitude toward themselves, their friends and learning. Those with special needs or aptitudes will be encouraged to expand or share their knowledge. Teaching methods will vary. At times students will be expected to work independently on their assignments, at other times competitively.

A major part of our classroom experience will involve cooperative small group learning. The capacity to work together is becoming even more important in the world in which we live. Of course, there is a significant difference between allowing students to work in groups and appropriately structuring small groups to facilitate both academic and social learning.

Cooperation is _not:_
- sitting close and talking as you work individually
- having students who finish first help slower students
- one person doing all the work and others getting credit

Cooperation _is_:
- being physically near each other
- discussing material together
- sharing materials in the group
- having common goals
- having individual accountability
- learning social skills
- sharing leadership roles
- expecting to provide help and be helped
- increasing knowledge of all members
- evaluating cooperative improvement
- sharing responsibility for each other

By using a variety of effective methods in the classroom, students will be learning individual, competitive, and cooperative skills that will help them throughout their school years, as well as in their adult lives.

Please feel free to become involved in our classroom. We welcome any questions you might have.

(Teacher's Name)

(Adapted from: Jean Bell, Tim Brewer, & Bob Hughes, 1988, Olympia School District, Olympia, Washington)

Your Draft Letter

Use this as a worksheet to draft your own letter to parents. Consider developing your letter cooperatively with other staff members. Be sure to share and discuss your letter with your principal, too!

> Given your students, school, and community: What do you predict will be the primary concerns of parents? Make a list. Star the concerns most important to acknowledge in your letter.

> What basic information about cooperative learning would you like parents to understand (e.g., your rationale for using cooperative groups, specific social skills students will be practicing, what cooperative learning is and is not)?

> In what ways would you like parents to be supportively involved (see the following page for ideas)? Extend an invitation in your letter!

B. Bennett, C. Rolheiser-Bennett, L. Stevahn (1991)
Cooperative Learning: Where Heart Meets Mind

Ideas for Involving Parents and the Community in Cooperative Learning

The following ideas may be used to meaningfully involve parents and the community in supporting cooperative learning. Discuss the ideas with other staff members --- and make plans to experiment with a variety of options appropriate to your context. What other ideas might you add?

- Invite parents to participate in a cooperative lesson by monitoring for use of social skills and recording observations.

- Invite business and community leaders to speak to the importance of developing social skills. Follow the talk with a forum where parents and students respond to the ideas presented.

- Provide references on cooperative learning for parents, perhaps highlighting certain sections.

- Clip current events and classified advertisements that validate the need for cooperative skills (this could be a home assignment that students and parents work on together). Use the "clippings" to create a "Cooperative News" bulletin board.

- Demonstrate cooperative learning during "School Open House" by involving parents in a brief cooperative activity (e.g., in groups of three, have parents list, rankorder, and reach agreement on learning outcomes they feel are most important for their children).

- Prepare a videotape of students in your classroom engaged in cooperative learning, then show the video to parents during conference week.

- Share cooperative class books or group projects with parents.

- Keep a current file of articles on cooperative learning in the parent library or resource corner.

- Have the students make a picture collage or videotape of their cooperative learning experiments. Invite parents in to view the product.

- Have parents experience and discuss cooperative learning during a parent evening. For example, involve parents in a jigsaw on the topic of effective study skills. Following the jigsaw, have parents reflect on their experience in the cooperative process. Be prepared to discuss parent questions related to study skills and cooperative learning.

"... Educational reform requires the conjoint efforts of families and schools. Parents and teachers should recognize the critical complementary importance of each other in the life of the student."

- Michael Fullan (1991) -

B. Bennett, C. Rolheiser-Bennett, L. Stevahn (1991)
Cooperative Learning: Where Heart Meets Mind

Chapter 17

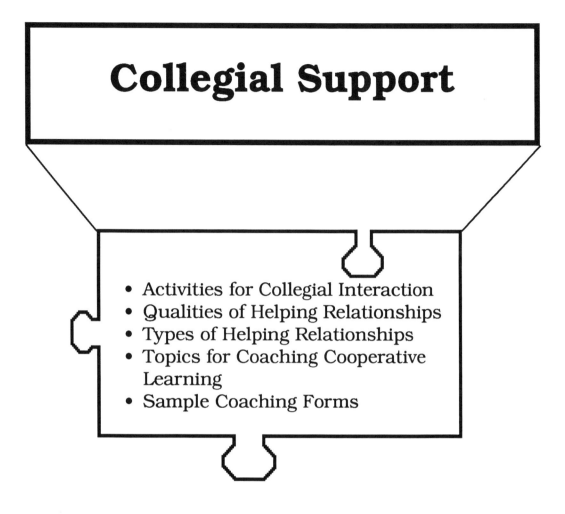

Collegial Support

- Activities for Collegial Interaction
- Qualities of Helping Relationships
- Types of Helping Relationships
- Topics for Coaching Cooperative Learning
- Sample Coaching Forms

Overview

This chapter considers the importance of supportive collegial interaction as an essential ingredient in professional growth. The questions that start the chapter initiate reflection about significant professional development experiences, followed by suggested activities for pursuing continued growth with cooperative learning. The chapter continues by focusing attention on qualities important to helping relationships. A range of professional helping relationships is briefly described. The chapter concludes by suggesting topics of focus for coaching cooperative learning, followed by sample forms for use throughout the process.

Professional Growth Through Collegial Interaction

The importance of supportive collegial interaction for professional growth cannot be overstated. For example, consider your own professional growth. What has been a highpoint for you in your development as an educator? What led to that highpoint? Were others involved? In what ways?

My thoughts...

Chances are that your "highpoint" experience involved supportive interaction with others.

With a colleague, make plans to pursue professional growth with cooperative learning by considering the Professional Stretching Activities listed on the following pages:

Together...

- Read through the ideas and decide where to start.

- Agree on a timetable for completing your activity.
  Will preplanning be necessary? When will you meet to share what you discovered and process your experience?

- After carrying out your initial plan, continue the process by deciding what your next steps will be.

B. Bennett, C. Rolheiser-Bennett, L. Stevahn (1991)
Cooperative Learning: Where Heart Meets Mind

Professional Stretching Activities

1. Reflect on the variety of competitive, individualistic, and cooperative experiences that you participated in last year --- last month --- last week. Describe how you felt in each situation. Which competitive, individualistic, and cooperative experiences were enjoyable, motivating, or satisfying? Why? Which experiences were unenjoyable? Describe the circumstances. What can you do as a teacher to ensure appropriate competitive, individualistic, and cooperative learning experiences?

2. Where do you already use small groups in your teaching? Analyze how you have structured positive interdependence into those group situations. How might you strengthen the positive interdependence in each situation? Discuss your ideas with a colleague.

3. Read/review an article or chapter on cooperative learning. Have a colleague do the same. React to the material by indicating what is most meaningful to you --- and explaining why. Also, jot down any questions or concerns that came to mind as you considered the material. Discuss those issues with your colleagues.

4. Draft a letter to parents that explains cooperative learning and why you are using it in your classroom. Within the letter, anticipate and address typical concerns. Share your letter with another teacher in your school -- and with your principal, too!

5. Develop some long range goals for using cooperative learning throughout the year. Discuss your plan with a colleague.

6. Conduct a formal conversation with your principal explaining why you are using cooperative learning groups and asking for assistance. Prepare an outline and decide what information you will share. Encourage questions and specify the kind of support you need. After talking with your principal, jot down the highlights of the conversation.

7. Develop a personal plan to gain and sustain support for using and refining your skill with cooperative learning. List the steps you can take to set yourself up for continued success with cooperative learning (e.g., With whom will you interact? When will you meet? What are possible agendas?).

8. Plan cooperative lessons! You may wish to use the Lesson Planning Guides in this book. Co-plan with a staff member or walk through your lesson(s) with a staff member.

9. Teach cooperative lessons! Have a colleague observe some of these, then together complete a Teaching Follow-up sheet (see Chapter 14).

10. Share students' cooperative products with colleagues and parents. Discuss your observations.

11. Collaboratively problem-solve! Identify frustrations, difficulties, and concerns. With supportive colleagues, brainstorm possible ways to deal with the issues (see Chapter 15). Make a personal decision about which option you will try -- and share the results with your colleagues! Keep experimenting with options until your expectations are met.

12. What other activities for growth with cooperative learning would you add to this list? How will you involve colleagues as you pursue the activities?

Helping Relationships

As you and your colleagues take steps to continue growing with cooperative learning, consider the interpersonal qualities that contribute to effective teaming.

Reflections

Think of someone who has significantly contributed to your professional development as an educator. What specifically did that person do to help you grow? How did that person empower you? What qualities or characteristics of that person enhanced the helping relationship? How was trust strengthened in the relationship?

Ask your colleagues to also reflect on the questions above and compare responses. What do your experiences have in common?

Together consider the **Collegial Support** diagram on the following page and discuss these questions:

- Where do you see aspects of your experiences illustrated on the diagram?

- What helpful qualities do you bring to collegial interactions for professional growth? What do you consider to be your strongest assets as a collaborator?

- How might you enhance your skill as a collaborator?

B. Bennett, C. Rolheiser-Bennett, L. Stevahn (1991)
Cooperative Learning: Where Heart Meets Mind

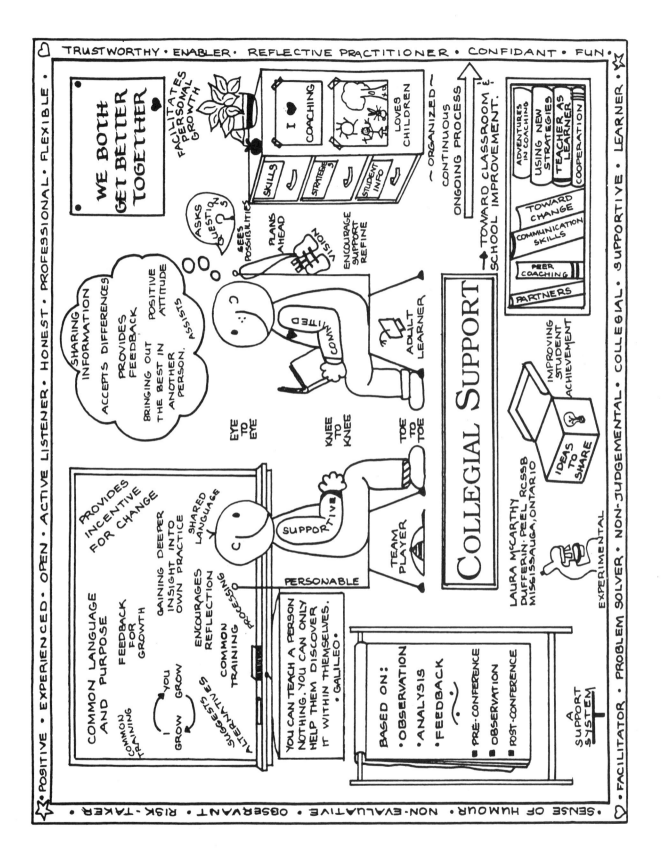

B. Bennett, C. Rolheiser-Bennett, L. Stevahn (1991)
Cooperative Learning: Where Heart Meets Mind

Page 315

Empowering Colleagues
Through Questions

When interacting for professional growth, consider ways you can empower others through questions (e.g., in pre- and post-conferences).

Ask Open-ended Questions:

Open-ended questions that foster reflections enable one to clarify thinking about skills and their applications as well as set goals for continued practice. Useful questions include:

- How did you feel during the lesson?
- What did you notice while students were working?
- What is your perception of student needs?
- What would you consider changing, if anything?

The following table may be used to formulate a variety of open-ended questions:

Question Starter...		Reflection...		Content...
What did you		think		the lesson
How do you		feel		the students
Could you		observe		instructional skills
Would you	**+**	analyze	**+**	adjustments
What is your		reflect		
Tell me		perceive		
		remember		
		notice		

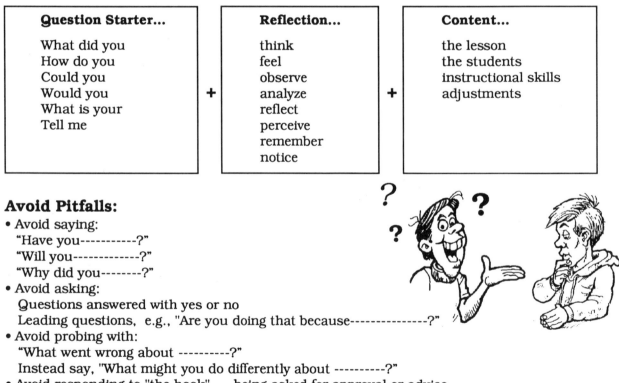

Avoid Pitfalls:

- Avoid saying:
  "Have you----------?"
  "Will you------------?"
  "Why did you--------?"
- Avoid asking:
  Questions answered with yes or no
  Leading questions, e.g., "Are you doing that because--------------?"
- Avoid probing with:
  "What went wrong about ----------?"
  Instead say, "What might you do differently about ----------?"
- Avoid responding to "the hook" --- being asked for approval or advice.

Remember To:

- Paraphrase ⇨ Check accuracy of your perception
- Reflect ⇨ Reflect feelings when there's a gap between what was said and how it was said
- Summarize ⇨ Along the way and at the end

Adapted from Cooper and Thompson (1990)

B. Bennett, C. Rolheiser-Bennett, L. Stevahn (1991)
Cooperative Learning: Where Heart Meets Mind

A Range of Supportive Relationships

There are a variety of ways that colleagues can interact to support one another in professional growth. Coaching is one option. When considering different types of coaching, remember...

All Coaching Relationships:

- Are built on trust and support
- Involve professionsls who have a common understanding of the skills, strategies, or other areas being coached
- Enable the sharing of teaching through activities that typically include co-planning lessons, classroom visitations, and follow-up discussions

Peer Coaching... implies reciprocal collegial interaction among colleagues (e.g., teachers). The mutual goal of all participants is further development of professional practice and all participants act as coaches.

Consultative Coaching... occurs when a consultant, specialist, or administrator collaboratively coaches a teacher for professional growth. Trust, support, and mutual respect characterize the relationship. Supervisory evaluation does not enter the relationship.

Mentor Coaching... occurs when experienced teachers coach new teachers. In addition to fostering supportive professional friendships with new teachers, mentors have opportunities to share practical insights gleaned from classroom experience.

In which type of coaching relationship would you like to be involved?
Who will you invite to be your coach?

Adapted from: North York Board of Education. (1991). *Supervision for Growth - Pathways to Professional Growth.* Toronto, Ontario.

Topics For Coaching Cooperative Learning

The following are *possible* topics of focus for coaching cooperative learning. What others would you add?

Basic Elements of Cooperative Learning:
    Positive Interdependence
    Individual Accountability
    Face-to-face Interaction
    Social Skills
    Processing of Social Skills

Today's Topic...

Teacher's Role:
    Organizational decisions prior to teaching
    Setting the lesson
    Monitoring and intervening during group work
    Evaluating the product and process of group work

Cooperative Structures:

Simpler:	Think-Pair-Share, Roundtable/Roundrobin, etc.
More Complex:	Jigsaw, Teams-Games-Tournaments, Group Investigation, etc.
Integration of Structures:	Using Think-Pair-Share to initiate a Jigsaw in one or more phases of Group Investigation, etc.

Integration of Other Instructional Skills:

Motivation:	• Was the lesson meaningful, interesting?
	• Did the students experience success?
	• Did the lesson link to the students' experiences?
Participation:	• When questions were asked, were all students in the group held accountable?
Thinking:	• What levels and types of thinking were being encouraged by the questions and activities?
	• Were the objectives clear and obtainable?

Student Learning:
    Appropriate use of social skills
    On-task behavior
    Ability to take responsibility for learning and resolving conflicts

---

The forms on the pages that follow may be useful as you proceed with professional interaction.

B. Bennett, C. Rolheiser-Bennett, L. Stevahn (1991)
Cooperative Learning: Where Heart Meets Mind

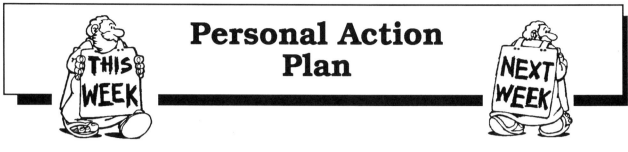

Personal Action Plan

1. A cooperative learning idea I'd like to act on is...

2. I plan to act on this idea by...

3. After carrying out my plan, I discovered...

Share your discoveries with a colleague!

This Week...

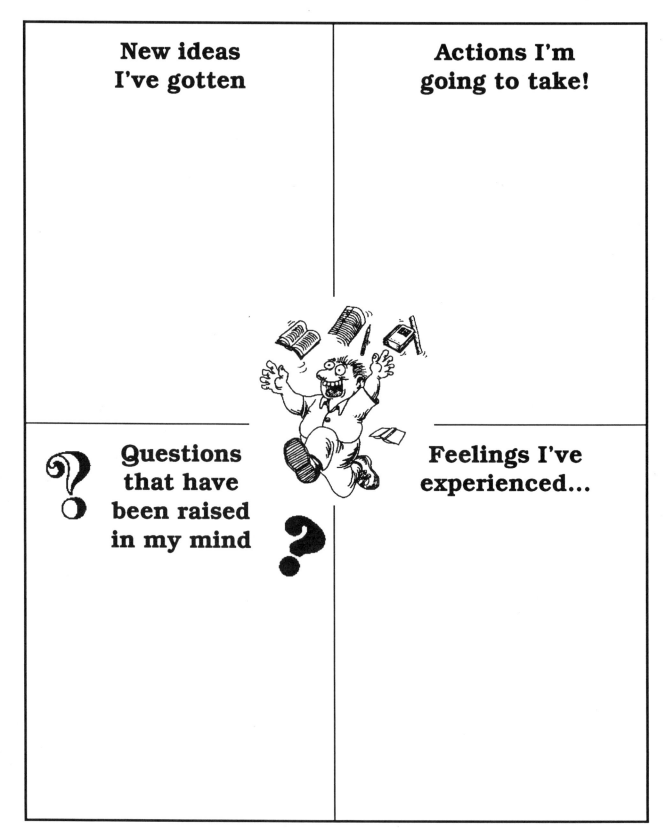

New ideas
I've gotten

Actions I'm
going to take!

Questions
that have
been raised
in my mind

Feelings I've
experienced...

(Adapted from Arthur Costa)

B. Bennett, C. Rolheiser-Bennett, L. Stevahn (1991)
Cooperative Learning: Where Heart Meets Mind

Reading Follow-Up

Name: _____

Article/Chapter: _____

Date: _____

1. **What are the major messages in the reading?**

2. **What ideas in the reading were most meaningful to you? Why?**

3. **How might you invite staff, students, or parents to consider these messages/ideas?**

"Professional growth means... working together!"

"Don't just stand there, do something!"

"If you don't risk anything, you risk even more."

"Experimentation is the key!"

"Chaotic action is preferable to orderly inaction."

"Ready. Fire. Aim." (Begin sooner than later!)

(Quotations from: Peters, T.J., & Waterman, Jr., R.H. (1982). *In Search of Excellence: Lessons From America's Best-Run Companies.* New York: Harper & Row.)

B. Bennett, C. Rolheiser-Bennett, L. Stevahn (1991)
Cooperative Learning: Where Heart Meets Mind

Chapter 18

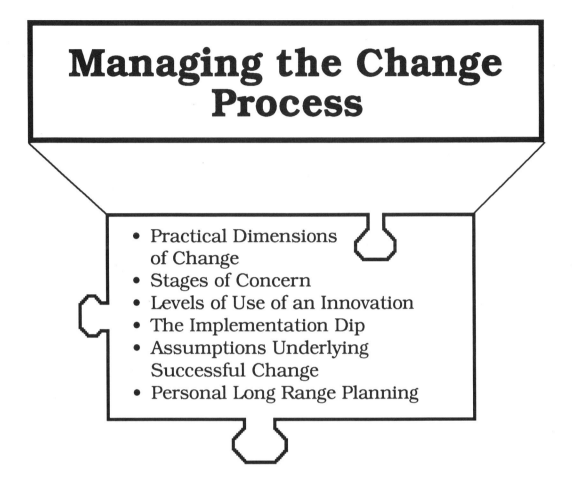

Managing the Change Process

- Practical Dimensions of Change
- Stages of Concern
- Levels of Use of an Innovation
- The Implementation Dip
- Assumptions Underlying Successful Change
- Personal Long Range Planning

Overview

This chapter considers important aspects of managing the change process. The questions that start the chapter initiate thinking about the process, followed by an examination of five important areas related to change: Practical Dimensions of Change, Stages of Concern, Levels of Use of an Innovation, The Implementation Dip, and Assumptions Underlying Successful Change. Throughout the chapter, questions challenge educators to reflect on personal experiences and concerns related to the implementation of cooperative learning. Those concerns include identifying present needs, as well as planning for the future. The chapter concludes with a worksheet for developing personal long range plans.

Thinking About Change

- When learning something new there is an adage: "Things get worse before they get better." Can you think of a situation when this was true for you (e.g., when learning a new golf swing, swimming stroke, or other skill)?

- What are the implications of that adage for using cooperative learning in your classroom and school?

Successful implementation of cooperative learning is a long-term endeavor involving changes in curricula, teacher behaviors and teacher attitudes or beliefs. Armed with basic knowledge of the change process, educators can more effectively plan ways to initiate, implement, and sustain change.

The pages that follow briefly examine several important areas related to change including: Practical Dimensions of Change, Stages of Concern, Levels of Use of an Innovation, the Implementation Dip, and Assumptions Underlying Successful Change. As you consider each area, determine how the information can help you as you continue to implement cooperative learning.

B. Bennett, C. Rolheiser-Bennett, L. Stevahn (1991)
Cooperative Learning: Where Heart Meets Mind

Practical Dimensions of Change

Implementing educational change is no simple matter. Realistically, perceiving educational change as a highly complex process is fundamental to any meaningful consideration of the process one goes through in implementing cooperative learning.

However, in a practical sense, we can briefly consider three dimensions of change (Fullan, 1991) to begin to gain insight into that complex process. Basically, effective implementation of an educational innovation (including cooperative learning) involves:

1. **Using new materials**
   (i.e., instructional resources)

2. **Employing new teaching behaviors**
   (i.e., classroom practices)

3. **Developing new beliefs and understandings about teaching and learning**
   (i.e., assumptions and conceptions that underlie the innovation)

Initiating, implementing, and sustaining an innovation will directly or indirectly involve change in all three dimensions. Importantly though, we don't know how much attention should be paid to each particular area or the advantages of starting in one area rather than another. For example, some argue that it's only through the adoption of new materials or a change in practice that ultimately effects a change in beliefs. On the other hand, it is also argued that a change in beliefs can drive the adoption of new materials or practices.

Regardless, it is important to consider all three dimensions. For example, if we change our beliefs about the value of cooperative groupwork, but fail to change our instructional practices; or if we change our practices when someone is watching, but fail to change our beliefs or fail to get support with appropriate materials, then we virtually guarantee that cooperative learning will not be effectively implemented.

There exists an endless number of ways for individuals to interact with the dimensions of change. The diagrams below represent different ways that an individual might interact with the three dimensions.

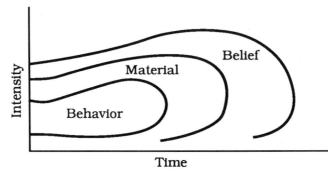

This diagram shows an individual who, over time, is changing teaching behavior, using new materials, and developing underlying beliefs that support the implementation.

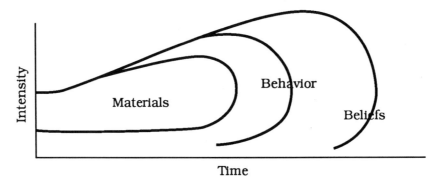

This diagram shows an individual who begins the change process with the adoption of new materials, which leads to a change in teaching behavior, and results in changed beliefs.

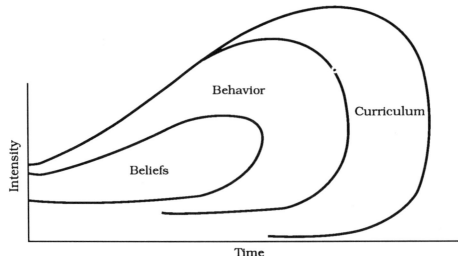

This diagram shows an individual whose changed beliefs have led to changes in teaching behavior and use of new curricular materials.

B. Bennett, C. Rolheiser-Bennett, L. Stevahn (1991)
Cooperative Learning: Where Heart Meets Mind

A Personal Reflection: Practical Dimensions of Change

In the process of implementing cooperative learning, how have you been involved with the Practical Dimensions of Change?

1. Using new materials
2. Employing new teaching behaviors
3. Developing new beliefs and understandings about teaching and learning

Discuss your reflections with a colleague.

What do the Practical Dimensions of Change imply for you as you contemplate future growth with cooperative learning? What steps can you take to continue to facilitate meaningful change in each dimension? Discuss possible steps with a colleague and list them below.

-
-
-

Stages of Concern

"The questions don't ever disappear... they just change."

– L. Stevahn (1991) –

From our experience and research, we know that teacher concerns about cooperative learning move from **information** concerns: "I need to know how cooperative learning differs from groupwork"; to **personal** concerns: "I don't have enough time to plan the lessons"; to **management** concerns: "I'm trying to figure out how to more effectively hold students accountable in the Jigsaw process" (Anderson, Bennett, & Rolheiser-Bennett, 1991). On the following page is a taxonomy of concerns (Hall & Hord, 1987; Hall & Loucks, 1977) that most teachers move through as they work at implementing an innovation. Importantly, the taxonomy assists teachers in understanding the nature of the concerns that are most likely to occur from when they first start to experiment with a new teaching practice to when they become more skilled. The important message is that as you become more skilled in your understanding and application of cooperative learning, your concerns change. Working through the implementation process ultimately means attending to those changing concerns.

B. Bennett, C. Rolheiser-Bennett, L. Stevahn (1991)
Cooperative Learning: Where Heart Meets Mind

Stages of Concern About the Innovation *

0 **Awareness:** Little concern about or involvement with the innovation is indicated (e.g., "I don't know what cooperative learning is.").

1 **Informational:** A general awareness of the innovation and interest in learning more detail about it is indicated. The person seems to be unworried about herself/himself in relation to the innovation. The individual is interested in substantive aspects of the innovation in a selfless manner such as general characteristics, effects, and requirements for use (e.g., "How is cooperative learning different from my present use of groupwork?").

2 **Personal:** The individual is uncertain about the demands of the innovation, one's inadequacy to meet those demands, and one's role with the innovation. This includes analysis of the individual's role in relation to the reward structure of the organization, decision-making, and consideration of potential conflicts with existing structures or personal commitment. Financial or status implications of the program for self and colleagues may also be reflected (e.g., "Am I doing it 'correctly'?").

3 **Management:** Attention is focused on the processes and tasks of using the innovation and the best use of information and resources. Issues related to efficiency, organizing, managing, scheduling, and time demands are utmost (e.g., "How can we manage the social conflict that arises in the groups?").

4 **Consequence:** Attention focuses on impact of the innovation on students in the teacher's immediate sphere of influence. The focus is on relevance of the innovation for students, evaluation of student outcomes, including performance and competence, and changes needed to increase student outcomes (e.g., "I wonder how cooperative learning is impacting the progress of my stronger students?").

5 **Collaboration:** The focus is on coordination and cooperation with others regarding use of the innovation (e.g., "I need more time to work with others in planning and observing cooperative learning lessons.").

6 **Refocusing:** The focus is on exploration of more universal benefits from the innovation, including the possibilities of major changes or replacement with a more powerful alternative. The individual has definite ideas about alternatives to the proposed or existing form of the innovation (e.g., "I have developed a new structure for cooperative learning that is really working well.").

* See: Hall, G.E., & Hord, S. (1987). *Change in Schools: Facilitating the Process.* Albany: State University of New York Press.

A Personal Reflection:
Stages of Concern

1. In the process of implementing cooperative learning, how have you evolved through various stages of concern (see the next page, 331)?

2. What significant incidents or experiences do you associate with particular stages?

3. What do the Stages of Concern imply for your continued growth with cooperative learning?

4. What predictions would you make about future personal concerns?

5. What support has been and will be necessary along the way? Share your reflections with a colleague who will support you in the change process.

A Personal Reflection...

B. Bennett, C. Rolheiser-Bennett, L. Stevahn (1991)
Cooperative Learning: Where Heart Meets Mind

Your Evolving Concerns
with Cooperative Learning

. . . Reflect on your initial concerns with cooperative learning.

. . . How have those concerns changed or been resolved?

. . . What are your current concerns?

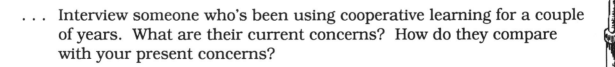

. . . Interview someone who's been using cooperative learning for a couple of years. What are their current concerns? How do they compare with your present concerns?

Levels of Use of an Innovation

Below is a list of stages that most educators move through as they work at implementing an innovation. Just like the Stages of Concern, the Levels of Use (Hall & Hord, 1987; Hall & Loucks, 1977) assist teachers in understanding the levels of competence and comfort that are most likely to occur from when they first start to experiment with a new practice to when they become more knowledgeable and skilled. The benefit of this taxonomy of stages is in helping teachers to appreciate that although they will begin by "skinning their knees", they will eventually master the new learning. As well, the cycle will continue. In their next experimentation with another innovation they will start the cycle anew.

Levels of Use

0 - **Non-Use:** no action is being taken with respect to the innovation

1 - **Orientation:** the user is seeking out information about the innovation

2 - **Preparation:** the user is preparing to use the innovation

3 - **Mechanical:** the user has not coordinated the use of the innovation; planning tends to be day-by-day versus long-term; organization is less than coordinated and no routines have been established

4 - **Routine:** the user has an established pattern of use, but is making few or no changes

5 - **Refinement:** the user is making changes to increase outcomes

6 - **Integration:** the user is making deliberate efforts to coordinate with others using the innovation to make learning more powerful for students

7 - **Renewal:** the user is seeking more effective alternatives to the established use of the innovation

B. Bennett, C. Rolheiser-Bennett, L. Stevahn (1991)
Cooperative Learning: Where Heart Meets Mind

A Personal Reflection: Levels of Use

1. In the process of implementing cooperative learning, how have you evolved through various levels of use?

2. What "highlights" come to mind as you have experienced various levels?

3. What do the Levels of Use imply for your continued growth with cooperative learning?

4. How might the Levels of Use be useful for measuring future progress of yourself or colleagues? Discuss your ideas and share your "stories" with a colleague.

A Personal Reflection...

The Implementation Dip

A simple and powerful link to both the Levels of Use of an Innovation and the Stages of Concern is Michael Fullan's (1991) idea related to:

The Implementation Dip

Basically, the diagram reminds us that when we learn something new or do something we know in a different way, we can expect things to get worse before they get better. Also, the dip is likely a lot less smooth than how it is portrayed in the diagram above. Note, that the more intensely committed you are, the deeper the dip will likely be – which means the more you try to explore and experiment, the more you can expect to be challenged. More importantly though, you rise meaningfully higher on the other side — the greater the input, the greater the output!

B. Bennett, C. Rolheiser-Bennett, L. Stevahn (1991)
Cooperative Learning: Where Heart Meets Mind

Assumptions Underlying Successful Change

"Change is a highly personal experience – each and every one of the teachers who will be affected by change must have the opportunity to work through this experience in a way in which the rewards at least equal the cost."

- Michael Fullan (1991) -

With a colleague, carefully consider the following assumptions that underlie successful change. Together discuss:

1. What does each assumption mean to you in your classroom and school?

2. What actions can you take to ensure and strengthen each assumption?

---

10 Assumptions About Change *

1. Do not assume that your version of what the change should be is the one that should or could be implemented.

2. Assume that any significant innovation, if it is to result in change, requires individual implementers to work out their own meaning.

3. Assume that conflict and disagreement are not only inevitable but fundamental to successful change.

4. Assume that people need pressure to change (even in directions that they desire). But, it will only be effective under conditions that allow them to react, to form their own position, to interact with other implementers, to obtain technical assistance, etc.

con't...

---

* See: Fullan, M., with Stiegelbauer, S. (1991). *The New Meaning of Educational Change.* New York: Teachers College Press.

5. Assume that effective change takes time; 2 - 3 years for specific innovations, 5 or more years for institutional reforms.

6. We should not assume that the reason for lack of implementation is outright rejection of the values embodied in the change, or hard core resistance to all change. There are a number of possible reasons: value rejection, inadequate resource to support implementation, insufficient time elapsed.

7. We should not expect all or even most people or groups to change. Progress occurs when we take steps that increase the number of people. Our reach should exceed our grasps... but not by such a margin that we fall flat on our face.

8. Assume that you will need a plan that is based on the above assumptions.

9. Assume that no amount of knowledge will ever make it totally clear what action should be taken.

10. We should assume that changing the culture of institutions is the real agenda, not implementing single innovations.

B. Bennett, C. Rolheiser-Bennett, L. Stevahn (1991)
Cooperative Learning: Where Heart Meets Mind

Long Range Implementation Plan

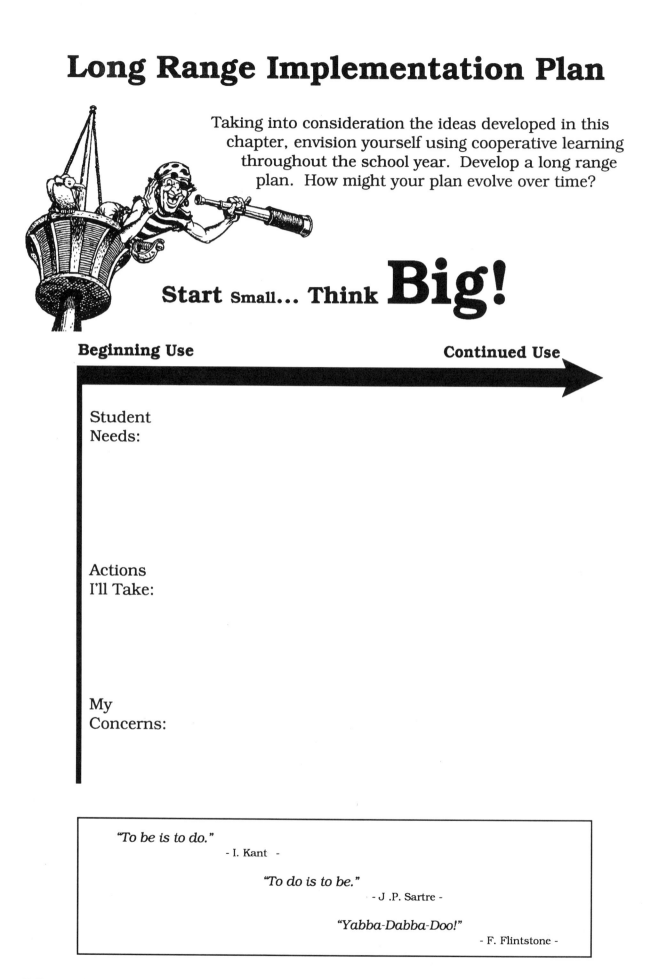

Taking into consideration the ideas developed in this chapter, envision yourself using cooperative learning throughout the school year. Develop a long range plan. How might your plan evolve over time?

Start Small... Think **Big!**

Beginning Use ———————————————→ **Continued Use**

Student
Needs:

Actions
I'll Take:

My
Concerns:

> *"To be is to do."*
>   - I. Kant -
>
>   *"To do is to be."*
>   - J.P. Sartre -
>
>   *"Yabba-Dabba-Doo!"*
>   - F. Flintstone -

Insights into the Change Process

DON'T FORGET:

- The necessity of combining pressure and support in the change process.

- The critical importance of reducing some of the early costs and increasing some of the early rewards for implementers.

- The need to think big, but start small, in order to achieve some manageability.

- The tendency for behavior to change before beliefs, and all that implies for inservice.

- The realization that achieving clarity, skill, and commitment, is a progressive process.

- Michael Fullan (1990) -

B. Bennett, C. Rolheiser-Bennett, L. Stevahn (1991)
Cooperative Learning: Where Heart Meets Mind

"The truly educated person
is the one who
has learned how to learn
and how to change."

- Carl Rogers (1969) -

> *"We are going to have to find ways of organizing ourselves cooperatively. sanely, scientifically, harmonically and in regenerative spontaneity with the rest of humanity around earth... We are not going to be able to operate our spaceship earth successfully nor for much longer unless we see it as a whole spaceship and our fate as common. It has to be everybody or nobody."*

- R. Buckminster Fuller -

B. Bennett, C. Rolheiser-Bennett, L. Stevahn (1991)
Cooperative Learning: Where Heart Meets Mind

References

Anderson, M. (1988). *Partnerships: Developing teamwork at the computer.* Santa Cruz, CA: Educational Apple-cations.

Anderson, S., Bennett, B., & Rolheiser-Bennett, C. (1991). *Teacher concerns in the first year of implementing cooperative learning* (submitted for publication).

Andrini, B. (1989). *Cooperative learning & mathematics: A multi-structural approach.* San Juan Capistrano, CA: Resources for Teachers.

Aronson, E. (1980). Training teachers to use jigsaw learning: A manual for teachers. In S. Sharan, P. Hare, C.D. Webb, & R. Hertz-Lazarowitz (Eds.), *Cooperation in education.* Provo, UT: Brigham Young University Press.

Aronson, E., & Goode, E. (1978). *The jigsaw classroom.* Beverly Hills, CA: Sage Publications.

Bellanca, J. (1990). *Keep them thinking: Level III.* Palatine, IL: Skylight Publishing.

Brandt, R.S. (Ed.). (1989/1990). Cooperative learning. *Educational Leadership, 47* (4).

Brubacher, M., Payne, R., & Rickett, K. (Eds.). (1990). *Perspectives on small group learning. Theory and practice.* Oakville, ON: Rubicon Publishing.

Buzan, T. (1983). *Use both sides of your brain* (rev. ed.). New York: E.P. Dutton.

Clarke, J., & Wideman, R. (1985). *Cooperative learning. The jigsaw strategy.* Scarborough, ON: Scarborough Board of Education.

Clarke, J., Wideman, R., & Eadie, S. (1990). *Together we learn.* Scarborough, ON: Prentice-Hall.

Coelho, E., Winer, L., & Winn-Bell Olsen, J. (1989). *All sides of the issue. Activities for cooperative jigsaw groups.* Hayward, CA: Alemany Press.

Cohen, E.G. (1986). *Designing groupwork: Strategies for the heterogeneous classroom.* New York: Teachers College Press.

Cohen, E.G., & Lotan, R.A. (1987). *Can classrooms learn?* Stanford University, CA.

Curran, L. (1990). *Cooperative learning lessons for little ones: Literature-based language arts and social skills.* San Juan Capistrano, CA: Resources for Teachers.

Davidson, N. (Ed.). (1989). *Cooperative learning in mathematics: A handbook for teachers.* Reading, MA: Addison-Wesley.

Dishon, D. & O'Leary, P.W. (1984). *A guidebook for cooperative learning: A technique for creating more effective schools.* Holmes Beach, FL: Learning Publications.

Duckworth, E. (1987). *"The having of wonderful ideas" and other essays on teaching and learning.* New York: Teachers College Press.

Fullan, M.G., Bennett, B., & Rolheiser-Bennett, C. (1990). Linking classroom and school improvement. *Educational Leadership, 47* (8), 13-19.

Fullan, M.G., with Stiegelbauer, S. (1991). *The new meaning of educational change* (2nd ed.). New York: Teachers College Press. Toronto: OISE Press.

Gibbs, J. (1987). *Tribes: A process for social development and cooperative learning.* Santa Rosa, CA: Center Source Publications.

Gibbs, J. (1990). The tribes process: Preparing students for tomorrow in the "here-and-now" of the cooperative learning community. *Cooperative Learning, 11* (2), 21-22.

Glasser, W. (1986). *Control theory in the classroom.* New York: Harper & Row.

Graves, T. (1991). The controversy over group rewards in cooperative classrooms. *Educational Leadership, 48* (7), 77-79.

Graves, N., & Graves, T. (1990). *What is cooperative learning? Tips for teachers and trainers.* Santa Cruz, CA: Cooperative College of California.

Graves, N., & Graves, T. (Eds.). (1990). Cooperative learning: A resource guide. *Cooperative Learning, 11* (1).

Hall, G.E., & Hord, S. (1987). *Change in schools: Facilitating the process.* Albany: State University of New York Press.

Hall, G., & Loucks, S. (1977). Developmental model for determining whether the treatment is actually implemented. *American Educational Research Journal, 14* (3), 263-276.

Hertz-Lazarowitz, R., & Davidson, J.B. (1990). *Six mirrors of the classroom: A pathway to cooperative learning.* Westlake Village, CA: Joan B. Davidson.

Highet, G. (1950). *The art of teaching.* Toronto, ON: Random House.

Holm, A., Schultz, D., Winget, P., & Wurzbach, L. (1987). *Cooperative activities for the home: Parents working with teachers to support cooperative learning.* Sacramento, CA: Resources in Special Education.

Johnson, D.W. (1986). *Reaching out: Interpersonal effectiveness and self-actualization* (3rd ed.). Englewood Cliffs, NJ: Prentice-Hall.

Johnson, D.W., & Johnson, F.P. (1991). *Joining together: Group theory and group skills* (4th ed.). Englewood Cliffs, NJ: Prentice-Hall.

Johnson, D.W., & Johnson, R.T. (1988). *Creative conflict.* Edina, MN: Interaction Book Company.

Johnson, D.W., & Johnson, R.T. (1989). *Leading the Cooperative School.* Edina, MN: Interaction Book Company.

Johnson, D.W., & Johnson, R.T. (1989). *Cooperation and competition: Theory and research.* Edina, MN: Interaction Book Company.

Johnson, D.W., & Johnson, R.T. (1991). *Learning together and alone: Cooperative, competitive, and individualistic learning* (3rd ed.). Englewood Cliffs, NJ: Prentice-Hall.

Johnson, D.W. & Johnson, R.T. (Eds.). (1991). *Learning mathematics and cooperative learning lesson plans for teachers.* Edina, MN: Interaction Book Company.

B. Bennett, C. Rolheiser-Bennett, L. Stevahn (1991)
Cooperative Learning: Where Heart Meets Mind

Johnson, D.W., Johnson, R.T., & Bartlett, J.K. (1990). *Cooperative learning lesson structures.* Edina, MN: Interaction Book Company.

Johnson, D.W., Johnson, R.T., Bartlett, J.K., & Johnson, L.M. (1988). *Our cooperative classroom.* Edina, MN: Interaction Book Company.

Johnson, D.W., Johnson, R.T., & Holubec, E.J. (1986). *Circles of learning: Cooperation in the classroom* (rev. ed). Edina, MN: Interaction Book Company.

Johnson, D.W., Johnson, R.T., & Holubec, E.J. (1990). *Circles of learning: Cooperation in the classroom.* (3rd ed.). Edina, MN: Interaction Book Company.

Johnson, D.W., Johnson, R.T., & Holubec, E.J. (1990). *Cooperation in the classroom* (rev. ed.). Edina, MN: Interaction Book Company.

Johnson, D.W., Johnson, R.T., & Holubec, E.J. (Eds.). (1987). *Structuring cooperative learning: Lesson plans for teachers.* Edina, MN: Interaction Book Company.

Joyce, B., & Weil, M. (1986). *Models of teaching* (3rd ed.). Englewood Cliffs, NJ: Prentice-Hall.

Kagan, S. (1990). *Cooperative learning resources for teachers.* San Juan Capistrano, CA: Resources for Teachers.

Kohn, A. (1990). The risks of rewards: Prizes and praise may send kids the wrong message. *Health, 22* (1), 28.

Kohn, A. (1991a). Caring kids: The role of the schools. *Phi Delta Kappan, 72* (7), 496-506.

Kohn, A. (1991b). Group grade grubbing versus cooperative learning. *Educational Leadership, 48* (5), 83-87.

Kohn, A. (1991c). Don't spoil the promise of cooperative learning. *Educational Leadership, 48* (5), 93-94.

Male, M., Johnson, D., Johnson, R., & Anderson, M. (1986). *Cooperative learning & computers. An activity guide for teachers* (3rd ed.). Santa Cruz, CA: Educational Apple-cations.

Mayo, P., & Waldo, P. (1986). *Scripting: Social communication for adolescents.* Eau Claire, WI: Thinking Publications.

McCabe, M.E., & Rhodes, J. (1988). *The nurturing classroom. Developing self-esteem, thinking skills and responsibility through simple cooperation.* Willits, CA: ITA Publications.

Millar, J. (1897). *School management and the principles and practice of teaching.* Toronto, ON: William Briggs.

Moorman, C., & Dishon, D. (1983). *Our classroom: We can learn together.* Bay City, MI: Personal Power Press.

Newmann, F.M., & Thompson, J.A. (1987). *Effects of cooperative learning on achievement in secondary schools: A summary of research.* Madison, WI: National Center on Effective Secondary Schools.

Ontario Secondary School Teachers' Federation. (1989). *Independent learning: Process to product.* Toronto, ON.

Orlick, T. (1978). *The cooperative sports and games book.* New York: Pantheon Books.

Orlick, T. (1981). *The second cooperative sports and games book.* New York: Pantheon Books.

Peters, T.J., & Waterman, Jr., R.H. (1982). *In search of excellence: Lessons from America's best-run companies.* New York: Harper & Row.

Reid, J., Forrestal, P., & Cook, J. (1989). *Small group learning in the classroom.* Portsmouth, NH: Heinemann Educational Books.

Rogers, C. (1969). *Freedom to learn.* Columbus, OH: C.E. Merrill.

Rolheiser-Bennett, C., Hundey, I., & Gooding, J. (1991). *Collegial support in a preservice program and induction program: Building norms for professional growth.* Paper presented at the annual meeting of the Canadian Society for Studies in Education, Kingston, ON.

Roy, P. (1990). *Cooperative learning: Students learning together.* Minneapolis, MN: Patricia Roy Company.

Schaps, E., & Lewis, C. (1991). Extrinsic rewards are education's past, not its future. *Educational Leadership, 48* (7), 81.

Schmuck, R.A., & Schmuck, P.A. (1988). *Group processes in the classroom.* Dubuque, IA: Wm. C. Brown Co.

Schwartz, S., & Pollishuke, M. (1990). *Creating the child-centred classroom.* Concord, ON: Irwin Publishing.

Sharan, D., & Hertz-Lazarowitz, R. (1980). A group investigation method of cooperative learning in the classroom. In S. Sharan, P. Hare, C.D. Webb, & R. Hertz-Lazarowitz (Eds.), *Cooperation in Education* (pp. 14-46). Provo, UT: Brigham Young University Press.

Sharan, Y. & Sharan, S. (1990). Group investigation expands cooperative learning. *Educational Leadership, 47* (4), 17-21.

Sharan, S. (Ed.). (1990). *Cooperative learning: Theory and research.* Westport, CT: Praeger Publishers.

Sharan, S., Hare, P., Webb, C.D. & Hertz-Lazarowitz, R. (Eds.). (1980). *Cooperation in education.* Provo, UT: Brigham Young University Press.

Slavin, R.E., et al. (Eds.). (1985). *Learning to cooperate, cooperating to learn.* New York: Plenum Press.

Slavin, R.E. (1986). *Using student team learning* (3rd ed.). Baltimore, MD: The Johns Hopkins Team Learning Project.

Slavin, R.E. (1989). *Cooperative learning. Theory, research, and practice.* Englewood Cliffs, NJ: Prentice-Hall.

Slavin, R.E. (1991a). Synthesis of research on cooperative learning. *Educational leadership, 48* (5), 71-82.

Slavin, R.E. (1991b). Group rewards make groupwork work. *Educational leadership, 48* (5), 89-91.

Stone, J.M. (1989). *Cooperative learning and language arts: A multi-structural approach.* San Juan Capistrano, CA: Resources for Teachers.

Yager, S. et al. (1986). The impact of group processing on achievement in cooperative learning groups. *Journal of Social Psychology, 126* (3), 389-397.

B. Bennett, C. Rolheiser-Bennett, L. Stevahn (1991)
Cooperative Learning: Where Heart Meets Mind

Order Form

Educational Connections
Station "P", 704 Spadina Ave.,
P.O. Box 249
Toronto, Ontario
CANADA M5S 2S8

Quantity	Item	Unit Price	Total
	Cooperative Learning: Where Heart Meets Mind	$29.00	$

Method of Payment:

☐ Check or Money Order enclosed (Made payable to **Educational Connections**)

☐ Purchase Order attached

For bulk orders Shipping & Handling will be reduced accordingly.

(10% Discount for 50-99 copies)   – $ _____

(20% Discount for 100 or more copies)   – $ _____

Subtotal $ _____

Shipping & Handling (10% of subtotal, $5.00 minimum)   + $ _____

Goods and Services Tax (GST) (Canadian residents add 7%)   + $ _____

TOTAL $ _____

(Price is effective August 1, 1991 and subject to change without notice.)
GST Reg# - 128224078

Bill To: (complete only if different from <u>Ship To</u> address below)

Name _____

Address _____

City _____

Province/State _____   Postal Code/Zip _____

Phone (_____) _____

Ship To:

Name _____

Address _____

City _____

Province/State _____   Postal Code/Zip _____

Phone (_____) _____

Contact **Merelyn Loates** for further information: Phone (416) 619-0161 or Fax (416) 619-0162.